AF559961

HOTEL ACCOUNTING

HOTEL ACCOUNTING

M. C. METTI

ANMOL PUBLICATIONS PVT. LTD.
NEW DELHI - 110 002 (INDIA)

ANMOL PUBLICATIONS PVT. LTD.

H.O.: 4374/4B, Ansari Road, Darya Ganj,
New Delhi-110 002 (India)
Ph.: 23278000, 23261597

B.O.: No. 1015, Ist Main Road, BSK IIIrd Stage
IIIrd Phase, IIIrd Block
Bangalore - 560 085 (India)
Visit us at: www.anmolpublications.com

Hotel Accounting

ISBN 978-81-261-3232-4

PRINTED IN INDIA

Printed at Mehra Offset Press, Delhi.

Contents

Preface

The success of every business in the hospitality industry depends on maximizing revenues and minimizing costs. This book is a presentation of fundamental concepts and analytical techniques that are essential to taking control of real-world accounting systems, evaluating current and past operations, and effectively managing finances toward increased profits. Complete with scores of helpful drawings, charts, and tables, *Hotel Accounting* is the ultimate resource for students who need to grasp the principles of accounting and learn to apply them to real-world hospitality management.

It offers hands-on coverage of computer applications and practical decision-making skills to successfully prepare readers for the increasingly complex and competitive hospitality industry. Offering a unique approach in the field, this book presents the principles of accounting from a corporate perspective. This provides readers with a real-world understanding of the concepts. The book then helps readers gain the skills, and the confidence they need to use those skills effectively in making hotel business decisions.

Author

Chapter 1

Accounting Cycle and Financial Statements

INTRODUCTION

A hotel is an establishment that provides paid lodging, usually on a short-term basis. Hotels often provide a number of additional guest services such as a restaurant, a swimming pool or childcare. Some hotels have conference services and meeting rooms and encourage groups to hold conventions and meetings at their location. Hotels differ from motels in that most motels have drive-up, exterior entrances to the rooms, while hotels tend to have interior entrances to the rooms, which may increase guests' safety and present a more upmarket image.

The hotel industry has a complex and fast paced accounting environment. The need to control sales revenue from a variety of sources received in cash, credit card and cheque by advance deposit or against sales invoices creates daily accounting issues not experienced in other industries. Furthermore specific taxation issues and reporting demands create a specialist requirement to ensure these needs are met.

A dedicated Accountant whose responsibility is to manage the accounting function supports each one of Hotels.

Duties include the balancing and auditing of the managers' and employees' work, maintenance of the hotel's accounts receivable and accounts payable, processing of employee payroll and ensuring adherence to accounting standard operating procedures by all departments within the hotel. In Hotels, the Accountants have the additional responsibility for the Human Resources function. While a Regional Director of Human Resources supports them, Accountants have the opportunity to develop their Human Resources skills including interviewing, recruiting, counseling, coaching, disciplining and motivating.

The accounting opportunities in the Hotel Group are as diverse as the properties themselves. Depending on the size of the property, the Accounting Department may include up to 75 people, specializing in a number of different areas. In large hotels, a separate department maintains the Human Resources function. Functions of the Accounting Department include Accounts Payable, Accounts Receivable, Payroll, Tax, Auditing, Internal Controls and Cashier. Opportunities exist for individuals at all levels of the organization.

In Australia, a hotel may also be an establishment that serves alcoholic drinks, and usually meals in a casual setting but which does not necessarily provide accommodation. This type of establishment would more usually be called a pub or bar in other countries. In general use in Australia the terms '"hotel" and *pub* are usually taken to be synonymous. In India, the word may also refer to a restaurant since the best restaurants were always situated next to a good hotel.

The word *hotel* derives from the French *hôtel,* which referred to a French version of a townhouse, not a place offering accommodation (in contemporary usage, *hôtel* has the meaning of "hotel", and *hôtel particulier* is used for the old meaning). The French spelling (with the circumflex) was once also used in English, but is now rare. The circumflex replaces the 's' once preceding the 't' in the earlier *hostel* spelling, which over time received a new, but closely related meaning.

Services and Facilities

Basic accommodation of a room with only a bed, a cupboard, a small table and a washstand has largely been replaced by rooms with en-suite bathrooms and climate control. Other features found may be a telephone, an alarm clock, a TV, and broadband Internet connectivity. Food and drink may be supplied by a mini-bar (which often includes a small refrigerator) containing snacks and drinks (to be paid for on departure), and tea and coffee making facilities (cups, spoons, an electric kettle and sachets containing instant coffee, tea bags, sugar, and creamer or milk).

In the United Kingdom a hotel is required by law to serve food and drinks to all comers within certain stated hours; to avoid this requirement it is not uncommon to come across "private hotels" which are not subject to this requirement. However, in Japan the capsule hotel supplies minimal facilities and room space.

Classification

The cost and quality of hotels are usually indicative of the range and type of services available. Due to the enormous increase in tourism worldwide during the last decades of the 20th century, standards, especially those of smaller establishments, have improved considerably. For the sake of greater comparability, rating systems have been introduced, with the one to five stars classification being most common.

Boutique Hotels

"Boutique Hotel" is a term originating in North America to describe intimate, usually luxurious or quirky hotel environments. Boutique hotels differentiate themselves from larger chain or branded hotels by providing an exceptional and personalized level of accommodation, services and facilities. Boutique hotels are furnished in a themed, stylish and/or aspirational manner. Although usually considerably smaller than a mainstream hotel (ranging from 3 to 100 guest rooms) boutique hotels are generally fitted with telephone and wi-fi Internet connections, honesty bars and often cable/pay

TV. Guest services are attended to by 24 hour hotel staff. Many boutique hotels have on site dining facilities, and the majority offer bars and lounges which may also be open to the general public. Of the total travel market a small percentage are discerning travellers, who place a high importance on privacy, luxury and service delivery. As this market is typically corporate travelers, the market segment is non-seasonal, high-yielding and repeat, and therefore one which boutique hotel operators target as their primary source of income.

THE ACCOUNTING CYCLE

In accountancy, an account is a label used for recording and reporting a quantity of almost anything. Most often it is a record of an amount of money owned or owed by or to a particular person or entity, or allocated to a particular purpose. It may represent amounts of money that have actually changed hands, or it may represent an estimate of the values of assets, or it may be a combination of these.

Types of Accounts

1. Asset accounts: represent the different types of economic resources owned by a business, common examples of Asset accounts are cash, cash in bank, building, inventory, prepaid rent, goodwill.
2. Liability accounts: represent the different types of economic obligations by a business, such as accounts payable, bank loan, bonds payable, accrued interest.
3. Equity accounts: represent the residual equity of a business (after deducting from Assets all the liabilities) including Retained Earnings and Appropriations.
4. Revenue accounts: represent the hotel's gross earnings and common examples include Sales, Service revenue and Interest Income.
5. Expense accounts: represent the hotel's expenditures to enable itself to operate. Common examples are electricity and water, rentals, depreciation, doubtful accounts, interest, insurance.

6. Contra-accounts: from the term contra, meaning to deduct, the value of which are opposite the 5 above mentioned types of accounts. For instance, a contra-asset account is Accumulated depreciation. This label represent deductions to a relatively permanent asset like Building.

The accounting process is a series of activities that begins with a transaction and ends with the closing of the books. Because this process is repeated each reporting period, it is referred to as the *accounting cycle* and includes these major steps:

1. Identify the transaction or other recognizable event.
2. Prepare the transaction's source document such as a purchase order or invoice.
3. Analyze and classify the transaction. This step involves quantifying the transaction in monetary terms (e.g. dollars and cents), identifying the accounts that are affected and whether those accounts are to be debited or credited.
4. Record the transaction by making entries in the appropriate journal, such as the sales journal, purchase journal, cash receipt or disbursement journal, or the general journal. Such entries are made in chronological order.
5. Post general journal entries to the ledger accounts.

The above steps are performed throughout the accounting period as transactions occur or in periodic batch processes. The following steps are performed at the end of the accounting period:

6. Prepare the trial balance to make sure that debits equal credits. The trial balance is a listing of all of the ledger accounts, with debits in the left column and credits in the right column. At this point no adjusting entries have been made. The actual sum of each column is not meaningful; what is important is that the sums be equal. Note that while out-of-balance

columns indicate a recording error, balanced columns do not guarantee that there are no errors. For example, not recording a transaction or recording it in the wrong account would not cause an imbalance.

7. Correct any discrepancies in the trial balance. If the columns are not in balance, look for math errors, posting errors, and recording errors. Posting errors include:
   - Posting of the wrong amount,
   - Omitting a posting,
   - Posting in the wrong column, or
   - Posting more than once.
8. Prepare adjusting entries to record accrued, deferred, and estimated amounts.
9. Post adjusting entries to the ledger accounts.
10. Prepare the adjusted trial balance. This step is similar to the preparation of the unadjusted trial balance, but this time the adjusting entries are included. Correct any errors that may be found.
11. Prepare the financial statements.
    - Income statement: prepared from the revenue, expenses, gains, and losses.
    - Balance sheet: prepared from the assets, liabilities, and equity accounts.
    - Statement of retained earnings: prepared from net income and dividend information.
    - Cash flow statement: derived from the other financial statements using either the direct or indirect method.
12. Prepare closing journal entries that close temporary accounts such as revenues, expenses, gains, and losses. These accounts are closed to a temporary income summary account, from which the balance is transferred to the retained earnings account (capital).

Any dividend or withdrawal accounts also are closed to capital.

13. Post closing entries to the ledger accounts.
14. Prepare the after-closing trial balance to make sure that debits equal credits. At this point, only the permanent accounts appear since the temporary ones have been closed. Correct any errors.
15. Prepare reversing journal entries (optional). Reversing journal entries often are used when there has been an accrual or deferral that was recorded as an adjusting entry on the last day of the accounting period. By reversing the adjusting entry, one avoids double counting the amount when the transaction occurs in the next period. A reversing journal entry is recorded on the first day of the new period.

    Instead of preparing the financial statements before the closing journal entries, it is possible to prepare them afterwards, using a temporary income summary account to collect the balances of the temporary ledger accounts (revenues, expenses, gains, losses, etc.) when they are closed. The temporary income summary account then would be closed when preparing the financial statements.

Accounting Information System

An accounting information system (AIS) is the system of records a business keeps to maintain its accounting system. This includes the purchase, sales, and other financial processes of the business. The purpose of an AIS is to accumulate data and provide decision makers (investors, creditors, and managers) with information to make decisions. While this was previously a paper-based process, most modern businesses now use accounting software. In an Electronic Financial Accounting system the steps in accounting cycle are dependent upon the system itself. Example: some systems allow direct journal posting to the various ledgers and others do not.

Accounting Reform

Accounting reform is an expansion to accounting rules that goes beyond the realm of financial measures for both individual economic entities and national economies. It is advocated by those who consider the focus of the present standards and practices wholly inadequate to the task of measuring and reporting the activity, success, and failure of modern enterprise, including government. The basic bookkeeping concepts underlying contemporary accounting date back about 500 years to Renaissance Italian practices. Obviously, the vast majority of articulations by modern standard setters have little in common with the accounting practices then used. Real debate concerns concepts such as whether to report transactions, such as asset acquisitions, at their cost or to report them at their current market values. The former, traditional approach, appeals for its reliability but can quickly lose its relevance due to inflation and other factors; the latter, increasingly common approach, appeals for its relevance but may be less reliable due to its resort to appraisals or other subjective measures. This trade off is essentially impossible to overcome. The relative virtue of either approach depends on the subject matter in question.

Business

Limited reforms within professional management circles have led in the past to activity-based costing, economic value added, regret and risk measures. Not only do most businesses raise capital based on numbers derived from current standards, there are extensive lobbying efforts by the accounting industry to keep those standards roughly as they are: complex, loopholed, and unable to be applied or audited easily by laymen.

Heads of the U.S. Securities and Exchange Commission since the 1980s have consistently complained that this lobbying makes it impossible for them to apply meaningful reform, even in the wake of accounting scandals, e.g. that which felled Arthur Andersen in 2002.

National Economies

Any comprehensive scheme of accounting reform is a major professional and academic enterprise; Typically it requires examination of the role of each of the fundamental factors of production, an analysis of capital indicating how many types there are and how each supports each factor of a production process. A comprehensive scheme that would affect, for instance, the United Nations standards for national accounts, the rules of the Bank for International Settlements, or listing requirements on the major stock exchanges, would have to defend any change against critics that advocated lesser reforms - making it extraordinarily difficult to achieve simultaneous consent.

Marilyn Waring, who deeply criticized the UN account system for systematically under-valuing the social and economic contributions of women, stated also that she had to read literally an entire room full of books in order even to understand the standards applied today. It seems unlikely that most advocates of reform have the stamina to do so, nor the background required to debate each issue with economists or accountants that build their careers on the detailed extension and improvement of standards that already exist. Most critics considered reform prospects bleak.

The critique from ecological economics was even more fundamental, claiming that most means of measuring well-being indicated that the developed nations were in a state of "uneconomic growth" through the 1980s and 1990s, due mostly to failures of measurement, most or all of which could be tracked back to the practice of using the Gross National Product as a means of making money supply decisions. This is perhaps the most obvious and widely-held critique of current national accounting and economic growth reporting systems - the creators of the GNP and GDP measures themselves advise against its use as a single measure of economic growth - but politicians and press typically do so without caveat nor apology.

Robert Costanza, Paul Hawken, Amory Lovins and others who advocate a consistent global system for valuing natural capital, note that failures in this area are particularly grim: promoting extinction, loss of biodiversity, climate change and destructive weather for the sake of such "growth". John McMurtry characterized this as "the cancer stage of capitalism". What makes "economic sense" under current standards, they argue, is in fact leading to ecological catastrophe, social conflict, and economic chaos.

One barrier to accounting reform are governments themselves. They have the authority to determine what are accepted accounting principles, while using questionable accounting practices themselves. Governments, for example, pay off operating costs with longer-term debt and thus overstate budgetary surpluses or conceal operating deficits. This is not unlike the allegedly fraudulent practices of some corporations.

Accounting Software

Accounting software is computer software that records and processes accounting transactions within functional modules such as accounts payable, accounts receivable, payroll and trial balance. It functions as an accounting information system. It may be developed in-house by the hotel or organization using it, may be purchased from a third party, or may be a combination of a third-party application software package with local modifications. It varies greatly in its complexity and cost. Since the mid 1990s, the market has been undergoing considerable consolidation, with many suppliers ceasing to trade or being bought by larger groups.

Modules

Accounting software is typically composed of various modules, different sections dealing with particular areas of accounting. Among the most common are:

Core Modules

- *Accounts receivable*—where the hotel enters money received

- *Accounts payable*—where the hotel enters its bills and pays money it owes
- *General ledger*—the hotel's "books"
- *Billing*—where the hotel produces invoices to clients/ customers
- *Stock/Inventory*—where the hotel keeps control of its inventory
- *Purchase Orders*—where the hotel orders inventory
- *Sales Orders*—where the hotel records customer order for the supply of inventory Non Core Modules
- *Debt Collection*—where the hotel tracks attempts to collect overdue bills (sometimes part of accounts receivable)
- *Expense*—where employee business-related expenses are entered
- *Inquiries*—where the hotel looks up information on screen without any edits or additions
- *Payroll*—where the hotel tracks salary, wages, and related taxes
- *Reports*—where the hotel prints out data
- *Timesheet*—where professionals (such as attorneys and consultants) record time worked so that it can be billed to clients

PERSONAL ACCOUNTING

Mainly for home users that use accounts payable type accounting transactions, managing budgets and simple account reconciliation at the inexpensive end of the market suppliers include:

Low End

At the low end of the business markets, inexpensive applications software allows most general business accounting functions to be performed. Suppliers frequently serve a single national market, while larger suppliers offer separate solutions in each national market.

Many of the low end products are characterized by being "single-entry" products, as opposed to double-entry systems seen in many businesses. Some products have considerable functionality but are not considered GAAP or FASB compliant. Some low-end systems do not have adequate security nor audit trails.

Mid Market

The mid-market covers a wide range of business software that may be capable of serving the needs of multiple national accountancy standards and allow accounting in multiple currencies. In addition to general accounting functions, the software may include integrated or add-on management information systems, and may be oriented towards one or more markets, for example with integrated or add-on project accounting modules.

Software applications in this market typically include the following features:

- Industry-standard robust databases (eg Microsoft SQL, Oracle, Pervasive)
- Industry-standard reporting tools (eg Cognos, Crystal)
- Tools for configuring or extending the application (eg an SDK, access to program code, the ability to be controlled via Visual Basic for Applications (VBA))

High End

The most complex and expensive business accounting software is frequently part of an extensive suite of software often known as Enterprise resource planning or *ERP* software. These applications typically have a very long implementation period, often greater than six months. In many cases, these applications are simply a set of functions which require significant integration, configuration and customisation to even begin to resemble an accounting system.

The advantage of a high-end solution is that these systems are designed to support individual hotel specific processes, as they are highly customisable and can be tailored to exact business requirements. This usually comes at a significant cost in terms of money and implementation time.

Vertical Market

Some business accounting software is designed for specific business types. It will include features that are specific to that industry. The choice of whether to purchase an industry-specific application or a general-purpose application is often very difficult. Concerns over a custom-build application or one designed for a specific industry include:

- Smaller development team
- Increased risk of vendor business failing
- Reduced availability of support

This can be weighed up against:

- Less requirement for customisation
- Reduced implementation costs
- Reduced end-user training time and costs

Some important types of vertical accounting software are:

- Banking
- Construction
- Medical
- Point of Sale (Retail)

Use by Non Accountants

With the increasing dominance of having financial accounts prepared with Accounting Software, as well as some suppliers claims that anyone can prepare their own books, accounting software can be considered at risk of not providing appropriate information as non-accountants prepare accounting information. As recording and interpretation is left to software and expert systems, the necessity to have a Systems Accountant overseeing the accountancy system becomes ever more important. The set up of the processes and the end result must be vigorously checked and maintained on a regular basis in order to develop and maintain the integrity of the data and the processes that manage this data.

MANAGEMENT ACCOUNTING

Management accounting is concerned with the provisions and use of accounting information to managers within organizations, to provide them with the basis in making informed business decisions that would allow them to be better equipped in their management and control functions. Unlike financial accountancy information (which, for the most part, is public information), management accounting information is used within an organization (typically for decision-making) and is usually confidential and access to which is only available to a select few.

According to CIMA, The Chartered Institute of Management Accountants, Management Accounting is "the process of identification, measurement, accumulation, analysis, preparation, interpretation and communication of information used by management to plan, evaluate and control within an entity and to assure appropriate use of and accountability for its resources. Management accounting also comprises the preparation of financial reports for non management groups such as shareholders, creditors, regulatory agencies and tax authorities" (CIMA Official Terminology)

Aims

1. Formulating strategies;
2. Planning and constructing business activities;
3. Making decisions;
4. Well use of resources;
5. Supporting financial reports preparation; and
6. Safeguarding assets.

Traditional vs. Innovative Management Accounting

In the late 1980s, accounting practitioners and educators were heavily criticized on the grounds that management accounting practices (and, even more so, the curriculum taught to accounting students) had changed little over the preceding 60 years, despite radical changes in the business environment. Professional accounting institutes, perhaps fearing that management accountants would increasingly be seen as superfluous in business organizations, subsequently devoted considerable resources to the development of a more innovative skills set for management accountants. The distinction between 'traditional' and 'innovative' management accounting practices can be illustrated by reference to cost control techniques. Traditionally, management accountants' principal technique was *variance analysis*, which is a systematic approach to the comparison of the actual and budgeted costs of the raw materials and Labour used during a production period.

While some form of variance analysis is still used by most manufacturing firms, it nowadays tends to be used in conjunction with innovative techniques such as *life cycle cost analysis* and *activity-based costing*, which are designed with specific aspects of the modern business environment in mind. *Lifecycle costing* recognizes that managers' ability to influence the cost of manufacturing a product is at its greatest when the product is still at the design stage of its product lifecycle (i.e., before the design has been finalised and production commenced), since small changes to the product design may lead to significant savings in the cost of manufacturing the product. *Activity-based costing* (ABC) recognizes that, in modern factories, most manufacturing costs are determined by the amount of 'activities' (e.g., the number of production runs per month, and the amount of production equipment idle time) and that the key to effective cost control is therefore optimizing the efficiency of these activities. Activity-based accounting is also known as *Cause and Effect accounting.*

Both lifecycle costing and activity-based costing recognize that, in the typical modern factory, the avoidance of disruptive events (such as machine breakdowns and quality control failures) is of far greater importance than (for example) reducing the costs of raw materials. Activity-based costing also deemphasizes direct Labour as a cost driver and concentrates instead on acitivities that drive costs, such as the provision of a service or the production of a product component.

Development of Throughput Accounting

The most significant recent direction in managerial accounting is throughput accounting, which recognizes the interdependencies of modern production processes and provide managers with a tool that will allow them to measure the contribution per unit of constrained resource for any given product, customer or supplier.

An Alternative View

A seldom expressed alternative view of management accounting is that it is neither a neutral or benign influence in organizations, rather a mechanism for management control through surveillance. This view locates management accounting specifically in the context of management control theory.

In throughput accounting, the cost accounting aspect of Theory of Constraints (TOC), operating expense is the money spent turning inventory into throughput. In TOC, operating expense is limited to costs that vary strictly with the quantity produced, like raw materials and purchased components. Everything else is a fixed cost, including labour unless there is a regular and significant chance that workers will not work a full-time week when they report on its first day.

FINANCIAL ACCOUNTANCY

Financial accountancy (or financial accounting) is the branch of accountancy concerned with the preparation of financial statements for decision makers, such as stockholders, suppliers, banks, government agencies, owners, and other stakeholders. The fundamental need for financial accounting is to reduce principal-agent problem by measuring and monitoring agents' performance and reporting the results to interested users. Financial Accountancy is used to prepare accounting information for people outside the organisation or not involved in the day to day running of the hotel. Managerial accounting provides accounting information to help managers make decisions to manage the business. Financial Accountancy is governed by both local and international accounting standards.

Basic Accounting Concepts

The accounting equation (Assets = Liabilities + Owners' Equity) and financial statements are the main topics of financial accounting. The trial balance which is usually prepared using the Double-entry accounting system forms the basis for preparing the financial statements. All the figures in the trial balance are rearranged to prepare a profit and loss statement and balance sheet. There are certain accounting standards that determine the format for these accounts (SSAP, FRS, IFS). The financial statements will display the income and expenditure for the hotel and a summary of the assets, liabilities, and shareholders or owners' equity of the hotel on the date the accounts were prepared to.

or

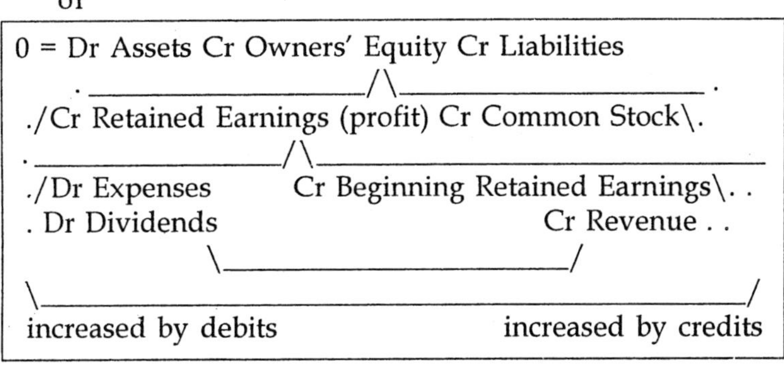

Thus —Crediting a credit / Debiting a debit→ account increases its absolute value (balance)

Thus —Debiting a credit / Crediting a debit→ account decreases its absolute value (balance)

Meaning of the Accounting Equation

The value of a hotel can be understood simply as the useful assets that ownership of a hotel entitles one to claim. This value is known as Owners' Equity. Some assets of a hotel, however, cannot be claimed as equity by the owners of a hotel because other people have legal claim to them - for example if the hotel has borrowed money from the bank. The value of a resource claimable by a non-owner is called a liability. All of the Assets of a hotel can be claimed by someone, whether owner or not, so the sum of a hotel's equity and its liabilities must equal the value of its Assets. Thus the accounting equation describes what portion of a hotel's assets can by claimed by the owners.

Various account types are classified as 'credit' or 'debit' depending on the role they play in the accounting equation.

Assets = Liabilities + Equity *or* Assets - Liabilities - Equity = 0

Another way of stating it is:

Equity = Assets - Liabilities

which can be interpreted as: "Equity is what is left if all assets have been sold and all liabilities have been paid".

FORENSIC ACCOUNTING

Forensic accounting is the specialty practice area of accounting that describes engagements which result from actual or anticipated disputes or litigation. 'Forensic' means suitable for use in Court, and it is to that standard and potential outcome that forensic accountants generally have to work. Forensic accountants often have to give expert evidence at the eventual trial. All of the larger accounting firms, as well as many medium-sized and boutique firms have specialist forensic accounting departments. Within these groups, there may be further sub-specialisations: some forensic accountants may for example just specialise in insurance claims, personal injury claims, fraud, construction, or royalty audits.

Engagements relating to civil disputes may fall into several categories: calculating and quantifying losses and economic damages, whether suffered through tort or breach of contract; disagreements relating to hotel acquisitions - perhaps earn outs or breaches of warranties; and business valuation. Forensic accountants often assist in professional negligence claims where they are assessing and commenting on the work of other professionals.

Engagements relating to criminal matters typically arise in the aftermath of fraud. They frequently involve the assessment of accounting systems and accounts presentation - in essence assessing if the numbers reflect reality.

Forensic accountants may be involved in recovering proceeds of crime and in relation to confiscation proceedings concerning actual or assumed proceeds of crime or money laundering. In the UK, relevant legislation is contained in the Proceeds of Crime Act 2002. Many forensic accountants are also Certified Fraud Examiners and/or Certified Public Accountants.

Forensic accountants utilize an understanding of business information and financial reporting systems, accounting and auditing standards and procedures, evidence gathering and investigative techniques, and litigation processes and procedures to perform their work. Forensic accountants are also increasingly playing more proactive risk reduction roles by designing and performing extended procedures as part of the statutory audit, acting as advisors to audit committees, and assisting in investment analyst research.

CREATIVE ACCOUNTING

Creative accounting and earnings management are euphemisms referring to accounting practices that may or may not follow the letter of the rules of standard accounting practices but certainly deviate from the spirit of those rules. They are characterized by excessive complication and the use of novel ways of characterizing income, assets or liabilities. The terms "innovative" or "aggressive" are also sometimes used.

The term as generally understood refers to systematic misrepresentation of the true income and assets of corporations or other organizations. "Creative accounting" is at the root of a number of accounting scandals, and many proposals for accounting reform - usually centering on an updated analysis of capital and factors of production that would correctly reflect how value is added. Newspaper and television journalists have hypothesized that the stock market downturn of 2002 was precipitated by reports of accounting irregularities at the Enron, Worldcom, and other business entities in the United States. One commonly accepted incentive for the systemic over-reporting of corporate income which came to light in 2002 was the granting of stock options as part of executive compensation packages. Since stock prices reflect earning reports, stock options could be most profitably exercised when income is exaggerated, and the stock can be sold at an inflated profit.

The most notable activist is Abraham Briloff (professor emeritus of CUNY Baruch) who for years wrote a column for *Barron's* that constantly analyzed breaches of ethics and audit professionalism among CPA firms. His most famous book is called *Unaccountable Accounting*. The profession, in turn, was not kind to Dr. Briloff but much of what he advocated has been forced on the industry in the wake of the Enron scandal. A lesser usage is in professional humor, when accountants poke fun at each other's more esoteric accountancy practices. According to critic David Ehrenstein, the term "Creative Accounting" was first used in 1968 in the film *The Producers* by Mel Brooks.

Creative Accounting Tactics

Although not technically wrong, many annual and quarterly reports and presentations dive heavily into theoretical scenarios where "one-time charges" to earnings are excluded. What this means is for example, a law suit settlement amount would be taken out of the reported profit in one big chunk, even if it is paid out little by little over time (this practice is called reserving). Often, when explaining the quarterly results, a CEO might say "Well if we didn't take this charge for the law suit, we would have made this much money". Very often, the hypothetical situations proposed get even more complicated. The main "creative" aspect to this is when a "one time" "exceptional" charge really is something that is very common to the business.

- Banks are able to lend out most of the money they receive in deposit (they also can lend money they borrow from other banks). However, to protect against bad loans, banks must keep aside a supply of money called a "reserve". The bank, within general guidelines, gets to set the size of this reserve to what it feels is prudent compared to how risky its outstanding loans are. However, when the bank wants to make it look like it made more money this quarter than last, one way to do that is to take money from the reserve and call it profit with the excuse that the loans are safer now than before and that amount was no longer needed.
- One of the main genres of "creative accounting" is known as slush fund accounting, whereby some earnings from this quarter are hidden away just in case the profit from next quarter is not enough for the management to make their bonuses. This happened most famously at Freddie Mac. As of 2004 there is a large investigation underway to see if retroactive insurance policies from insurers such as General Re of Berkshire Hathaway were used for slush fund accounting. The question is if these insurance policies truly transferred some risk or were merely a slush fund.
- Creative accounting is not limited to large firms with banks of accountants. Smaller companies often use creative accounting, but for tax saving purposes rather than meeting bonuses or shareholder expectations. Salaries are sometimes included in profits to benefit from corporation tax rates being lower than personal tax rates and spouses are sometimes put on the books as employees though they may never have worked for the hotel. As smaller companies are generally subject to less onerous rules - and many of them fall below the limit required for a full annual audit every year - much of the creative accounting in this sector does not get a lot of publicity.

TRIAL BALANCE

If the journal entries are error-free and were posted properly to the general ledger, the total of all of the debit balances should equal the total of all of the credit balances. If the debits do not equal the credits, then an error has occurred somewhere in the process. The total of the accounts on the debit and credit side is referred to as the *trial balance.*

To calculate the trial balance, first determine the balance of each general ledger account as shown in the following example:

General Ledger

Cash						*Accounts Receivable*					
Sep	1	7500	Sep	15	100	Sep	17	700	Sep	25	425
	17	400		28	500						
	25	425									
Bel.		6825				Bel.	275				
Parts Inventory						*Accountable payble*					
Sep	8	250C	Sep	18	275	Sep	28	500	Sep		8 250C
Bal.		2225							Bal.		2000
Capital						*Revenue*					
Sep	1	750C				Sep	17	1100			
Bal.		7500				Bal.		1100			
Expenses											
Sep	15	1000									
Sep	18	275									
Bal.		1275									

Once the account balances are known, the trial balance can be calculated as shown:

Trial Balance

Account Title	*Debits*	*Credits*
Cash	6825	
Accounts Receivable	275	
Parts Inventory	2225	
Accounts Payable		2000
Capital		7500
Revenue		1100
Expenses	1275	
	10600	10600

In this example, the debits and credits balance. This result does not guarantee that there are no errors. For example, the trial balance would not catch the following types of errors:

- Transactions that were not recorded in the journal
- Transactions recorded in the wrong accounts
- Transactions for which the debit and credit were transposed
- Neglecting to post a journal entry to the ledger

If the trial balance is not in balance, then an error has been made somewhere in the accounting process. The following is listing of common errors that would result in an unbalanced trial balance; this listing can be used to assist in isolating the cause of the imbalance.

1. Summation error for the debits and credits of the trial balance
2. Error transferring the ledger account balances to the trial balance columns
    - Error in numeric value
    - Error in transferring a debit or credit to the proper column
    - Omission of an account
3. Error in the calculation of a ledger account balance
4. Error in posting a journal entry to the ledger
    - Error in numeric value
    - Error in posting a debit or credit to the proper column
5. Error in the journal entry
    - Error in a numeric value
    - Omission of part of a compound journal entry

The more often that the trial balance is calculated during the accounting cycle, the easier it is to isolate any errors; more frequent trial balance calculations narrow the time frame in which an error might have occurred, resulting in fewer transactions through which to search.

JOURNAL ENTRIES

Closing Entries

At the end of the accounting period, the balances in temporary accounts are transferred to an income summary account and a retained earnings account, thereby resetting the balance of the temporary accounts to zero to begin the next accounting period.

First, the revenue accounts are closed by transferring their balances to the income summary account. Consider the following example for which September 30 is the end of the accounting period. If the revenue account balance is $1100, then the closing journal entry would be:

Date	*Accounts*	*Debit*	*Credit*
9/30	Revenue	1100	
	Income Summary	1100	

Next, the expense accounts are closed by transferring their balances to the income summary account. If the expense account balance is $1275, then the closing entry would be:

Date	*Accounts*	*Debit*	*Credit*
9/30	Income Summary	1275	
	Expenses		1275

At this point, the net balance of the income summary account is a $175 debit (loss). The income summary account then is closed to retained earnings:

Date	*Accounts*	*Debit*	*Credit*
9/30	Retained Earnings	175	
	Income Summary		175

Finally, the dividends account is closed to retained earnings. For example, if $50 in dividends were paid during the period, the closing journal entry would be as follows:

Date	*Accounts*	*Debit*	*Credit*
9/30	Retained Earnings	50	
	Dividends		50

Once posted to the ledger, these journal entries serve the purpose of setting the temporary revenue, expense, and dividend accounts back to zero in preparation for the start of the next accounting period.

Note that the income summary account is not absolutely necessary - the revenue and expense accounts could be closed directly to retained earnings. The income summary account offers the benefit of indicating the net balance between revenue and expenses (i.e. net income) during the closing process.

Reversing Entries

When an adjusting entry is made for an expense at the end of the accounting period, it is necessary to keep track of this expense so that the transaction will be allocated properly between the two periods. *Reversing entries* are a way to handle such transactions.

Consider the case in which a note is issued on the 16th of September, with interest payable on the 15th of October. If the total interest to be paid at the end of the 30 day period is $100, then half of the amount would be allocated to the month of September using the following adjusting journal entry:

Period-End Adjusting Entry

Date	*Accounts Title*	*Debit*	*Credit*
9/30	Interest Expense	50	
	Interest Payable		50
	15 days of accrued interest.		

On October 15, the 30 days of interest will be paid as a $100 lump sum. If the bookkeeper remembers that half of that interest already was recorded as an expense in September, then he or she can record only $50 as the interest expense for October. Alternatively, a *reversing entry* can be made at the beginning of October as follows:

Reversing Entry

Date	*Accounts Title*	*Debit*	*Credit*
10/1	Interest Payable	50	
	Interest Expense		50
	Reversing entry for		
	15 days of interest accrued in Sep.		

Note that the above journal entry is exactly the reverse of the adjusting entry made on September 30. Once this reversing entry is posted, the affected ledger accounts will appear as follows:

Ledger Accounts After Reversing Entry

Interest Payable

Oct	1	50	Sep	3C	50
				Bal.	0

Interest Expense

			Oct	1	50
				Bal.	50

The interest payable account carried a credit balance of $50 over to the new period, and this balance became zero when the October 1 reversing entry was posted. Because the interest expense ledger account was closed at the end of the reporting period on September 30 (as were all expense accounts), its balance was reset to zero at that time. After the posting of the reversing entry on October 1, the interest expense ledger account had a credit balance (i.e. a negative expense balance) of $50.

On Oct 15, the note matures and the $100 interest is due. Because the reversing entry was made on Oct 1, the Oct 15 entry is for the full $100 that is due on the note, and is recorded as follows:

October 15 Journal Entry

Date	*Accounts Title*	*Debit*	*Credit*
10/15	Interest Expense	100	
	Interest Payable		100
	Interest for Sep 16 through Oct 15.		

The ledger accounts will appear as follows once the journal entries through October 15 are posted:

Interest Payable

Oct	1	50	Sep	3C	50
			Oct	15	100
				Bal.	100

Interest Expense

Oct	15	100	Oct	1	50
	Bal.	50			

The net interest expense for October then is $50, as it should be since the other $50 already was reported in September.

As can be seen in the ledger accounts, the net effect is that a $50 interest expense will be realized in October, and the full $100 of interest will be paid to the holder of the note.

Reversing entries are a useful tool for dealing with certain accruals and deferrals. Their use is optional and depends on the accounting practices of the particular firm and the specific responsibilities of the bookkeeping staff.

LEDGER

A ledger (from the English dialect forms *liggen* or *leggen*, to lie or lay; in sense adapted from the Dutch substantive *logger*), is the principal book for recording transactions in the hotel. Originally, the term referred to a book remaining regularly in one place, and so it was used of the copies of the Scriptures and service books kept in a church. According to Charles Wriothesley's *Chronicle* (1538):

> *The curates should provide a booke of the bible in Englishe, of the largest volume, to be a lidger in the same church for the parishioners to read on.*

It is an application of this original meaning that is found in the commercial usage of the term for the principal book of account in a business house. Apart from these applications to various forms of books, the word is used for

- A small line immediately above or below the musical staff to contain a note such as middle C on the leger line just below the a staff with a treble clef, or an octave higher than concert A, or Hi A on the highland bagpipe, just above the staff with a treble clef. (often spelled leger)
- The horizontal timbers in a scaffold lying parallel to the face of a building, which support the "put logs" (also known by ligger);
- A flat stone to cover a grave, often inscribed as a memorial;
- A stationary form of tackle and bait in angling.

In the form "lieger", the term was formerly frequently applied to a "resident", as distinguished from an "extraordinary" ambassador.

LEDGER POSTINGS

The process of posting account payable transactions in Peoplesoft creates balanced accounting entries that can be transferred to a General Ledger system. Peoplesoft creates accounting entries for all payments. Posting payments in Peoplesoft Payables creates balanced accounting entries for all payment-related transactions. Payment-related transactions include manual payments, drafts, electronic funds transfers, system created and cancelled payments. After these accounting entries are generated, they are available for General Ledger journal generation.

The Payment posting run is activated by the production of cheques. Debits are made to creditor control accounts and the corresponding credit is made to the bank account. Note the accounting examples shown below. Entries are also made as necessary to foreign currency gain and loss accounts. Overall, the effect of this run is a 'clearing' of the creditors control to the extent of the total amount being paid in the cheque run. The Voucher posting run carried out by the Accounts Payable System posts transactions for claims and credit notes that have been budget checked. The creditors control accounts are recorded and the various expense accounts indicated by individual document lines are charged. The document posting run reports expenditure movements on non-salary expense account codes within each cost centre.

The University cash flow is monitored to ensure that sufficient funds are available to cover the cheques. The following examples illustrate the current accounting treatment for authorised and verified accounts payable.

1. A voucher claim is processed for the supply of five different items purchased for direct use. The claim has a system status of *postable* and is automatically selected by the system for posting to the ledger and acquittal of commitment.

DR Expense (e.g., materials, services, publications, etc.) $1,000

CR Creditors Control $1,000

Individual document lines are posted to department/ section and by expense account.

2. Two of the five items purchased are found to be faulty and are returned to the supplier. A credit note is issued for the full cost of the two items, and is authorised and verified.

   DR Creditors Control $400

   CR Expense $400

   The credit note line amount produces a credit adjustment to the account charging of the associated claim line. The vouchers are posted to the actuals (cash) ledger.

3. A cheque is drawn to pay the supplier the net amount owing.

   DR Creditors Control $600

   CR Bank $600

   The vouchers are posted to the actuals (cash) ledger.

Voucher Processing

In order for a voucher to be eligible for posting, it must meet the following criteria.

- All save validations passed
- Passed budget checking
- If Purchase Order Voucher - Matched (if applicable)
- Purchase Order must be posted (if applicable)
- Approved
- Entry Status set to postable
- The post checkbox clicked on
- Not already posted

Once a voucher has been posted, only its non-accounting information can be modified. If a change to accounting information is required for a posted voucher, you must first unpost it.

Payment Posting-Processing

Running payment posting allows you to create accounting entries for payments applied to vouchers. These accounting entries are then available for general ledger journal creation using the Journal generator. The Vouchers and Payments should be posted on any weeknight. Journal generators and General Ledger Interfaces should also be run on weeknights. If a voucher is unposted, any posted payments for that voucher will be automatically unposted.

To post a payment, use the following path in ESP Go ® Administer Procurement ® Create Payments ® Process ® Payment Posting Request ® Add or Update/Display

GENERAL LEDGER

The general ledger, sometimes known as the nominal ledger, is the main accounting record of a hotel business which uses double-entry bookkeeping. It will usually include accounts for such items as current assets, fixed assets, liabilities, revenue and expense items, gains and losses. The general ledger is a summary of all of the transactions that occur in the hotel. It is built up by posting transactions recorded in the general journal. There are seven basic categories in which all accounts are grouped:

1. Asset
2. Liability
3. Owner's equity
4. Revenue
5. Expense
6. Gains
7. Losses

The balance sheet and the income statement are both derived from the general ledger. Each account in the general ledger consists of one or more pages. The general ledger is where posting to the accounts occurs. Posting is the process of recording amounts as credits, (right side), and amounts as debits, (left side), in the pages of the general ledger. The listing of the account names and the sum of the account balances is called a trial balance. The purpose of the trial balance is, at a preliminary stage of the financial statement preparation process, to ensure the equality of the total debits and credits.

The general ledger should include the date, description and balance or total amount for each account. It is usually divided into at least seven main categories. These categories generally include assets, liabilities, owner's equity, revenue, expenses, gains and losses. The main categories of the general ledger may be further subdivided into sub-ledgers to include additional details of such accounts as cash, accounts receivable, accounts payable, etc. Because each bookkeeping entry debits one account and credits another account in an equal amount, the double-entry bookkeeping system will ensure that the general ledger will always be in balance; thus maintaining the accounting equation:

Assets = Liabilities + Shareholders' Equity

The accounting equation is the mathematical structure of the balance sheet.

FINANCIAL STATEMENTS

Financial statements (or financial reports) are a record of a hotel financial flows (revenues/expenses) and levels (assets/liabilities). Because these statements are often complex an extensive set of Notes to the Financial Statements and management discussion and analysis is usually included. The notes will typically describe each item on the Balance Sheet, Income statement and Cash flow statement in further detail. In many cases the notes are much longer than the financial statement they are elucidating.

The reason financial statements are required by many statutes is to require management of the enterprise to report to the owners and government. Debtholders, suppliers and employees, as well as internal mangement are other users of the statements. The POV of the statements though, is for the owner's use. Accounting is the language of finance. Financial statement presentation rules are the grammar. The statements are necessary for owners to asses management and make rational economic decisions.

Once the adjusting entries have been made or entered into a worksheet, the financial statements can be prepared using information from the ledger accounts. Because some of the financial statements use data from the other statements, the following is a logical order for their preparation:

- Income statement
- Statement of retained earnings
- Balance sheet
- Cash flow statement

Income Statement

The income statement reports revenues, expenses, and the resulting net income. It is prepared by transferring the following ledger account balances, taking into account any adjusting entries that have been or will be made:

- Revenue
- Expenses
- Capital gains or losses

Statement of Retained Earnings

The retained earnings statement shows the retained earnings at the beginning and end of the accounting period. It is prepared using the following information:

- Beginning retained earnings, obtained from the previous statement of retained earnings.
- Net income, obtained from the income statement
- Dividends paid during the accounting period

Balance Sheet

Balance sheet which describes a hotel's assets, liabilities and net equity at both a specific point of time and at the beginning of the period of time. It is constructed using the following information:

- Balances of all asset accounts such cash, accounts receivable, etc.
- Balances of all liability accounts such as accounts payable, notes, etc.
- Capital stock balance
- Retained earnings, obtained from the statement of retained earnings

Cash Flow Statement

The cash flow statement explains the reasons for changes in the cash balance, showing sources and uses of cash in the operating, financing, and investing activities of the hotel. Because the cash flow statement is a cash-basis report, it cannot be derived directly from the ledger account balances of an accrual accounting system. Rather, it is derived by converting the accrual information to a cash-basis using one of the following two methods:

- *Direct method:* Cash flow information is derived by directly subtracting cash disbursements from cash receipts.
- *Indirect method:* Cash flow information is derived by adding or subtracting non-cash items from net income.

Analogy of Financial statements

Knowing is not the same as understanding, so it is helpful to present an analogy.

- Think of an investment as a water reservoir. The value of the investment is the volume of water in it. The shareholder equity on the balance sheet measures this value.

- Streams empty into the reservoir, adding more water. These inflows are measured by revenues on the income statement.
- Streams run out of the reservoir, depleting it. These outflow are measured by expenses on the income statement.
- When a neighbour joins in the investment as a partner, he digs a canal from his own reservoir so it drains into yours. This additional water is measured by an increase in the share capital.
- When employees install an underground pipe to drain the reservoir into one of their own, the value of the investment falls. This draw is for stock options. Historically this drain has not been measured, and even now is not fully measured.

While measuring the volume of water in the reservoir at a point in time (balance sheet) is relatively easy, keeping track of the streams' volumes at every second of the year is difficult. Accountants may choose to ignore some streams: they may not know some streams exist: water may be evaporating, and unmeasurable. As a result the income statement is easily wrong. Regardless, the net sum of inflows less outflows should equal the difference in the reservoir (beginning vs. ending). The statement of changes in shareholder equity attempts this reconciliation.

None of the financial statements measures your own personal share of the reservoir when you have partners. It is up to the individual investor to measure, not the business totals, but his share. The methods to use 'equity per share' is shown at shareholders' equity.

Government Financial Statements

The rules for measurement and presentation of a government's financials may be different from those required for business and even for non-profit organizations. They may use either accrual accounting, or cash accounting, or a combination of the two. Because most governments may not lawfully spend money previously approved in a budget, the financial results are usually presented side by side with the budget.

Audit

Although the legal statues differ, most jurisdictions require an audit of the financials, by independent accountants, of all hotel businesses. Private ones can waive the requirement. Note that the auditors do not certify financial statements, that is done by the hotel's directors. All an auditor does is give an opinion on whether they are "true and fair" (or meet other particular requirements that the auditor is engaged to opine on).

There has been much legal debate over who an auditor is liable to. Since audit reports tend to be addressed to the current shareholders, it is commonly thought that they owe a legal duty of care to them. But this may not be the case as determined by common law precedent. In Canada, auditors are liable only to investors using a prospectus to buy shares in the primary market. In the UK, they have been held liable to potential investors when the auditor was aware of the potential investor and how they would use the information in the financial statements. Nowadays auditors tend to include in their report liability restricting language, discouraging anyone other than the addressees of their report from relying on it. Liability is an important issue: in the UK, for example, auditors have unlimited liability.

In the United States, especially in the post-Enron era there has been substantial concern about the accuracy of financial statements. Corporate officiers (the CEO and CFO) are personally liable for attesting that financial statements "do not contain any untrue statement of a material fact or omit to state a material fact necessary to make the statements made, in light of the circumstances under which such statements were made, not misleading with respect to the period covered by th[e] report". Making or certifiing misleading financial statements exposes the people involved to substantial civil and criminal liability. For example Bernie Ebbers (former CEO of WorldCom) was sentenced to 25 years in federal prison for allowing WorldCom's revenues to be overstated by $11 billion over five years.

Standards and Regulation

To ensure that financial statements prepared by different companies can be adequately compared, they must be prepared according to certain rules. Countries under the common law legal system usually follow guidelines set in generally accepted accounting principles ("GAAP"). National accounting bodies in each country have developed their own specific sets of accounting principles. Different countries have developed their own accounting principles over time, making international comparisons of companies difficult. Recently there has been a push towards standardising accounting rules made by the International Accounting Standards Board ("IASB"). IASB develops International Financial Reporting Standards that have been adopted by Australia, Canada and the European Union (for publicly quoted companies only), are under consideration in South Africa and other countries. The United States Federal Accounting Standards Board has made a commitment to converge the US GAAP and IFRS over time.

Inclusion in Annual Report

To entice new investors, most public companies assemble their financial statements on fine paper with pleasing graphics and photos in an annual report to shareholders, attempting to capture the excitement and culture of the organization in a "marketing brochure" of sorts. Usually the hotel's chief executive will write a letter to shareholders, describing the financial year in the most favorable light. In the United States, prior to the advent of the internet, the annual report was the main way that a corporation communicated with individual shareholders. Blue chip companies went to great expense to produce and mail out attractive annual reports to every shareholder. The annual report was often prepared in the style of a coffee table book. Financial statements and records have been produced for as far back as there has been human writing. The people in the old Mesopotamian societies operated both insurance and credit corporations, and had the obvious need of record keeping.

Chapter 2

Statement of Income and Balance Sheet of Hotel

INCOME

Income, generally defined, is the money that is received as a result of the normal business activities of a hotel business. For example, for individuals income usually means the gross amount on their payslips, i.e. amount before any tax and other deductions has been made by their employer. Internationally, the accounting term income is synonymous to term revenue. One of the best accounting definitions of income is the one used by International Accounting Standards Board (quotation from IFRS Framework):

> *Income is increases in economic benefits during the accounting period in the form of inflows or enhancements of assets or decreases of liabilities that result in increases in equity, other than those relating to contributions from equity participants.*

Meaning within U.S. Accountancy

In U.S. business and accounting, however, income most often means the amount of money that a hotel earns after paying for all its costs. Outside the U.S., the term is usually profit or earnings. To calculate a hotel's income, it starts with its amount of revenue, deducts all costs, including such things as employees' salaries and depreciation, and the number that results is its income, which may be a negative number. This money is typically reinvested in the business, paid in corporate tax and used to pay the owners (the shareholders) a dividend.

All public companies are required to provide financial statements on a quarterly basis. The statement of income is an important part of this. Some companies also provide a more rosy financial report of their income, with *pro forma* reporting, or, EBITDA reporting. *Pro forma* income is an estimate of how much the hotel would have earned without including the negative effect of exceptional "one-time events", supposedly in order to show investors how much money the hotel would have made under normal circumstances if these exceptional, one-time events had not occurred. Critics charge that, in most cases, the "one-time events" are normal business events, such as an acquisition of another hotel or a write off of a cancelled project or division, and that *pro forma* reporting is an attempt to mislead investors by painting a rosy financial picture. Besides that, when discussing results with analysts and shareholders, CEOs and CFOs have a tendency to do even more "hypothetical accounting". EBITDA stands for "earnings before interest, taxes, depreciation, and amortisation", and is also criticised for being an attempt to mislead investors. Warren Buffett has criticised EBITDA reporting, famously asking, "Does management think the tooth fairy pays for capital expenditures?"

It is common for some other companies, such as real estate investment trusts, to present reports using a standard called FFO, or "Funds From Operations". Like EBITDA reporting, FFO ignores depreciation and amortization. This is widely accepted in the industry, as real estate values tend to increase rather than decrease over time, and many data sites report earnings per share data using FFO.

Meaning within Economic Science

In Economics, income is the constraint to unlimited consumer purchases. Consumers can purchase a limited number of goods represented by their "budget constraint". The basic equation for this is Y = Px × x + Py × y, where Px is the price of good x, x is the quantity of good x, and Y is the income (Py and y are similar to Px and x). If you need to examine more than two goods, you can add more on. This equation tells us two things. First, if you buy one more of good x, you get Px/Py less of good y. Here, Px/Py is known as the rate of substitution. Secondly, if the price of x changes, then the rate of substitution changes. This causes demand curves to slope down. While it may make some sense to suppose that an individual has a limited income for the time being, the level of income is not fixed over time. The same person can gain more productive skills or acquire more productive income-earning assets to earn a higher income. This part is the subject of theory of economic development. Again, something may happen to the economy beyond the control of the individual to reduce (or increase) the flow of income. This would be studied by theory of business cycle.

Distribution of Income

The distribution of income within a society can be measured by the Lorenz curve and the Gini coefficient. This may reveal the existence of politically unacceptable inequality of income. There may be strong political pressure to adopt policies of income redistribution by taxing the richer people at a higher rate than the middle class and giving subsidies or income-support to the very poor in a variety of ways. Political economy tends to be highly controversial because people have conflicting opinion regarding income redistribution.

National income, measured by statistics such as the Net National Income (NNI), measures the total income of all individuals in the economy.

Optimal Gini-coefficient

In their study for the World Institute for Development Economics Research, Giovanni Andrea Cornia and Julius Court (2001) reach policy conclusions as to the optimal distribution of wealth. The authors recommend to pursue moderation also as to the distribution of wealth and particularly to avoid the extremes. Both very high egalitarianism and very high inequality cause slow growth. Extreme egalitarianism leads to incentive-traps, free-riding, high operation costs and corruption in the redistribution system, all reducing a country's growth potential.

However also extreme inequality diminishes growth potential through the erosion of social cohesion, increasing social unrest and social conflict causing uncertainty of property rights. Therefore public policy should target an 'efficient inequality range'. The authors claim that such efficiency range roughly lies between the values of the Gini coefficients of 25 (the inequality value of a typical Northern European country) and 40 (that of countries such as China and the USA). The precise shape of the inequality-growth relationship depicted in the Chart obviously varies across countries depending upon their resource endowment, history, remaining levels of absolute poverty and available stock of social programmes, as well as on the distribution of physical and human capital.

Income as Moral

Throughout history, many scholars have written about the impact of income growth on morality and society. In particular, a number of scholars have come to the conclusion that material progress and prosperity, as manifested in continuous income growth at both individual and national level, provide the indispensable foundation for sustaining any kind of morality. This argument was explicitly given by Adam Smith in his *Theory of Moral Sentiments,* and has more recently been developed in depth by Harvard economists Benjamin Friedman in his well-acclaimed recent book *The Moral Consequences of Economic Growth.*

INCOME STATEMENT

Income statements for hotels indicate how Net Revenue (money received from the sale of products and services before expenses are taken out, also known as the "top line") is transformed into Net Income (the result after all revenues and expenses have been accounted for, also known as the "bottom line"). The purpose of the income statement is to show managers and investors whether the hotel made or lost money during the period being reported. Also called Profit and Loss Statement (PandL), outside the USA or in reference to charitable organizations Statement of Activities and Changes in Net Assets.

Usefulness and Limitations of Income Statement

Income statement should help investors and creditors:

- Evaluate the past performance of the enterprise
- Predict future performance
- Assess the risk of achieving future cash flows.

However, information in an income statement has several limitations:

- Items that might be relevant but cannot be reliably measured are not reported (e.g. brand recognition and loyalty)
- Some numbers depend on accounting methods used (e.g. using FIFO or LIFO accounting to measure inventory level)
- Some numbers depend on judgments and estimates (e.g. depreciation expense depends on estimated useful life and salvage value).

Single-step Income Statement

In the single-step statement, just two groups exist: revenues and expenses. Expenses are deducted from revenues to get net income (single step). Its main advantage is simplicity, but more and more companies choose multiple-step statements. The basic format is shown below.

Revenues

Net sales	$3,400,000
Rent revenue	40,000
Interest revenue	12,000
Total revenue	3,452,000

Expenses (usually sorted by amount)

Cost of goods sold	2,000,000
Selling expenses	450,000
Administrative expenses	350,000
Interest expense	45,000
Total expense	2,845,000
Income before taxes	607,000
Income taxes	182,100
Net income	424,900
Earnings per share	$4.20

Based on 100,000 shares.

Multiple-step Income Statement

It is argued that multiple-step income statement provides more useful information because it separates operating and non-operating activities and classifies expenses by function. It allows instant comparisons and ratio computations which evaluate performance of the hotel. The basic sections are shown below.

	Net Revenue	
-	Cost of Sales (or Cost of Goods Sold)	>Operating Section
=	*Gross Margin or Profit*	
-	Selling Expenses	
-	General and Administrative Expenses	
=	*Operating Profit*	>Non-Operating Section
-	Interest Expense	
+	Other Revenues or Gains	
-	Other Expenses or Losses	
=	*Earnings Before Taxes*	
-	Taxes	

=	*Earnings Before Irregular Items*	
-/+	Discontinued Operations	Irregular Items
-/+	Extraordinary Items	
-/+	Changes in Accounting Principle	
=	*Net Income*	
	Earnings Per Share	

Items on Income Statement

Operating Section

1. *Net Revenue*—Inflows or other enhancements of assets of an entity or settlements of its liabilities during a period from delivering or producing goods, rendering services, or other activities that constitute the entity's ongoing major or central operations. Usually presented as sales minus sales discounts, returns, and allowances.
2. *Expenses*—Outflows or other using-up of assets or incurrence of liabilities during a period from delivering or producing goods, rendering services, or carrying out other activities that constitute the entity's ongoing major or central operations.
   - *Cost of goods sold* - represents the amount a product cost you to produce.
   - *General and administrative expenses* (G and A) - represent expenses to manage the business (officer salaries, legal and professional fees, utilities, insurance, depreciation of office building and equipment, stationery supplies).
   - *Selling expenses* - represent expenses needed to sell products (e.g., sales salaries and commissions, advertising, freight, shipping, depreciation of sales equipment).
   - *R and D expenses* - represent expenses included in research and development.
   - *Depreciation* - represents costs associated with depreciated assets.

Non-operating section

- *Other revenues or gains* - revenues and gains from other than primary business activities (e.g. rent, patents). It also includes unusual gains and losses that are either unusual or infrequent, but not both (e.g. sale of securities or fixed assets).
- *Other expenses or losses* - expenses or losses not related to primary business operations.

Irregular items

They are reported separately because this way users can better predict future cash flows - irregular items most likely won't happen next year. These are reported net of taxes.

- Discontinued operations is the most common type of irregular items. Shifting business location, stopping production temporarily, or changes due to technological improvement do not qualify as discontinued operations.
- Extraordinary items are both unusual (abnormal) and infrequent, for example, unexpected nature disaster, expropriation, prohibitions under new regulations. Note: nature disaster might not qualify depending on location (e.g. frost damage in Canada would not qualify whereas in tropics would).
- Changes in accounting principle is, for example, changing method of computing depreciation from straight-line to sum-of-the-years'-digits. However, changes in estimates (e.g. estimated useful life of a fixed asset) do not qualify.

Earnings per share

Because of its importance, earnings per share (EPS) are required to be disclosed on the face of the income statement. A hotel which reports any of the irregular items must also report EPS for these items either in the statement or in the notes.

Earnings per share =

$$\frac{\text{net income–preferred stock dividends}}{\text{weighted average of common stock shares outstanding}}$$

There are two forms of EPS reported:

- *Basic*: in this case "weighted average of shares outstanding" includes only actual stocks outstanding.
- *Diluted*: in this case "weighted average of shares outstanding" is calculated as if all stock options, convertible bonds, and other securities that could be transformed into shares *are* transformed. This way number of shares increases and EPS decreases. Diluted EPS is considered to be a more accurate way to measure EPS.

Alternative setup of Multiple-step Income Statement

Setups of income statements come in many shapes and forms. Below is an alternative definition which carries a direct relationship to terminology commonly used in financial analysis. On the right hand side of the table several alternative suggestions for terminology are listed - economics and accounting is by no means a discipline with a single standard definition of terms used. Hence, part of the skill in understanding income statements and balance sheets is to see through the words.

Income statement item terminology	Acronym spelled out	Alternauve
Revenues		Sales, Income,
Turnover		
-CoGS	Cost of Goods Sold	Cost of sales
EBITDA	Earnings before I+T+D+A	Gross margin,
Gross profit, Operating margin		
- Depreciation		
- Amortization		
EBIT	Earnings before I+T	
- Interest		Financial items, Financial income, Financial expense

EBT	Earnings before Taxes	Pretax net income
- Taxes		
E	Earnings	Net income

Simple example: Colgate-Palmolive income statement

Colgate-palmolive hotel consolidated statements of income
(Dollars in Millions Except Per Share Amounts)

For the years ended December 31,	*2004*	*2003*	*2002*
Net sales	$ 10,584.2	$ 9,903.4	$ 9,294.3
Cost of sales	4,747.2	4,456.1	4,224.2
Gross profit	5,837.0	5,447.3	5,070.1
Selling, general and administrative expenses	3,624.6	3,296.3	3,034.0
Other (income) expense, net	90.3	(15.0)	23.0
Operating profit	2,122.1	2,166.0	2,013.1
Interest expense, net	119.7	124.1	142.8
Income before income taxes	2,002.4	2,041.9	1,870.3
Provision for income taxes	675.3	620.6	582.0
Net income	$ 1,327.1	$ 1,421.3	$ 1,288.3
Earnings per common share, basic	$ 2.45	$ 2.60	$ 2.33
Earnings per common share, diluted	$ 2.33	$ 2.46	$ 2.19

Complex example: Viacom, Inc. Income Statement

Viacom inc. And subsidiaries consolidated statements of operations
(In millions, except per share amounts)

Year Ended December 31,	*2004*	*2003*	*2002*
Revenues	$ 22,525.9	$ 20,827.6	$19,186.8
Expenses: Operating	12,545.8	11,879.8	10,735.5
Selling, general and administrative	4,142.1	3,732.3	3,498.6
Depreciation and amortization	809.9	741.9	711.8
Impairment charge (Note 3)	17,997.1		
Total expenses	35,494.9	16,354.0	14,945.9
Operating income (loss)	(12,969.0)	4,473.6	4,240.9
Interest expense	(718.9)	(742.9)	(799.1)
Interest income	25.3	11.7	12.0
Other items, net	7.6	(3.0)	(32.9)

Earnings (loss) from continuing operations before income taxes, equity in earnings (loss) of affiliated companies and minority interest	(13,655.0)	3,739.4	3,420.9
Provision for income taxes	(1,378.6)	(1,497.0)	(1,338.3)
Equity in earnings (loss) of affiliated companies, net of tax	(20.8)	.1	(37.3)
Minority interest, net of tax	(5.1)	(4.7)	(3.3)
Net earnings (loss) from continuing operations	(15,059.5)	2,237.8	2,042.0
Discontinued operations (Note 2):			
Earnings (loss) from discontinued operations	(1,182.7)	(718.8)	255.3
Income taxes, net of minority interest	92.4	(83.6)	(90.7)
Net earnings (loss) from discontinued operations	(1,090.3)	(802.4)	164.6
Net earnings (loss) before cumulative effect of accounting change	(16,149.8)	1,435.4	2,206.6
Cumulative effect of accounting change, net of minority interest and tax (Note 1)	(1,312.4)	(18.5)	(1,480.9)
Net earnings (loss)	$ (17,462.2)	$ 1,416.9	$ 725.7
Basic earnings (loss) per common share:			
Net earnings (loss) from continuing operations	$ (8.78)	$ 1.28	$1.16
Net earnings (loss) from discontinued operations	$ (.64)	$ (.46)	$ .09
Net earnings (loss) before cumulative effect of accounting change	$ (9.42)	$ .82	$ 1.26
Cumulative effect of accounting change	$ (.77)	$ (.01)	$ (.84)
Net earnings (loss)	$(10.19)	$ .81	$ .41
Diluted earnings (loss) per common share:			
Net earnings (loss) from continuing operations	$ (8.78)	$ 1.27	$ 1.15
Net earnings (loss) from discontinued operations	$ (.64)	$ (.46)	$ .09
Net earnings (loss) before cumulative effect of accounting change	$ (9.42)	$ .82	$ 1.24
Cumulative effect of accounting change	$ (.77)	$ (.01)	$ (.83)
Net earnings (loss)	$(10.19)	$ .80	$ .41

Weighted average number of common shares outstanding:			
Basic	1,714.4	1,744.0	1,752.8
Diluted	1,714.4	1,760.7	1,774.8
Dividends per common share	$ -	$ .25	$ .12

BALANCE SHEET

A balance sheet, in formal bookkeeping and accounting, is a statement of the book value of a hotel business at a particular date, at the end of a period such as a "fiscal year," as distinct from an income statement, also known as a profit and loss account (P and L), which records revenue and expenses over a specified period of time. A balance sheet is often described as a "snapshot" of the hotel's financial condition on a given date. Of the four basic financial statements, the balance sheet is the only statement which applies to a single point in time, instead of a period of time.

A simple hotel business operating entirely in cash could measure its profits by simply withdrawing the entire bank balance at the end of the period, plus any cash in hand. However, real businesses are not paid immediately; they build up inventories of goods to sell and they acquire buildings and equipment. In other words: businesses have assets and so they could not, even if they wanted to, immediately turn these into cash at the end of each period. Real businesses also owe money to suppliers and to tax authorities, and the proprietors do not withdraw all their original capital and profits at the end of each period. In other words businesses also have liabilities.

A modern balance sheet usually has three parts: assets, liabilities and shareholders' equity. The main categories of assets are usually listed first and are followed by the liabilities. The difference between the assets and the liabilities is known as the 'net assets' or the 'net worth' of the hotel. The net assets shown by the balance sheet equals the third part of the balance sheet, which is known as the shareholders' equity. This balance is not a coincidence. Records of the values of each account in the balance sheet are maintained using a system of accounting known as double-entry bookkeeping.

Balance Sheet Structure

The following Balance Sheet structure is just an example. It does not show all possible kinds of assets, equity and liabilities, but it shows the most usual ones. Because it shows Goodwill it could be a consolidated balance sheet. Monetary values are not shown, summary (total) rows are missing as well.

Balance Sheet of XYZ, Ltd. as on 31 December 2005

ASSETS

Current Assets
Cash and cash equivalents
Marketable Securities
Accounts receivable
Inventories
Prepaid Expenses

Investments held for trading

Other current assets
Non-Current Assets (Fixed Assets)
Property, plant and equipment
Less : Accumulated Depreciation
Goodwill
Other intangible fixed assets
Investments in associates
Deferred tax assets

Liabilities and equity
Current liabilities
Accounts payable
Current income tax liabilities
Current portion of bank loans payable
Short-term provisions
Other current liabilities

Long term Liabilities (Fixed Liabilities)
Bank loans
Issued debt securities
Deferred tax liability

Provisions
Minority interest

Capital and Reserves

Share capital
Capital reserves
Revaluation reserve
Translation reserve
Retained earnings

Equity Valuation

The real value to a purchaser of the business or a shareholder may be different from the net assets shown by the balance sheet. This is because factors that affect the value of a business may not be recorded yet. For example, a purchaser will be interested in the future earnings of the business, whether assets such as property have been revalued recently, and whether there are potential liabilities in the future such as lawsuits. The value of the assets in the balance has also been based on the assumption that the business is a going concern, otherwise the break-up value of the assets may be far less than the value in the balance sheet.

Constructing a Balance Sheet

Case Study

1.1 A new business starts up as a limited hotel called Sunrise Ltd by raising $10,000 from the owners i.e. share holders. The money is put in to a new bank account. What would the assets, liabilities and equity be?

Assets:	
Bank Balance	10,000
Equity and Liabilities:	
Share Capital	10,000

1.2 They then use 6,000 of its bank account to buy a delivery van. Assets and liabilities after this transaction:

Assets:	
Bank Balance	4,000

Delivery Van	6,000
Equity and Liabilities:	
Share Capital	10,000

1.3 Sunrise Ltd then buys some inventory at 3,000 on credit. Assets and liabilities after this transaction:

Assets:	
Bank Balance	4,000
Delivery Van	6,000
Inventory	3,000
Liabilities:	
Accounts Payable	3,000 (to be paid to creditors)
Equity:	
Share Capital	10,000

Total assets must always equal total liabilities (and equity). It is inevitable as the liabilities (and equity) are providing the funds that we are spending on these assets.

1.4 Shortly afterwards, after selling 1,000 of inventory for 2,500, payment of 2,600 of the accounts payable and the purchase of 2,200 of machinery financed by a 2,200 bank loan, the assets and liabilities change to the following:

Sunrise Ltd.
Balance Sheet
As of December 31, 2005

Fixed Assets	
Delivery Van	6,000
Machinery	2,200
Total fixed assets	8,200
Current Assets	
Bank Balance	1,400
Inventory	2,000
Accounts Receivable	2,500
Total	5,900
Accounts Payable	400

Net current assets	*5,500*
Long-Term Liabilities	
Loans Repayable	2,200
Total Long Term Liabilities	*2,200*
NET ASSETS	*11,500*
Shareholders' Equity	
Share Capital	10,000
Retained profits	1,500
Total shareholders' equity	**11,500**

Points to note:

- Must be headed with the name of the reporting entity (e.g. Sunrise Ltd) and the date.
- The van has not been depreciated and there are no other trading expenses
- The terms 'Current Liability' and 'Long-Term Liability' are the traditional names possibly used by sole traders or partnerships. Limited companies may use the phrases 'Liabilities: Amounts falling due within 1 year' and 'Liabilities: Amounts falling due after 1 year'.
- The Total Equity may also be called the 'Net Worth'.
- The Net Worth is in principle what the hotel is worth, it shows the monetary amount that would effectively be left, if all assets were sold and all liabilities paid off.

CURRENT LIABILITY

In hotel accounting, current liabilities are considered liabilities of the hotel business that are to be settled in cash within the fiscal year. For example accounts payable for goods, services or supplies that were purchased for use in the operation of the business and payable within a normal period of time would be current liabilities.

Bonds, mortgages and loans that are payable over a term exceeding one year would be fixed liabilities. However the payments due in the current fiscal year could be considered current liabilities if the amount were material. The proper classification of liabilities is essential when considering a true picture of an organization's fiscal health.

ASSET

In business and accounting by asset is meant economic resources controlled by an entity as a result of *past* transactions or events and from which future economic benefits may be obtained.

Asset Characteristics

Assets have three essential characteristics:

- They embody a future benefit that involves a capacity, singly or in combination with other assets, in the case of profit oriented enterprises, to contribute directly or indirectly to future net cash flows, and, in the case of not-for-profit organizations, to provide services;
- The entity can control access to the benefit; and,
- The transaction or event giving rise to the entity's right to, or control of, the benefit has already occurred.

It is not necessary, in the financial accounting sense of the term, for control of access to the benefit to be legally enforceable for a resource to be an asset, provided the entity can control its use by other means. It is important to understand that in an accounting sense an asset is not the same as ownership. In accounting, ownership is described by the term "equity,". Assets are equal to "equity" plus "liabilities."

The accounting equation relates assets, liabilities, and owner's equity:

Assets = Liabilities + Owners' Equity,

The accounting equation is the mathematical structure of the balance sheet. Assets are usually listed on the balance sheet. It has a normal balance, or usual balance, of debit (i.e., asset account amounts appear on the left side of a ledger). Similarly, in economics an asset is any form in which wealth can be held.

Probably the most accepted accounting definition of asset is the one used by the International Accounting Standards

Board. The following is a quotation from the IFRS Framework: "An asset is a resource controlled by the enterprise as a result of past events and from which future economic benefits are expected to flow to the enterprise." Assets are formally controlled and managed within larger organizations via the use of asset tracking tools. These monitor the purchasing, upgrading, servicing, licensing, disposal etc., of both physical and non-physical assets.

Classification of Assets

Assets may be classified in many ways. In a hotel's balance sheet certain divisions are required by generally accepted accounting principles (GAAP), which vary from country to country.

US GAAP

U.S. Generally Accepted Accounting Principles (GAAP) are currently promulgated and codified by the Financial Accounting Standards Board (FASB) at the pleasure of the Securities and Exchange Commission (SEC), the government body authorized by the Securities Acts of 1933 and 1934 to prescribe accounting principles to be employed in public financial transactions. Under US GAAP, the fundamental definition of an asset is as follows: "Assets are probable future economic benefits obtained or controlled by a particular entity as a result of past transactions or events." The following is an example of classification according to US GAAP.

Current Asset

In accounting, a current asset is an asset on the balance sheet which is expected to be sold or otherwise used up in the near future, usually within one year, or one business cycle - whichever is longer. On the balance sheet, assets will typically be classified into current assets and long-term assets. Current assets are cash and other assets expected to be converted to cash, sold, or consumed either in a year or in the operating cycle. These assets are continually turned over in the course of a business during normal business activity. There are 5 major items included into current assets:

1. *Cash*—It is the most liquid asset, which includes currency, deposit accounts, and negotiable instruments (e.g., money orders, checks, bank drafts).
2. *Short-term investments*—Include securities bought and held for sale in the near future to generate income on short-term price differences (trading securities).
3. *Receivables*—Usually reported as net of allowance for uncollectible accounts.
4. *Inventory*—Trading these assets is a normal business of a hotel. The inventory value reported on the balance sheet is usually the historical cost or fair market value, whichever is lower. This is known as the "lower of cost or market" rule.
5. *Prepaid expenses*—These are expenses paid in cash and recorded as assets before they are used or consumed (a common example is insurance).

The phrase *net current assets* (also called *working capital*) is often used and refers to the total of current assets less the total of current liabilities. The current ratio is calculated by dividing total current assets by total current liabilities. It is frequently used as an indicator of a hotel's liquidity, its ability to meet short-term obligations.

Long-term Investments

Often referred to simply as "investments." Long-term investments are to be held for many years and are not intended to be disposed in the near future. This group usually consists of four types of investments:

1. Investments in securities, such as bonds, common stock, or long-term notes.
2. Investments in fixed assets not used in operations (e.g., land held for sale).
3. Investments in special funds (e.g., sinking funds or pension funds).
4. Investments in subsidiaries or affiliated companies.

Different forms of insurance may also be treated as long term investments.

Fixed Assets

Fixed asset, also known as property, plant, and equipment (PP&E), is a term used in accountancy for assets and property which cannot easily be converted into cash. This can be compared with current assets such as cash or bank accounts, which are described as liquid assets. In most cases, only tangible assets are referred to as fixed.

Fixed assets normally include items such as land and buildings, motor vehicles, furniture, office equipment, computers, fixtures and fittings, and plant and machinery. These often receive favourable tax treatment (deprecation allowance) over short-term assets because they depreciate over time. these are purchased for continued and long-term use in earning profit in a business. This group includes land, buildings, machinery, furniture, tools, and certain wasting resources e.g., timberland and minerals. They are written off against profits over their anticipated life by charging depreciation expenses (with exception of land). Accumulated depreciation is shown in the face of the balance sheet or in the notes. These are also called capital assets in management accounting.

Intangible Assets

Intangible assets lack physical substance and usually are very hard to evaluate. They include patents, copyrights, franchises, goodwill, trademarks, trade names, etc. These assets are (according to US GAAP) amortized to expense over 5 to 40 years with the exception of goodwill. Some assets such as websites are treated differently in different countries and may fall under either tangible or intangible assets.

This section includes a high variety of assets, most commonly:

- Long-term prepaid expenses
- Long-term receivables
- Intangible assets (if they represent just a very small fraction of total assets)
- Property held for sale.

In a lot of cases this section is too general and broad, because assets could be classified into four above categories.

Fixed Assets Management

Fixed assets management is an accounting process that seeks to track fixed assets for the purposes of financial accounting, preventive maintenance, and theft deterrence. Many organizations face a significant challenge to track the location, quantity, condition, maintenance and depreciation status of their fixed assets. A popular approach to tracking fixed assets utilizes serial numbered Asset Tags, often with bar codes for easy and accurate reading. Periodically, the owner of the assets can take inventory with a mobile barcode reader and then produce a report.

Off-the-shelf software packages for fixed asset management are marketed to businesses small and large. Some Enterprise Resource Planning systems are available with fixed assets modules.

LIABILITY

In the most general sense, a liability is anything that is a hindrance, or puts individuals at a disadvantage. In financial accounting, a liability is defined as an *obligation* of an entity arising from *past* transactions or events, the settlement of which may result in the transfer or use of assets, provision of services or other yielding of economic benefits in the future.

Liabilities have three essential characteristics:

- They embody a duty or responsibility to others that entails settlement by future transfer or use of assets, provision of services or other yielding of economic benefits, at a specified or determinable date, on occurrence of a specified event, or on demand;
- The duty or responsibility obligates the entity leaving it little or no discretion to avoid it; and,
- The transaction or event obligating the entity has already occurred.

Liabilities in financial accounting need not be legally enforceable; but can be based on equitable obligations or constructive obligations. An equitable obligation is a duty based on ethical or moral considerations. A constructive obligation is an obligation that can be inferred from a set of facts in a particular situation as opposed to a contractually based obligation.

"A liability is a present obligation of the enterprise arising from past events, the settlement of which is expected to result in an outflow from the enterprise of resources embodying economic benefits."

Regulations as to the recognition of liabilities are different all over the world, but are roughly similar to those of the IASB. Examples of types of liabilities include: money owing on a loan, money owing on a mortgage, or an IOU.

Classification of liabilities

Liabilities are reported on a balance sheet and are usually divided into two categories:

- *Current liabilities*—These liabilities are reasonably expected to be liquidated within a year. They usually include payables such as wages, accounts, taxes, and accounts payables, unearned revenue when adjusting entries, portions of long-term bonds to be paid this year, short-term obligations (e.g. from purchase of equipment), and others.
- *Long-term liabilities*—These liabilities are reasonably expected not to be liquidated within a year. They usually include issued long-term bonds, notes payables, long-term leases, pension obligations, and long-term product warranties.— In these liabilities a hotel has to pay after a fixed or long period For ex:- Long term bank loans up to 1yr or more than one 1yr.

In Law

- In law a legal liability is a situation in which a person is liable, such in situations of tort concerning property or reputation and is therefore responsible to pay compensation for any damage incurred; liability may be civil or criminal. Under English law, with the passing of the Theft Act 1978, it is an offense to dishonestly evade a liability. Compensation for damages usually resolved the liability. Vicarious liability arises under the common law doctrine of agency - *respondeat superior* - the responsibility of the superior for the acts of their subordinate.

- In commercial law, limited liability is a form of business ownership in which business owners are legally responsible for no more than the amount that they have contributed to a venture. If for example, a business goes bankrupt an owner with limited liability will not lose unrelated assets such as a personal residence (assuming they do not give personal guarantees). This is the standard model for larger businesses, in which a shareholder will only lose the amount invested (in the form of stock value decreasing). For an explanation see business entity.
- Manufacturer's liability is a legal concept in most countries that reflects the fact that producers have a responsibility not to sell a defective product.

Bank Account

Money deposited with a bank becomes a liability of the bank, because the bank has an obligation to pay the depositor the money deposited; usually on demand. (The money deposited is an asset for the depositor; but this asset will not be recorded by the bank because it is not the bank's asset. If the depositor maintains accounting records separate and apart from the bank account maintained by the bank, only then will the asset be recorded.) A debit increases an *asset*; and a credit decreases an *asset*. A debit decreases a *liability*; and credit increases a *liability*.

When a bank receives a deposit it credits a liability account called "Deposits" and credits the depositor's bank account for the same amount (the bank's "Deposits" account is the sum of all of the amounts credited to all of its customer's individual bank accounts). A deposit received by a bank is credited because the bank's liability to its customer, the depositor, increases. When a bank informs its depositor that it has debited the depositor's bank account, it means that the depositor's bank account has been decreased by the amount debited.

PAYROLL

In a hotel, payroll is the sum of all financial records of salaries, wages, bonuses, and deductions.

Paycheck

A paycheck is traditionally a paper document issued by an employer to pay an employee for services rendered. While most common being used in the United States, recently the physical paycheck has been increasingly replaced by electronic direct deposit. In most countries with a developed wire transfer system, e.g. in Europe, using a physical cheque for paying wages and salaries is most uncommon for the past several decades. However, vocabulary referring to the figurative "paycheck" does exist in some languages, e.g. German (*Gehaltsscheck*), partially due to the influence of US popular media.

Payroll Savings Programme

A payroll savings program is a method of automatically deducting money from one's paycheck and depositing it into a savings account. Since these funds are made less available there is a reduced chance that they will be spent.

Payroll Card

A payroll card is a card that allows an employee to access their paycheck by using a card that looks like a bank debit card. A payroll card can be more convenient than using a check casher, because it can be used at participating automatic teller machines to withdraw cash, or in retail environments to make purchases. Some payroll cards also are cheaper than Payday loans available from retail check cashing stores, but others are not. Most payroll cards will charge a fee if used at an ATM more than once per pay period.

The payroll card account usually is held as a single account in the employer's name. That account holds the payroll funds for all employees using the payroll card system. Some payroll card programs establish a separate account for each employee, but others do not.

Payroll Professionals

In Canada Payroll Professionals are Certified by the Canadian Payroll Association. They are qualified as either 'Payroll Compliance Practitioners(PCP)' or as 'Certified Payroll Managers(CPM)' Upon completion of the required course material and with continuing Education and membership fees the person is then entitled to the Post-nominal letters associated with their current level of accomplishment.

Chapter 3

Hotel Accounting and Revenue

ACCOUNTING METHODS

Cash Basis

Cash-basis accounting is a method of bookkeeping that records financial events based on cash flows and cash position. Revenue is recognized when cash is received and expense is recognized when cash is paid. In cash-basis accounting, revenues and expenses are also called cash receipts and cash payments. Cash-basis accounting does not recognize promises to pay or expectations to receive money or service in the future, such as payables, receivables, and prepaid expenses.

This is simpler for individuals and organizations that do not have significant amounts of these transactions, or when the time lag between the initiation of the transaction and the cash flow is very short. Two types of cash-basis accounting exist: *strict* and *modified*. Strict cash-basis follows the cash flow exactly. Modified cash-basis includes some elements from accrual-basis accounting such as inventory and property capitalization.

Issues with Cash Basis

Cash-basis accounting fails to meet GAAP requirements because it does not adhere to the following two GAAP principles:

- *Revenue recognition principle*—Revenue should be recognized when it is realized (e.g. a credit sale)
- *Matching principle*—Revenue should be matched to the expense if possible (e.g. sales to COGS)

Additionally, cash-basis accounting is not viable for cost accounting in manufacturing operations because expenses cannot always be correctly associated with product costs.

Example: When you pay your rent, your landlord would record an income event at the time he receives your payment. The landlord would subsequently record an expense event when he pays the rental agent their fee for your apartment. It is the accounting method used by most individuals, and by some businesses, that have limited payables or receivables or whose income and expense cash flows are closely associated with each other in time.

A simplified Income Statement and Balance Sheet for cash basis accounting might look like the following:

Vandalay Industries
Income Statement
For the year ended December 31, 2004

Revenue	$1,000
Expense	$ 800
Net income	$ 200

Vandalay Industries
Balance Sheet
For the year ended December 31, 2004

Assets	
Cash	$5,500
Total assets	$5,500
Liabilities and Stockholders' Equity	
Common stock	$5,500
Total liabilities and Equity	$5,500

Accrual Basis

Accrual-basis accounting records financial events based on events that change your net worth (the amount owed to you minus the amount you owe others). Standard practice is to record and recognize revenues in the period which they incur and to match them with related expenses in a process known as matching or expense matching. Even though cash is not received or paid in a credit transaction, they are recorded because they are consequential in the future income and cash flow of the hotel. Accrual-basis is GAAP compliant.

Example: Your landlord would record an income event on the day your rent comes due (you owe it to him). He records an expense event when the fee owed to the rental agent comes due for your apartment that month (he owes it to the agent). The details of the actual cash flows and their timing are tracked by bookkeeping.

A simplified Income Statement and Balance Sheet for accrual basis accounting will look like the following (note the existence of receivable and payable):

Vandalay Industries
Income Statement
For the year ended December 31, 2004

Revenues	$1,200
Expenses	$ 800
Net income	$ 400

Vandalay Industries
Balance Sheet
For the year ended December 31, 2004

Assets	
Cash	$5,500
Accounts receivable	$ 200
Total assets	$5,700
Liabilities and Stockholders' Equity	
Accounts payable	$ 100
Common stock	$5,600
Total liabilities and Equity	$5,700

Comparison

- Using cash-basis accounting, income and expenses are recognized only when cash is received or paid out.

- Using accrual-basis accounting, receivables and payables are recognized when a sale is agreed to, even though as yet, no cash has been received or paid out.
- Cash-basis accounting defers all credit transactions to a later date. It is more conservative for the seller in that it does not record revenue until cash receipt. In a growing hotel, this results in a lower income compared to accrual-basis accounting.

A simple example

- A small business such as a fruit stand, which buys its inventory daily for cash at a wholesale market, sells the inventory for cash, and throws away what didn't sell, can get an accurate picture of its profits or losses using cash-basis accounting.
- A remodeling business that gives customers 90 days to pay and that procures materials on account at the lumber yard, must use the accrual method to gain an accurate picture of its financial condition.
- Either business will probably get a relatively accurate picture using either method over a long period of time, except for the transactions that have already begun that are not yet closed.

Standard accrual-basis financial statements (profit statements and balance sheets) do not indicate the cash inflows and outflows of a hotel. The Statement of Cash Flows is created to indicate that information for accrual-basis accounting. Accrual-basis accounting is more costly to maintain, because it requires the bookkeeper to record many more transactions. However, the advent of accounting software has made the difference between the reporting methods less significant.

Companies that have extended or used credit significantly should use (and in the United States may be required by the Internal Revenue Service to use) the accrual-basis method of accounting. The U.S. Securities and Exchange Commission requires that all publicly traded companies follow GAAP, thus all publicly traded companies publish their financial statements using accrual-basis method. Three kind of external stakeholders should be considered when deciding the reporting method:

- Creditors
- Stockholders
- Taxation authorities

For the creditors and stockholders of large enterprises, cash basis accounting is financially inadequate. It does not project the future cash flow of the hotel.

For tax purposes, cash basis accounting is highly favored because it defers tax burdens until the cash is received. It is often used by small businesses and organizations that are not required to use the accrual method, both for tax reasons and for its simplicity.

HOTEL REVENUE

Revenue is a U.S. business term for the amount of money that a hotel earns from its activities in a given period, mostly from sales of products and/or services to customers. In Europe (including the UK) the term is turnover. For individuals, the equivalent term is *income*. For government, revenues refers to the gross proceeds received from taxes, fees, and the like. For non-profit organizations, revenue from products and services can be expanded to include proceeds from donations, grants, trade in lieu of cash, and other liquid assets.

Revenue is often referred to as the "top line" due to its position on the income statement at the very top. This is to be contrasted with the "bottom line" which denotes net income, revenues after all applicable costs. At times, the term "Sales" is used interchangeably, but is only accurate when the amount described is denoted in currency as opposed to units ($100,000 of iPod sales vs. 500 iPods sold).

Revenue is often simplified in economics or basic finance projections to "Price x Quantity" (the price of a good times the number of goods sold) though it is rarely this simple in actuality. Net revenue (revenue - returns) is used when sales returns are a factor in the business. Revenue, like all income statement accounts, can only be presented in terms of a period, for example, the revenues a hotel earned between January 1, 2005 and December 31, 2005. Alternatively, one could express it in terms of the following examples: 2005 revenue, Q1 (1st quarter) revenue, or March revenue. This periodicity is in contrast to a balance sheet account, which would be given as of the date of the statement. To simply say that a hotel earned revenue of $5 million without giving a period is meaningless (however, saying that a hotel has $5 million cash certainly has meaning). Internally, companies break revenue down by operating segment, geographic region, and product line.

Revenue Recognition and Unearned Revenue

Conflicts abound as to when revenue should be recognized. The Financial Accounting Standards Board's (FASB) Statement of Financial Accounting Concept 5 states that revenues should be recognized when they are "realized or realizable" and "earned". Revenues are "realized or realizable" when products are exchanged for assets (such as cash) or claims to assets (such as promises to pay). Revenues are "earned" when the entity has performed all duties necessary to the purchaser.

Oftentimes one of the two situations will arise but not both. If assets are received before revenue is earned, a liability account is created called "Unearned Revenue". An example of when this would happen is in the event of magazine subscriptions: suppose a hotel sold 12 month magazine subscriptions on July 1, 2005 for $10,000 cash. At the hotel's year end, December 31, the hotel is still obligated to deliver 6 months, or $5,000, worth of magazines to subscribers. In this case, the hotel would recognize $5,000 as revenue for 2005, and $5,000 would be seen in the liability account "Unearned Revenue."

In general, for US GAAP purposes, revenue should be recognized at time of delivery of the goods or performance of the service. If cash is received prior to this time, revenue is unearned as explained above. If cash has not yet been received at time of performance, the asset account "Accounts Receivable" will show this. This is in contrast to IRS revenue recognition policies, which call for revenues to be recognized on a "cash received" basis. In the above magazine example, the hotel would have to pay taxes on $10,000 of "revenue" for 2005.

Revenue is a crucial part of any financial analysis. A hotel's performance is measured to the extent to which its asset inflows (revenues) compare with its asset outflows (expenses). Net Income is the result of this equation, but revenue typically enjoys equal attention during a standard earnings call. If a hotel displays solid "top-line growth," analysts could view the period's performance as positive even if earnings growth, or "bottom-line growth" is stagnant. Conversely, high income growth would be tainted if a hotel failed to produce significant revenue growth. Consistent revenue growth, as well as income growth, is considered essential for a hotel's publicly traded stock to be attractive to investors.

Revenue is used as an indication of quality of earnings. There are several financial ratios attached to it, the most important being Price / Sales, Gross Margin, and Net Income / Sales (profit margin). Also, companies use revenue to determine bad debt expense using the income statement method.

Price / Sales is sometimes used as a substitute for a Price to earnings ratio when earnings are negative and the P/E is meaningless. Though a hotel may have negative earnings, it almost always has positive revenue. Gross Margin is a calculation of revenue less Cost of Goods Sold, and is used to determine how well sales cover direct variable costs relating to the production of goods. Net Income / Sales, or Profit margin, is calculated by investors to determine how efficiently a hotel turns revenues into profits.

BOOKKEEPING

Bookkeeping is the recording of all financial transactions undertaken by a business (or an individual). A bookkeeper (or accounting clerk) is a person *who keeps the books* of an organization. The organization might be a business, a charity or a local sports club. Two methods are widely in use: single-entry accounting system and double-entry bookkeeping system.

The system most commonly used in bookkeeping is the double-entry bookkeeping system. A bookkeeper is usually responsible for writing up the "daybooks". The daybooks consist of purchase, sales, receipts and payments. The bookkeeper is responsible for ensuring that all transactions are recorded in the correct daybook, suppliers ledger, customer ledger and general ledger. The bookkeeper will bring the *books* to the trial balance stage for a financial accountant. This accountant will prepare the profit and loss statement and balance sheet using the trial balance and ledgers prepared by the bookkeeper.

Bookkeeping can also consist of simply listing payments on a page, e.g. recording deposits received from people (single entry bookkeeping). Bookkeeping is an essential part of any business. Without bookkeeping no accounting information can be compiled. Bookkeeping is the first level of financial data gathering.

Manual Bookkeeping System

Books, Daybooks, Ledgers are the main stay of manual entry bookkeeping. The picture of a person leaning over a big leather bound ledger, with an ink quill pen in their hand, portrays the historical image of the bookkeeper performing their bookkeeping entries. The painstaking accuracy required to ensure that a bookkeeping system was kept properly may have attracted the type of person who were unfairly portrayed as "boring" or a perfectionist. The skillset required to be a bookkeeper requires accuracy and perfectionism. A knowledge of Debits and Credits ensured that the bookkeeper understood how any financial transactions would affect the financial presentation of a hotel's accounts. An invoice received or a cheque paid out were recorded in the correct daybooks by the bookkeeper and transferred to the relevant nominal ledger account.

The Computerisation of Bookkeeping

The computerisation of Bookkeeping has removed many of the "Books" that were used to record transactions. Computer software has deskilled the job of a bookkeeper and opened it up to more people. The software ensures that no entries are omitted from the ledger by performing the automatic double entry of every transaction. Computer software has also improved the speed at which the bookkeeping can be performed.

Gross Profit Method

The gross profit method assumes that the ratio of gross margin for a business remains relatively stable from year to year. It is used in place of the retail method when records of the retail prices of beginning inventory and purchases are not kept. It is considered acceptable for estimating the cost of inventory for interim reports, but is not acceptable for valuing inventory in the annual financial statements. It is also useful in estimating the amount of inventory lost or destroyed by theft, fire, or other disasters.

Using the gross profit method, you would first calculate the Cost of Goods Available for Sale by adding your purchases at cost to your beginning inventories. Second, you would subtract the estimated gross margin from the net sales to calculate the estimated Cost of Goods Sold. Third, subtract the estimated Cost of Goods Sold from the Cost of Goods Available for Sale. This will provide you the estimated cost of ending inventory.

The Gross Profit Method of Inventory Valuation

1.	Beginning Inventory at Cost	$ 50,000	
	Purchases at Cost		290,000
	Cost of Goods Available for Sale	$340,000	
2.	Less Estimated Cost of Goods Sold		
	Sales at Selling Price	$400,000	
	Less Estimated Gross Margin of 30%	120,000	
	Estimated Cost of Goods Sold		280,000
3.	Estimated Cost of Ending Inventory		$60,000

ACCOUNTS PAYABLE

Accounts payable is one of a series of accounting transactions covering payments to suppliers owed money for goods and services. The average household performs this task by writing cheques each month to such suppliers to the electric hotel, telephone company, cable television or satellite dish service, newspaper subscription, and other such regular services.

Business organisations which have become too large to perform such tasks by hand, or who prefer not to do them by hand will generally use accounting software on a computer to perform this task. Accounts payable is classified as a liability account and as such normally has a credit balance. Accounts payable is classified as a Current Liability because the obligation is generally due within 12 months from the initial transaction date. Other types of accounting transactions include accounts receivable, payroll, and trial balance.

One of the most difficult and time-consuming tasks can be reconciling hotel records of invoices and payments against vendors' statements of outstanding invoices. If the two companies have applied invoices to different sets of credit memos and checks, and the situation has been going on for a long time, it can become very difficult to untangle. For instance, if a hotel cuts a check for invoice #3, and the vendor applies the check to invoices #1 and #2, the vendor may continue asking for a payment for invoice #3. If this situation is multiplied over hundreds of invoices, it can take hours or days to resolve the discrepancies.

Expense Administration

Expense administration is usually closely related to accounts payable, and sometimes those functions are performed by the same employee. The expense administrator verifies employees' expense reports, confirming that receipts exist to support airline, ground transportation, meals and entertainment, telephone, hotel, and other expenses. This documentation is necessary for tax purposes and to prevent reimbursement of inappropriate or erroneous expenses. Airline expenses are, perhaps, the most prone to fraud because of the high cost of air travel and the confusing nature of airline-related documentation, which can consist of an array of reservations, receipts, and actual tickets.

Petty cash is also usually paid out by AP personnel in the form of a check made out to an employee, who cashes the check at the bank and puts the cash in the petty cashbox.

Internal controls

A variety of checks against abuse are usually present to prevent embezzlement by Accounts Payable personnel. Separation of duties is a common control. Nearly all companies have a junior employee process and print the checks and a senior employee review and sign the checks. Often, the accounting software will limit each employee to performing only the functions assigned to them, so that there is no way any one employee - even the controller - can singlehandedly make a payment.

Some companies also separate the functions of adding new vendors and entering vouchers. This makes it impossible for an employee to add himself as a vendor and then cut a check to himself without colluding with another employee. In addition, most companies require a second signature on checks whose amount exceeds a specified threshold.

Accounts payable personnel must watch for fraudulent invoices. In the absence of a purchase order system, the first line of defense is the approving manager. However, AP staff should become familiar with a few common problems, such as "Yellow Pages" ripoffs in which fraudulent operators offer to place an advertisement. The walking-fingers logo has never been trademarked, and there are many different Yellow Pages-style directories, most of which have a small distribution. According to an article in the Winter 2000 American Payroll Association's *Employer Practices*, "Vendors may send documents that look like invoices but in small print they state 'this is not a bill'. These may be charges for directory listings or advertisements. Recently, some companies have begun sending what appears to be a rebate or refund check; in reality, it is a registration for services that is activated when the document is returned with a signature."

In accounts payable, a simple mistake can cause a large overpayment. A common example involves duplicate invoices. A invoice may be temporarily misplaced or still in the approval status when the vendors calls to inquire into its payment status. After the AP staff member looks it up and finds it has not been paid, the vendor sends a duplicate invoice; meanwhile the original invoice shows up and gets paid. Then the duplicate invoice arrives and inadvertently gets paid as well, perhaps under a slightly different invoice number. As Mary S. Scheiffer points out in *Accounts Payable: A Guide to Running an Efficient Department*, "Depending on the controls in place, the second payment may or may not be caught! The phenomenal growth of payment recovery firms gives testimony to the fact that this is a serious issue in corporate America today."

Audits of Accounts Payable

Auditors often focus on the existence of approved invoices, expense reports, and other supporting documentation to support checks that were cut. In the real world, it is not uncommon for some of this documentation to be lost or misfiled by the time the audit rolls around. An auditor may decide to expand the sample size in such situations.

FINANCIAL AUDIT

A financial audit, or more accurately, an audit of financial statements, is the examination by an independent third party of the financial statements of a hotel or any other legal entity (including governments and individuals), resulting in the publication of an independent opinion on whether or not those financial statements are relevant, accurate, complete, and fairly presented.

Financial audits are typically performed by firms of *practising accountants* due to the specialist financial reporting knowledge they require. The financial audit is one of many *assurance* or *attestation* functions provided by accounting and auditing firms, whereby the firm provides an independent opinion on published information. Many organisations separately employ or hire internal auditors, who do not attest to financial reports but focus mainly on the internal controls of the organisation. External auditors may choose to place limited reliance on the work of internal auditors.

Financial audits exist to add credibility to the implied assertion by an organization's management that its financial statements fairly represent the organization's position and performance to the firm's *stakeholders* (interested parties). The principal stakeholders of a hotel are typically its *shareholders*, but other parties such as tax authorities, banks, regulators, suppliers, customers and employees may also have an interest in ensuring that the financial statements are accurate. The audit is designed to reduce the possibility of a *material misstatement*. A *misstatement* is defined as false or missing information, whether caused by fraud (including deliberate misstatement) or error. *Material* is very broadly defined as being large enough or important enough to cause stakeholders to alter their decisions. The exact 'audit opinion' will vary between countries, firms and audited organisations.

In the US, the CPA firm provides written assurance that financial reports are 'fairly presented in conformity with generally accepted accounting principles (GAAP).' The measure for 'fairly presented' is that there is less than 5%

chance (5% audit risk) that the financial statements are 'materially misstated'. In England and Wales, the Registered Auditors including Chartered Certified Accountant (ACCA) and Chartered Accountant (CA or ACA) provide 'reasonable assurance' that the financial statements are 'free from material misstatement', and that they give 'a true and fair view' of the state of the hotel's affairs as at a particular date, and of its profit/loss for the period then ended, and have been 'properly prepared in accordance with the Companies Act 1985' or other relevant legislation.

CHARTERED ACCOUNTANT

Chartered Accountant is the title of members of a certain professional accountancy associations in the Commonwealth countries and Ireland. The term *chartered* refers to the charter under which these bodies were incorporated. Subjects examined include financial accounting, management accounting, auditing, taxation and hotel law. Chartered Accountants work in all fields of business and finance. Some are engaged in public practice work, others work in the private sector and some are employed by government bodies.

AUDIT OF GOVERNMENT EXPENDITURE

The earliest surviving mention of a public official charged with auditing government expenditure is a reference to the Auditor of the Exchequer in England in 1314. The Auditors of the Imprest were established under Queen Elizabeth I in 1559 with formal responsibility for auditing Exchequer payments. This system gradually lapsed and in 1780, Commissioners for Auditing the Public Accounts were appointed by statute. From 1834, the Commissioners worked in tandem with the Comptroller of the Exchequer, who was charged with controlling the issue of funds to the government.

As Chancellor of the Exchequer, William Ewart Gladstone initiated major reforms of public finance and Parliamentary accountability. His 1866 Exchequer and Audit Departments Act required all departments, for the first time, to produce annual accounts, known as appropriation accounts. The Act also established the position of Comptroller and Auditor

General (C&AG) and an Exchequer and Audit Department (E&AD) to provide supporting staff from within the civil service. The C&AG was given two main functions - to authorise the issue of public money to government from the Bank of England, having satisfied himself that this was within the limits Parliament had voted - and to audit the accounts of all Government departments and report to Parliament accordingly. Auditing of UK government expenditure is now carried out by the National Audit Office and Audit Commission.

Audit of Hotels and Regulation of Auditors

In the US, prior to the 1930s, corporations were required neither to submit annual reports to government agencies or shareholders nor to have such reports audited. In the United States, the Securities Exchange Act of 1934 required all publicly traded companies to disclose certain financial information, and that financial information be audited. The establishment of the Securities and Exchange Commission (SEC) created a body to enforce the audit requirements.

In the United States, the SEC has generally deferred to the accounting industry (acting through various organizations throughout the years) as to the accounting standards for financial reporting, and the U.S. Congress has deferred to the SEC. This is also typically the case in other developed economies. In the UK, auditing guidelines are set by the institutes (including ACCA, ICAEW, ICAS and ICAI) of which auditing firms and individual auditors are members.

Accordingly, financial auditing standards and methods have tended to change significantly only after auditing failures. The most recent and familiar case is that of Enron. The hotel succeeded in hiding some important facts, such as off-book liabilities, from banks and shareholders. Eventually, Enron filed for bankruptcy, and (as of 2006) is in the process of being dissolved. One result of this scandal was that Arthur Andersen, then one of the five largest accountancy firms worldwide, lost their ability to audit public companies, essentially killing off the firm.

A recent trend in audits (spurred on by such accounting scandals as Enron and Worldcom) has been an increased focus on internal control procedures, which aim to ensure the completeness, accuracy and validity of items in the accounts, and restricted access to financial systems. This emphasis on the internal control environment is now a mandatory part of the audit of SEC-listed companies, under the auditing standards of the Public Hotel Accounting Oversight Board (PCAOB) set up by the Sarbanes-Oxley Act.

STAGES OF AN AUDIT

A financial audit is performed before the release of the financial statements (typically on an annual basis), and will overlap the 'year-end' (the date which the financial statements relate to). The following are the stages of a typical audit:

Planning and Risk Assessment

Timing: before year-end
Purpose:

- To understand the business of the hotel and the environment in which it operates.
- To determine the major audit risks (i.e. the chance that the auditor will issue the wrong opinion). For example, if sales representatives stand to gain bonuses based on their sales, and they account for the sales they generate, they have both the incentive and the ability to overstate their sales figures, thus leading to overstated revenue. In response, the auditor would typically plan to increase the rigour of their procedures for checking the sales figures.

Internal controls testing

Timing: before and/or after year-end
Purpose:

- To assess the internal control procedures (e.g. by checking computer security, account reconciliations, segregation of duties). If internal controls are assessed as strong, this will reduce (but not entirely eliminate) the amount of 'substantive' work the auditor needs to do.

Notes:

- In some cases an auditor may not perform any internal controls testing, because he/she does not expect internal controls to be reliable. When no internal controls testing is performed, the audit is said to follow a substantive approach.

Substantive procedures

Timing: after year-end

Purpose:

- To collect audit evidence that the actual figures and disclosures made in the Financial Statements are reliable and in accordance with required standards and legislation.

Methods:

- Where internal controls are strong, auditors typically rely more on Substantive Analytical Procedures (the comparison of sets of financial information, and financial with non-financial information, to see if the numbers 'make sense' and that unexpected movements can be explained)
- Where internal controls are weak, auditors typically rely more on Substantive Tests of Detail (selecting a sample of items from the major account balances, and finding hard evidence (e.g. invoices, bank statements) for those items)

Notes:

- Some audits involve a 'hard close' or 'fast close' whereby certain substantive procedures can be performed before year-end. For example, if the year-end is 31st December, the hard close may provide the auditors with figures as at 30th November. The auditors would audit income/expense movements between 1st January and 30th November, so that after year end, it is only necessary for them to audit the December income/expense movements and the 31st December balance sheet. In some countries and accountancy firms these are known as 'rollforward' procedures.

Finalisation

Timing: at the end of the audit
Purpose:

- To compile a report to management regarding any important matters the came to the auditor's attention during performance of the audit,
- To evaluate and review the audit evidence obtained, ensuring sufficient appropriate evidence was obtained for every material assertion and
- To consider the type of audit opinion that should be reported based on the audit evidence obtained.

SIGNIFICANT AUDIT FIRMS

These firms are the 'Big 4' multinational accountancy firms which audit the majority of large quoted/listed companies. In addition to providing audits, they also provide other services including tax advice and strategic consultancy.

Firm	*2005 global revenue (US dollars)*
PricewaterhouseCoopers (corporate website)	20.3bn
Deloitte (corporate website)	18.2bn
Ernst and Young (corporate website)	16.9bn
KPMG (corporate website)	15.7bn

Commercial Relationships versus Objectivity

One of the major issues faced by private auditing firms is the need to provide independent auditing services while maintaining a business relationship with the audited hotel. The auditing firm's responsibility to check and confirm the reliability of financial statements may be limited by pressure from the audited hotel, who pays the auditing firm for the service. The auditing firm's need to maintain a viable business through auditing revenue may be weighed against its duty to examine and verify the accuracy, relevancy, and completeness of the hotel's financial statements.

ACCOUNTS RECEIVABLE

Accounts receivable is one of a series of accounting transactions dealing with the billing of customers who owe money to a person, hotel or organization for goods and services that have been provided to the customer by the hotel. This is typically done in a one person organization by writing an invoice and mailing or delivering it to each customer. On a hotel's balance sheet, accounts receivable is the amount that customers owe a business. Sometimes called trade receivables, they are classified as current assets. To record a journal entry for a sale on account, one must debit a receivable and credit a revenue account. When the customer pays off their accounts, one debits cash and credit the receivable in the journal entry. The ending balance on the trial balance sheet for accounts receivable is always debit.

Business organizations which have become too large to perform such tasks by hand (or small ones that could but prefer not to do them by hand) will generally use accounting software on a computer to perform this task. Associated accounting issues include recognizing accounts receivable, valuing accounts receivable, and disposing of accounts receivable. Accounts receivable departments use the *Sales Ledger.* Other types of accounting transactions include accounts payable, payroll, and trial balance. Since not all customer debts will be collected, businesses typically record an allowance for bad debts which is subtracted from total accounts receivable. When accounts receivable are not paid, some companies turn them over to collection agencies. However, many debtors still do not pay; in those cases, some creditors turn to collection attorneys.

AMORTIZATION (BUSINESS)

Amortization is the distribution of a single lump-sum cash flow into many smaller cash flow installments, as determined by an amortization schedule. Unlike other repayment models, each repayment installment consists of both principal and interest. Amortization is chiefly used in loan repayments (a common example being a mortgage) and in sinking funds. Payments are divided into equal amounts for the duration of the loan, making it the simplest repayment model. A greater amount of the payment is applied to interest at the beginning of the amortization schedule, while more money is applied to principal at the end.

The amortization calculator formula is: $(1-v^n)/r$, where n = number of years, v = 1/(1+r), and r = interest rate / 100.

Divide by (1+r) if a payment is due at the beginning.

Another method of writing this kind of formula is:

$$A = P\frac{i(1+i)^m}{(1+i)^m - 1}$$

where: P = principal amount borrowed i = periodic interest rate m = number of periods each year (vs."t"= number of periods over the life of the loan, or t=n*m) A = periodic payment. Negative amortization (also called deferred interest) occurs if the payments made do not cover the interest due. The remaining interest owed is added to the outstanding loan balance, making it larger than the original loan amount.

In Accounting

In accounting, amortization refers to expensing the acquisition cost less the residual value of intangible assets such as trademarks and copyrights in a systematic manner over their estimated useful economic lives so as to reflect their consumption, expiration, obsolescence or other decline in value as a result of use or the passage of time. A corresponding concept for tangible assets is depreciation. Methodologies for allocating amortization to each accounting period are generally the same as for depreciation. However, many intangible assets such as goodwill or certain brands may be deemed to have an indefinite useful life and are therefore not subject to amortization.

Amortization is recorded in the financial statements of an entity as a reduction in the carrying value of the intangible asset in the balance sheet and as an expense in the income statement. Under International Financial Reporting Standards, guidance on accounting for the amortization of intangible assets is contained in International Accounting Standard 38, Intangible Assets. Under United States generally accepted accounting principles, the primary guidance is contained in Statement of Financial Accounting Standards No. 142, Goodwill and Other Intangible Assets.

ANNUAL REPORT

An annual report is a document which a hotel presents at its Annual General Meeting for approval by its shareholders. The report is made up of reports and of financial statements, including the following:

- Chairman's report
- CEO's report
- Auditor's report on the financial statements
- Auditor's report on corporate governance
- Balance sheet
- Statement of changes in equity
- Income statement
- Cash Flow statement
- Notes to the financial statements
- Mission statement
- Accounting policies
- Corporate governance statement of compliance
- Statement of directors' responsibilities

Other information deemed relevant to stakeholders may also be included, such as a report on operations for manufacturing firms. In the case of larger companies, it is usually a sleek, colorful, high gloss publication. The details provided in the report are of use to investors in gaining an understanding of the hotel's financial position and future direction. The report is usually compiled in compliance with

IFRSs and/or the domestic GAAP, as well as domestic legislation (e.g. the SOX in the U.S.). In the United States, a more-detailed version of the report, called a Form 10-K, is submitted to the U.S. Securities and Exchange Commission.

THROUGHPUT

In communication networks, throughput is the amount of digital data per time unit that is delivered to a certain terminal in a network, from a network node, or from one node to another, for example via a communication link. The throughput is usually measured in bit per second (bit/s or bps). The system throughput or aggregate throughput is the sum of the data rates that are delivered to all terminals in a network.

Often maximum throughput is implied by the term throughput. The maximum throughput of a node or communication link is synonym to its capacity. The maximum throughput is defined as the asymptotic throughput when the load (the amount of incoming data) is very large. In packet switched systems where the load and the throughput are equal (where there are no packet drops), the maximum throughput may be defined as the load in bit/s when the delivery time (the latency) asymptotically reaches infinity.

Channel Utilization

The channel utilization in percentage is the achieved throughput related to the physical data rate in bit/s of a digital communication channel (also known as the network access connection speed, the digital bandwidth or the channel capacity). For example, if the the throughput is 70 Mbit/s in a 100 Mbit/s Ethernet connection, the channel utilization is 70%. In a point-to-point or point-to-multipoint communication link, where only one terminal is transmitting, the maximum throughput is often equivalent to or very near the physical data rate (the channel capacity), since the channel utilization can be almost 100% in such a network, except for a small inter-frame gap.

For example in Ethernet, the interframe gap is 12 bytes, and the maximum frame size 1538 bytes (1500 byte payload + 12 byte interframe gap + 8 byte preamble + 14 byte header + 4 Byte trailer). This corresponds to a maximum channel utilization of (1538–12)/1538•100% = 99.2%, or a maximum throughput of 99.2 Mbit/s in a 100 Mbit/s Ethernet connection.

In a computer network, the throughput that is achieved from one computer to another may be lower than the maximum throughput, and than the network access channel capacity, for several reasons, for example:

1. The channel capacity may be shared by other users. If a bottle neck communication link physical data rate R is shared by N, every user typically achieves a throughput of approximately N/R if fair queuing best-effort communication is assumed.
2. Flow control, for example in the TCP protocol, affects the throughput if the bandwidth delay product is larger than the TCP window, i.e. the buffer size. In that case the sending computer must wait for acknowledgement of the data packets before it can send more packets.
3. Packet loss due to Network congestion. Packets may be dropped in switches and routers when the packet queues are full due to congestion.
4. Packet loss due to bit errors.
5. TCP congestion avoidance controls the data rate. So called "slow start" occurs in the beginning of a file, and after packet drops caused by router congestion or bit errors in for example wireless links.
6. Scheduling algorithms in routers and switches. If fair queuing is not provided, users that send large packet will get higher bandwidth. Some users may be prioritized in a weighted fair queuing (WFQ) algorithm if differentiated or guaranteed quality of service (QoS) is provided.
7. Ethernet "backoff" waiting time after collisions.

Throughput, Goodput and Overhead

The maximum throughput is often an unreliable measurement of perceived speed, for example the file transmission speed in bits per seconds. As pointed out above, the achieved throughput is often lower than the maximum throughput. Also, the protocol overhead affect the perceived speed.

The throughput is not a well-defined measure when it comes to how to deal with protocol overhead. The most simple definition is the number of bits per second that are physically delivered. A typical example where this definition is practised is an Ethernet network. In this case the maximum throughput is the gross bitrate or raw bitrate.

However, in schemes that include forward error correction codes (channel coding), the redundant error code is normally excluded from the throughput. An example in modem communication, where the throughput typically is measured in the interface between the PPP protocol and the circuit switched modem connection. In this case the maximum throughput is often called net bitrate or useful bitrate.

To determine the actual speed of a network or connection, the goodput measurement definition may be used. For example in file transmission, the goodput corresponds to the file size (in bits) divided by the file transmission time. The goodput is the amount of useful information that is delivered per second to the application layer protocol. Dropped packets, packet retransmissions and protocol overhead are not counted. Because of that, the goodput is lower than the throughput. Technical factors that affect the difference are presented in the goodput article.

Throughput over Analog Channels

The maximum throughput of a point-to-point or point-to-multipoint physical transmission medium, is equal to or near the channel capacity. This is affected by modulation method and physical layer protocol overhead such as error correction coding, bit synchronization and equalizer training sequences. The maximum throughput may be related to the analog bandwidth of a physical transmission medium, measured in Hertz. The link spectral efficiency in bit/s/Hz is the maximum throughput divided by the analog bandwidth. It is a measure of the efficiency of the digital transmission scheme.

In wireless networks or cellular systems, the system spectral efficiency in bit/s/Hz/area unit, bit/s/Hz/site or bit/s/Hz/cell, is the maximum system throughput (aggregate throughput) divided by the analog bandwidth and some measure of the system coverage area.

Throughput and Latency

Normally throughput and latency are opposed goals. To improve latency you typically want to increase how much the computer checks to see if you are trying to interact. This checking overhead slows you down. However, there is one very common exception to this rule. Network protocols and programs tend to synchronize both ends regularly. If these synchronizations are slow, then throughput can suffer tremendously.

The perceived speed is mostly based on the speed of requests made or responsiveness. As such, responsiveness has far less to do with throughput than latency. To illustrate this, consider a truck full of magnetic tape en route from Moscow to Paris. The time or latency it takes to deliver the data may be several days, but the amount or throughput of data delivered will exceed the throughput of a broadband connection. In contrast, the broadband connection, which has a throughput many times less than that of the truck, has a relatively low latency and can deliver smaller amounts of data much faster. For a user, surfing the Internet for instance, the latter which has a lower latency is perceived as "faster".

Latency is measured from the time a request (e.g. a single packet) leaves the client to the time the response (e.g. An Acknowledgment) arrives back at the client from the serving entity. The unit of latency is time. Throughput on the other hand is the amount of data that is transferred over a period of time. For example if over ten seconds twenty packets are transferred then the throughput would be 20/10=2 packets per second. Throughput can have many units (for example: "bits/second," "bytes/second," or "packets/second"), but it is always measured in a volume-per-time ratio.

Throughput Accounting

Throughput accounting (TA) is an alternative to cost accounting proposed by Eliyahu M. Goldratt. It is not based on Standard Costing or Activity Based Costing (ABC). Throughput Accounting is not costing and it does not allocate costs to products and services. It can be viewed as business intelligence for profit maximization. Conceptually throughput accounting seeks to increase the velocity at which products move through an organization by eliminiating bottlenecks within the organization.

Cost (or Management) accounting is an organization's internal method used to measure efficiency. Since no one outside the organization uses such internal accounts for investment or other decisions, any methods that an organization finds helpful can be used. Outside parties to a business depend on accounting reports prepared by financial (public) accountants who apply Generally Accepted Accounting Practices (GAAP) issued by the Financial Accounting Standards Board (FASB) and enforced by the U.S. Securities and Exchange Commission (SEC) and other regulatory agencies.

Throughput accounting improves profit performance with better management decisions by using measurements that more closely reflect the effect of decisions on three critical monetary variables (throughput, inventory, and operating expense — defined below).

When cost accounting was developed in the 1890's, Labour was the largest fraction of product cost and workers might not know how many hours they would work in a week when they reported on Monday morning. Cost accountants, therefore, concentrated on how efficiently managers used Labour since it was their most important variable resource. Now, however, workers who come to work on Monday morning almost always work 40 hours or more; their cost is fixed rather than variable. Many managers are still evaluated on their Labour efficiencies, though, and many "downsizing," "rightsizing," and other Labour reduction campaigns are based on them.

Goldratt argues that, under current conditions, Labour efficiencies lead to decisions that harm rather than help organizations. Throughput accounting, therefore, removes standard cost accounting's reliance on efficiencies in general and Labour efficiency in particular from management practice. Many cost and financial accountants agree with Goldratt's critique, but they have not agreed on a replacement of their own and there is enormous inertia in the installed base of people trained to work with existing practices.

The recent development of TA is constraints accounting, which focuses more strongly on the role of the constraint in decision making.

The Concept of Throughput Accounting

Goldratt's alternative begins with the idea that each organization has a goal and that better decisions increase its value. The goal for a profit maximizing firm is easily stated, to increase profit, now and in the future. Throughput accounting applies to not-for-profit organizations too, but they have to develop a goal that makes sense in their individual cases. Throughput Accounting also pays particular attention to the concept of bottlenecks in the manufacturing or servicing processes.

Throughput accounting uses three measures of income and expense:

1. *Throughput* (T) is the rate at which the system produces "goal units." When the goal units are money (in for-profit businesses), throughput is sales revenues less the cost of the raw materials (T = S - RM). Note that T only exists when there is a sale of

the product or service. Producing materials that sit in a warehouse does not count. ("Throughput" is sometimes referred to as "Throughput Contribution" and has similarities to the concept of "Contribution" in Marginal Costing which is sales revenues less "variable" costs - "variable" being defined according to the Marginal Costing philosophy.)

2. *Investment* (I) is the money tied up in the system. This is money associated with inventory, machinery, buildings, and other assets and liabilities. In earlier TOC documentation, the "I" was interchanged between "Inventory" and "Investment." The preferred term is now only "investment." Note that TOC recommends inventory be valued strictly on totally variable cost associated with creating the inventory, not with additional cost allocations from overhead.
3. *Operating expense* (OE) is the money the system spends in generating "goal units." For physical products, OE is all expenses except the cost of the raw materials. OE includes maintenance, utilities, rent, taxes, payroll, etc.

Organizations that wish to increase their attainment of The Goal should therefore require managers to test proposed decisions against three questions. Will the proposed change:

Increase Throughput? How?

Reduce Investment (Inventory) (money that cannot be used)? How?

Reduce Operating expense? How?

The answers to these questions determine the effect of proposed changes on system wide measurements:

Net profit (NP) = Throughput - Operating Expense = T-OE

Return on investment (ROI) = Net profit / Investment = NP/I

Productivity (P) = Throughput / Operating expense = T/OE

Investment turns (IT) = Throughput / Investment = T/I

These relationships between financial ratios as illustrated by Goldratt are very similar to a set of relationships defined by DuPont and General Motors financial executive Donaldson Brown about 1920. Brown did not advocate changes in management accounting methods, but instead used the ratios to evaluate traditional financial accounting data. Throughput Accounting is an important development in modern accounting that allows managers to understand the contribution of constrained resources to the overall profitability of the enterprise.

Chapter 4

Debit and Credit

CREDIT (FINANCE)

Credit as a financial term, used in such terms as credit card, refers to the granting of a loan and the creation of debt. Any movement of financial capital is normally quite dependent on credit, which in turn is dependent on the reputation or creditworthiness of the entity which takes responsibility for the funds. A similar usage is in commercial trade, where *credit* is used to refer to the approval for delayed payments for goods purchased. Sometimes if a person has financial instability or difficulty, credit is not granted. Companies frequently offer credit to their customers as part of the terms of a purchase agreement. Organizations that offer credit to their customers frequently employ a credit manager.

Credit is denominated by a unit of account. Unlike money (by a strict definition), credit itself cannot act as a unit of account. However, many forms of credit can readily act as a medium of exchange. As such, various forms of credit are frequently referred to as *money* and are included in estimates of the money supply.

Credit is also traded in the market. The purest form is the "Credit Default Swap" market, which is essentially a traded market in credit insurance. A credit default swap represents the price at which two counterparties will exchange this risk

– the protection "seller" takes the risk of default of the credit in return for a payment, commonly denoted in basis points (one basis point being 1/100 of a percent) of the notional amount to be referenced, while the protection "buyer" pays this premium and in the case of default of the underlying (a loan, bond or other receivable), delivers this receivable to the protection seller and receives from the seller the par amount (i.e., is made whole).

DEBITS AND CREDITS AND DEBT

Debit and Credit are formal bookkeeping and accounting terms that have opposite meanings and come from Latin. Debit comes from *debere,* which means "to owe". The Latin *debitum* means "debt". Credit comes from the Latin word *credere,* which means "to believe". It is more common to use the terms in the plural, Debits and Credits. Debit is abbreviated as *Dr.,* while credit is abbreviated as *Cr.*

"Debit" also refers to the left side of a general ledger account, while "Credit" refers to the right side. Due to the proliferation of bookkeeping and accounting computer software, it is now common for Debits to be mistakenly treated as positive values and Credits to be mistakenly treated as negative values. This allows for mathematical calculations. This has lead to confusion as people do not understand why a Sales amount is treated as an negative value (Credit) and an expense is treated as a positive value (Debit). If the value of the debits are greater than the value of the credits, then the balance on the account is a debit and should not be described as a positive value balance.

Debits or Credits are neither positive or a negative values. The balance on an account is either a debit or a credit not a positive or a negative value. Asset and expense accounts increase in value when debited and decrease when credited. Whereas liability, equity, and revenue accounts decrease in value when debited and increase when credited.

This distinction is somewhat counterintuitive, until the nature of those accounts is more closely scrutinized. For example, revenue is coded as a credit. After recording a day's sales invoices, the hotel will have credited a certain amount in revenue, but the customers ledger will hold a debit balance being the amount of the unpaid invoices. To fully understand this see Double-entry bookkeeping system where Debits and Credits form the core of that system.

For instance, the journal entry for paying the telephone bill might look like this:

Description	*Debits*	*Credits*
Phone expense	$200	
Cash		$200

The telephone company would record the exact same transaction (from their side) like this:

Description	*Debits*	*Credits*
Cash	$200	
Revenue		$200

Confusion also arises where the term debit is also informally referred to as a "charge" as in a charge card or Debit Card and that Credit is a limit set or an amount granted by a hotel to its customers as in a credit limit. They are ι sed in a different context in these two cases.

It is often assumed that a debit decreases a balance, and a credit increases it, because this is how the terms are used on bank statements and using a debit card decreases the balance in one's bank acco7unt. However, this is because bank statements are traditionally written from the bank's perspective, where the customer's account is a liability. By withdrawing money, the customer is decreasing the bank's liability. Since liability accounts normally have a credit balance, the withdrawal of cash from a banking account is reflected on the bank's balance sheet as a debit.

TRADE CREDIT

Trade credit exists when one provides goods or services to a customer with an agreement to bill them later, or receive a shipment or service from a supplier under an agreement to pay them later. It can be viewed as an essential element of capitalization in an operating business because it can reduce the required capital investment to operate the business if it is managed properly. Trade credit is the largest use of capital for a majority of business to business (B2B) sellers in the United States and is a critical source of capital for a majority of all businesses. For example, Wal-Mart, the largest retailer in the world, has used trade credit as a larger source of capital than bank borrowings; trade credit for Wal-Mart is 8 times thc amount of capital invested by shareholders. (Trade credit is the second largest source of capital for Wal-Mart; retained earnings is the largest.)

There are many forms of trade credit in common use. Various industries use various specialized forms. They all have, in common, the collaboration of businesses to make efficient use of capital to accomplish various business objectives.

For example: Let's say you operate an ice cream stand under a franchise which agrees to provide you with ice cream stock under the terms Net 60 with a ten percent discount on payment within 30 days, and a 20 % discount on payment within 10 days. This means that you have 60 days to pay the invoice in full. If you sell a sufficient amount of ice cream at your markup within a week, then you can dispatch a cheque for 80 % of the invoice, and make an extra 20 % on the ice cream sold. However, if sales are slow, leading to a month of low cash flow, then you may decide to pay 90 % within 30 days or use the money another 30 days and pay the full invoice amount within 60 days.

The ice cream distributor can do the same thing. Receiving trade credit from milk and sugar suppliers on terms of Net 30, 2 % discount, if paid within ten days, means he is apparently taking a loss or disadvantageous position in this web of trade credit balances. Why would he do this? First, remember he has a substantial markup on the ingredients and other costs of production of the ice cream he sells to you. There are many reasons and ways to manage trade credit terms for the benefit of a business. The ice cream distributor may be well capitalized either by steady profits or recent new investments and may be looking to expand his markets. In this case he is being aggressive in attempting to locate new customers or to help them get established. Having experienced a few customers going out of business from cash flow instabilities he has decided on financial terms to accomplish two things:

- Allow startup ice cream parlors the ability to mismanage their investment in inventory for a while, while learning their markets without having a dramatic negative balance in their till or bank account, which could put them out of business. This is in effect, a short term business loan made to help expand the distributor's market and customer base.

By tracking who pays, and when, the distributor can see potential problems developing and take steps to reduce or increase the allowed amount of trade credit he extends to prospering or faltering businesses. This limits the exposure to losses from customers going bankrupt who would never pay for the ice cream delivered. It is better to have a $5,000 loss than a $30,000 loss.

PETTY CASH

Hotel Businesses often need small amounts discretionary funds in the form of cash known as petty cash for expenditures where it is not practical to make the disbursement by check. The most common way of accounting for these expenditures is to use the imprest system. The initial fund would be created by issuing a check for the desired amount. Usually $100 would be sufficient for most small business needs, however larger businesses may have several thousand dollars in discretionary funds available as petty cash. The entry for this initial fund would be to debit Petty Cash and credit cash.

As expenditures are made, the custodian of the fund will reimburse employees and secure a petty cash voucher in return. At any given time the total of cash on hand plus reimbursed vouchers must equal the original fund. When the fund gets low the custodian submits the vouchers for reimbursement. Assuming the vouchers add up to $80 and that the majority of expenditures were for office supplies, an $80 check is issued and an $80 debit towards office expenses is marked. Once the check is cashed, the custodian has cash at the original amount.

Oversight of petty cash is important because of the potential for abuse. Examples of petty cash controls include a limit (such as 10% of the total fund) on disbursements and monthly audits by someone other than the custodian. Use of petty cash is sufficiently widespread that vouchers for use in reimbursement are available at any office supply store.

CASH FLOW STATEMENT

People and groups interested in cash flow statements include:

- Accounting personnel, who need to know whether the organization will be able to cover payroll and other immediate expenses
- Potential lenders/creditors, who want a clear picture of a hotel's ability to repay
- Potential investors who need to judge whether the hotel is financially sound
- Potential employees or contractors who need to know whether the hotel will be able to afford compensation

Cash flow statements are particularly important for start-up companies with limited liquid assets. These companies are vulnerable to devastating cash shortages, even when Accounts Receivable balances point to long-term financial health.

Statement of Cash Flows

Statement of Cash Flow for the period 12/31/2005 to 12/31/2006

Cash flow from operations (CFO) +/- x x

Cash flow from investing (CFI)	+/- y y
Cash flow from financing (CFF)	+/- z z
Equals change in cash account	= change of cash flow
+ Beginning of period cash	+ Beginning cash
= Ending cash balance	= Ending cash

Operating Activities

Operating activities include the production, sales and delivery of the hotel's product as well as collecting payment from its customers. This could include purchasing raw materials, building inventory, advertising and shipping the product. Items under Operating activities include:

- Net income from income statement
- Depreciation
- Non-cash items
- Deferred tax
- Interest amortization
- Accrual items, such as wages payable
- Working Capital

Investing activities

Investing activities focus on the purchase of the long-term assets a hotel needs in order to make and sell its products, and the selling of any long-term assets that are no longer needed by the hotel. Items under Investing Activities include:

- Capital expenditures, includes purchases of equipment on account.
- Investments.

Financing activities

Financing activities include the influx of cash from investors such as banks and shareholders, as well as the outflow of cash to investors as the hotel generates income. Other activities which impact the long-term liabilities and equity of the hotel are also listed in the financing activities section of the cash flow statement. Items under the Financing activities section include:

- Dividends paid
- Sale purchase of stock
- Net borrowings

Preparation Methods

Direct Method

Shows the major classes of gross cash receipts and payments. This method starts with Net Income and mirrors the Income Statement while also including Current Assets and Current Liabilities.

Indirect Method

Shows the net profit or loss as a starting point and makes adjustments for all transactions of a non-cash items

COST OF SERVICES DONE

In hotel accounting, the cost of services done (also, cost of sales or cost of revenue) describes the *direct* expenses incurred in producing a particular good for sale, including the actual cost of materials that comprise the good, and direct Labour expense in putting the good in salable condition. Cost of goods sold does *not* include indirect expenses such as office expenses, accounting, shipping department, advertising, and other expenses that can not be attributed to a particular item for sale.

Subtracting the *cost of goods sold* from the amount billed when selling the good (*sales revenue*) produces the *gross profit* on the good. The *net profit*, what most people understand as the business' income or profit, is determined by subtracting the *cost of goods sold* and the *indirect expenses* from the *sales revenue*.

Accounting method

The revenue from merchandise sold must be matched with the cost of goods sold. Cost of sales or cost of goods sold is the identification of the cost of those items sold in the most recent accounting period. It can be done by specific identification, taking inventory, or different methods using estimates such as the "retail" method.

Cost of Goods sold is also the determining factor in arriving at *gross profit* and is determined under the periodic method as follows:

Sales	$100,000
Cost of Goods Sold	
Inventory 01/01/03	$ 5,000
Purchases	45,000
Direct Labour	30,000
	80,000
Less: Inventory 12/31/03	10,000
Net Cost of Goods Sold	70,000
Gross Profit on Sales	$30,000

To determine the net profit, one would then compute the indirect expenses such as office expenses, light, heat, etc. Determining the cost of goods sold is the first step in arriving at the net profit.

If the cost of goods sold is too high gross profit will not support the indirect expenses and will result in a loss for the accounting period.

EARNINGS MANAGEMENT

According to Healy and Wahlen (1999), "Earnings Management" occurs when managers use judgement in financial reporting and in structuring transactions to alter financial reports to either mislead some stakeholders about the underlying economic performance of a hotel or to influence contractual outcomes that depend on reported accounting numbers. Earnings management usually involves the artificial increase (or decrease) of revenues, profits, or earnings per share figures through aggressive accounting tactics. Aggressive earnings management is a form of fraud and differs from reporting error.

Management wishing to show earnings at a certain level or following a certain pattern seek loopholes in financial reporting standards that allow them to adjust the numbers as far as is practicable to achieve their desired aim or to satisfy projections by financial analysts. These adjustments amount to fraudulent financial reporting when they fall 'outside the bounds of acceptable accounting practice'. Drivers for such behaviour include market expectations, personal realisation of a bonus, and maintenance of position within a market sector. In most cases conformance to acceptable accounting practices is a matter of personal integrity. Aggressive earnings management becomes more probable when a hotel is affected by a downturn in business.

Earnings management is seen as a pressing issue in current accounting practice. Part of the difficulty lies in the accepted recognition that there is no such thing as a single 'right' earnings figure and that it is possible for legitimate business practices to develop into unacceptable financial reporting.

It is relatively easy for an auditor to detect error but earnings management can involve sophisticated fraud that is covert. The requirement for management to assert that the accounts have been prepared properly offers no protection where those managers have already entered into conscious deceit and fraud. Auditors need to distinguish fraud from error by identifying the presence of intention.

The main forms of earnings management are as follows:

- Unsuitable revenue recognition
- Inappropriate accruals and estimates of liabilities
- Excessive provisions and generous reserve accounting
- Intentional minor breaches of financial reporting requirements that aggregate to a material breach.

ENGAGEMENT LETTER

An engagement letter defines the legal relationship (or engagement) between a professional firm (e.g., law, investment banking, consulting, advisory or accountancy firm) and its client(s). This letter states the terms and conditions of the engagement, principally addressing the scope of the engagement and the terms of compensation for the firm. Most engagement letters follow a standard format. The example given below refers to the engagement of an accountancy firm.

Standard format for letters of Engagement

- *Addressee*: Typically addressed to the senior management (e.g. CEO) of the client.
- *Identification of the service to be rendered*: One type of service is a financial statement audit. Provided in this section is a brief descri ption of the nature of the particular service. Other services that are planned for the audit (e.g. evaluation of internal control, preparation of regulatory reports) are also identified in this section.
- *Specification of the responsibilities of the auditor of the hotel*: This section refers to the specific professional standards and responsibilities of the auditor.
- *Constraints on the accounting firm*: For example, timing of access to client facilities and accounting records may delay the engagement.
- *Deadlines*: This section lays out the estimated date of completion and release of the financial statements, as well as the general guidelines for the timing of the audit work.
- *Description of any assistance to be provided by the client*: Typically, the client's personnel will prepare some schedules (e.g. bank reconciliations) and retrieve documents from files. The letter should describe the assistance of client personnel. If the assistance is not provided and the auditors must complete the work themselves, this section of the letter would provide justification for additional fees to the client.
- *Interactions with specialists, internal auditors, and the predecessor auditor needed to conduct the audit*: Some

specialists needed on an audit may include engineers to verify the stage of completion of electronic components, real estate appraisers to appraise realizable value of real estate used as collateral for loans, actuaries to evaluate the funding requirements and future cash flows associated with pensions or post-retirement health costs, and attorneys to evaluate the likely disposition of contingent losses arising from litigation.

- *A disclaimer*: Describing the limits of the audit. Typically this expresses that an audit is not designed to detect all forms of fraud or illegal acts; rather, an audit checks the financial position of a client with reference to generally accepted accounting principles.
- *A description of the basis for fees*: This may include a fixed fee or an estimate of fees based on expected completion time and billing rates of firm employees assigned to the engagement.
- Ownership and accessibility of the auditor's files to outsiders.

EXPENSE

In hotel accounting, an expense represents an event in which an asset is used up or a liability is incurred. In terms of the accounting equation, expenses reduce owners' equity. The official definition of *expense* used by International Accounting Standards Board is (quotation from IFRS Framework):

> *Expenses are decreases in economic benefits during the accounting period in the form of outflows or depletions of assets or incurrences of liabilities that result in decreases in equity, other than those relating to distributions to equity participants. [F.70]*

One specific use of the term in accounting is whether a particular expenditure is classified as an expense, which is reported immediately to the investing public in the business's income statement; or whether it is classified as a capital expenditure or an expenditure subject to depreciation, which is not. These latter types of expenditures are reported as expenses eventually, but not immediately, by businesses that use accrual-basis accounting, meaning all large businesses.

In investing, one controversy that mounted throughout 2002 and 2003 was whether companies should report the granting of stock options to employees as an expense on the income statement, or should not report this at all in the income statement, which is what had previously been the norm.

OWNERSHIP EQUITY

In hotel business accounting, ownership equity is the owners' interest in all assets after all liabilities are paid. There is a greater discussion at shareholders' equity (when the owners are shareholders). Ownership equity is also known as *equity, risk capital,* and *liable capital.* In a bankruptcy court, creditors have the first claim on assets, and ownership equity is the last or residual claim against assets, paid only after all other creditors are paid. In real estate the owner's equity in a property is the difference between the market price of a property and the owner's mortgage debt, or the owner's 'home equity loan'.

EQUIVALENT ANNUAL COST

In finance the equivalent annual cost (EAC) is the cost per year of owning and operating an asset over its entire lifespan. EAC is often used as a decision making tool in capital budgeting when comparing investment projects of unequal lifespans. For example if project A has an expected lifetime of 7 years, and project B has an expected lifetime of 11 years it would be improper to simply compare the net present values (NPVs) of the two projects, unless neither project could be repeated.

EAC is calculated by dividing the NPV of a project by the *present value of an annuity* factor. Equivalently, the NPV of the project may be multiplied by the *loan repayment factor.*

$$EAC=NPV$$

The use of the EAC method implies that the project will be replaced by an identical project.

A Practical Example

A manager must decide on which machine to purchase:

Machine A
Investment cost $50,000
Expected lifetime 3 years
Annual maintenance $13,000

Machine B
Investment cost $150,000
Expected lifetime 8 years
Annual maintenance $7,500

The cost of capital is 5%.

The EAC for machine A is: ($50,000*$A_{3,5}$)+$13,000=$31,360
The EAC for machine B is: ($150,000*$A_{8,5}$)+$7,500=$30,780

Where A is the loan repayment factor for t years and 5% cost of capital.

The conclusion is to invest in machine B since it has a lower EAC.

Alternative method:

The manager calculates the NPV of the machines:

Machine A EAC=$85,400*$A_{3,5}$=$31,360
Machine B EAC=$19,847*$A_{8,5}$=$30,780

The result is the same, although the first method is easier it is essential that the annual maintenance cost is the same each year.

Alternatively the manager can use the NPV method under the assumption that the machines will be replaced with the same cost of investment each time. This is known as the *chain method* since 8 repetitions of machine A are chained together and 3 repetitions of machine B are chained together. Since the time horizon used in the NPV comparison must be set to 24 years (3*8=24) in order to compare projects of equal length, this method can be slightly more complicated than calculating the EAC. In addition, the assumption of the same cost of investment for each link in the chain is essentially an assumption of zero inflation, so a real interest rate rather than a nominal interest rate is commonly used in the calculations.

FREE CASH FLOW

Free cash flow measures a firm's net increase in

- Cash from operations (this includes the reduction for interest),
- Less the dividends paid to preferred shareholders, and
- Less expenditures necessary to maintain assets.

Increases in non-cash current assets may, or may not be deducted, depending on whether they are considered to be maintaining the status quo, or to be investments for growth.

Problems with CapX

1. The expenditures for maintenance of assets is only part of the capx reported on the Statement of Cash Flows. It must be separated from the expenditures for growth purposes. This split is not a requirement under GAAP, and is not audited. Management is free to disclose maintenance capx or not. Therefore this input to the calculation of free cash flow is easy to manipulate. Since it is a very large number, maintenance capx's questionable validity is the basis for some people's dismissal of 'free cash flow'.
2. A second problem with the maintenance capx measurement is its intrinsic 'lumpyness'. By their nature, expenditures for capital assets that will last decades are infrequent, but costly when they occur. 'Free cash flow', in turn, will be very different from year to year. No particular year will be a 'norm' that can be expected to be repeated.

Uses of the metric

1. Free cash flow measures the ease with which businesses can grow and pay dividends to shareholders. Even profitable businesses may have negative cash flows. Their requirement for increased financing will result in increased financing costs

reducing future income. It is easier to grow with organic cash flows than with additional financing.

2. According to the discounted cash flow valuation model, the intrinsic value of a hotel is the present value of all future free cash flows, plus the cash proceeds from its eventual sale. The presumption is that the cash flows are used to pay dividends to the shareholders. Bear in mind the lumpyness discussed above.
3. Some investors prefer using free cash flow instead of net income to measure a hotel's financial performance, because free cash flow is more difficult to manipulate than net income. The problems with this presumption are itemized at cash flow and return of capital.
4. The payout ratio is a metric used to evaluate the sustainability of distributions from REITs, Oil and Gas Royalty Trusts, and Income Trust. The distributions are divided by the free cash flow. Distributions may include any of income, flowed-through capital gains or return of capital.

This metric is used only by shareholders. Debt holders are not concerned with maintaining the operating capital assets, or with growing the business. Nor are they concerned with taxes paid since their payments come first. The appropriate metric for debt holders is EBITDA.

GAIN

In electronics, gain is usually taken as the mean ratio of the signal output of a system to the signal input of the system. A gain of five would imply that either the voltage or power is increased by a factor of five. It has wide application in amplifiers.

Logarithmic units and Decibels

In electronics, it is common to use logarithmic units to measure gain. Originally, the bel was used:

$$\text{Gain} = \log_{10}(P_2/P_1) \text{ bel}$$

where P1 and P2 are the input and output *powers* respectively.

Using the bel unit, however, results in small numbers, so the decibel (one tenth of a bel) became popular in its place. As there are ten decibels (dB) in a bel:

$$\text{Gain} = 10 * \log_{10}(P_2/P_1) \text{ dB}$$

(A similar unit using natural logarithms is called the neper.)

When gain is calculated using voltage instead of power, making the substitution ($P=V^2/R$), the formula is:

- $\text{Gain} = 10 * \log ((V_2^2/R) / (V_1^2/R))$ dB
- $\text{Gain} = 10 * \log ((V_2/V_1)^2)$ dB
- $\text{Gain} = 20 * \log (V_2/V_1)$ dB

This formula only holds true if the load impedances are identical. In many modern electronic devices, output impedances are low enough and input impedances high enough that load can be ignored without significantly affecting the calculation.

Example: If an amplifier produces an output of 1 volt into a 1 ohm load, then it is providing 1 watt of output power. If the amplifier is then altered to produce an output of 10 volts into the same load, it is now providing 100 watts of output power ($P = V^2/R$). Therefore:

voltage gain = 10 times (10 dB)

power gain = 100 times (20 dB)

A gain of factor 1 or (equivalent to 0 dB) where both input and output are at the same voltage level is also known as *unity gain.*

INTEREST

Interest is the "rent" paid to borrow money. The lender receives a compensation for deferring their own consumption. The original amount lent is called the "principal," and the percentage of the principal which is paid/payable over a period of time is the "interest rate."

Calculations

Simple interest: Add up all the interest paid/payable in a period. Divide that by the principal at the beginning of the period. E.g. on $100 (principal):

- Credit card debt where $1/day is charged. 1/100 = 1%/day.
- Corporate bond where $3 is due after six months, and another $3 is due at year end. (3+3)/100 = 6%/year.
- Certificate of deposit (GIC) where $6 is paid at year end. 6/100 = 6%/year.

There are three problems with simple interest.

- The time periods used for measurement can be different, making comparisons wrong. You cannot say the 1%/day credit card interest is 'equal' to a 365%/year GIC.
- The time value of money means that $3 paid every six months hurts more than $6 paid only at year end. So you cannot 'equate' the 6% bond to the 6% GIC.
- When interest is due, but not paid, it must be clear what happens. Does it remain 'interest payable', like the bond's $3 payment after six months? Or does it get added to the original principal, like the 1%/day on the credit card? Each time it is added to the principal it 'compounds'. The interest from that time forward is calculated on that (now larger) principal. The more frequent the compounding, the faster the principal grows, and the greater the interest.

Compound interest: In order to solve these three problems, there is a convention that interest rates will be disclosed as if the term is one year and the compounding is yearly. The discussion at compound interest shows how to convert to and from the different measures of interest.

Real interest: This is calculated as (nominal interest rate) - (inflation). It attempts to measure the value of the interest in units of stable purchasing power.

Cumulative interest/return: This calculation is (FV/PV)-1. It ignores the 'per year' convention and assumes compounding at every payment date. It is usually used to compare two long term opportunities. Since the difference in rates gets magnified by time, so the speaker's point is more clearly made.

Rule of 78: Some consumer loans calculate interest by the "Rule of 78" or "Sum of digits" method. Seventy-eight is the sum of the numbers 1 through 12, inclusive. And the practice enabled quick calculations of interest in the pre-computer days. In a loan with interest calculated per the Rule of 78, the total interest over the life of the loan is calculated as either simple or compound interest and amounts to the same as either of the above methods. Payments remain constant over the life of the loan; however, payments are allocated to interest in progressively smaller amounts. In a one-year loan, in the first month, 12/78 of all interest owed over the life of the loan is due; in the second month, 11/78; progressing to the twelfth month where only 1/78 of all interest is due. The practical effect of the Rule of 78 is to make early pay-offs of term loans more expensive. Approximately 3/4 of all interest due on a one year loan is collected by the sixth month, and pay-off of the principal then will cause the effective interest rate to be much higher than than the APY used to calculate the payments.

The United States outlawed the use of "Rule of 78" interest in loans over five years in term. Certain other jurisdictions have outlawed application of the Rule of 78 in certain types of loans, particularly consumer loans.

Rule of 72: The "Rule of 72" is a "quick and dirty" method for finding out how fast money doubles for a given interest rate. For example, if you have an interest rate of 6%, it will take 72/6 or 12 years for your money to double, compounding at 6%. This is an approximation that starts to break down above 10%.

DEBT

Debt is that which is owed; usually referencing assets owed, but the term can cover other obligations. In the case of assets, debt is a means of using future purchasing power in the present before a summation has been earned. Some companies and corporations use debt as a part of their overall corporate finance strategy. A debt is created when a creditor agrees to loan a sum of assets to a debtor. In modern society, debt is usually granted with expected repayment; in many cases, plus interest. Historically, debt was responsible for the creation of indentured servants.

Payment

Before a debt can be had, both the debtor and the creditor must agree on the manner in which the debt will be repaid, known as the standard of deferred payment. This payment is usually denominated as a sum of money in units of currency, but can sometimes be denominated in terms of goods. Payment can be made in increments over a period of time, or all at once at the end of the loan agreement.

Types of debt

There are numerous types of debt, including basic loans, syndicated loans, bonds, and promissory notes. Debt, especially large sums of debt, can also be secured through a mortgage or other security interest over some of the debtor's property, in which case the creditor will have some rights over that property in the event that the debtor becomes unable to repay the debt and defaults on the loan.

A basic loan is the simplest form of debt. It consists of an agreement to lend a principal sum for a fixed period of time, to be repaid by a certain date. In commercial loans interest, calculated as a percentage of the principal sum per annum, will also have to be paid by that date. A syndicated loan is a loan that is granted to companies that wish to borrow more money than any single lender is prepared to risk in a single loan, usually many millions of dollars. In such a case, a syndicate of banks can each agree to put forward a portion of the principal sum.

A bond is a debt security issued by certain institutions such as companies and governments. A bond entitles the holder to repayment of the principal sum, plus interest. Bonds are issued to investors in a marketplace when an institution wishes to borrow money. Bonds have a fixed lifetime, usually a number of years; with long-term bonds, lasting over 30 years, being less common. At the end of the bond's life the money should be repaid in full. Interest may be added to the end payment, or can be paid in regular instalments (known as coupons) during the life of the bond. Bonds may be traded in the bond markets, and are widely used as relatively safe investments in comparison to stocks.

Accounting debt

In national accounting debts are added according to those who are indebted. Household debt is the debt held by households. "National" or Public debt is the debt held by the various governmental institutions (federal government, states, cities ...). Business debt is the debt held by businesses. Financial debt is the debt held by the financial sector (from one financial institution to another). Total debt is the sum of all those debts, excluding financial debt to prevent double accounting. These various types of debt can be computed in debt/GDP ratios. Those ratios help to assess the speed of variations in the indebtness and the size of the debt due. For example the USA has a high consumer debt and a low public debt, while in European countries the opposite tends to be true.

There are differences in the accounting of debt for private and public agents. If a private agent promises to pay something later, it has a debt, and this debt is enforceable by public agents. If a public body passes a law stating that it'll pay something later (a kind of promise), it keeps the right to change the law later (and not to pay). This is why for instance the money governments promised to pay for retirements does not show up in the public debt assessment, whereas the money private companies promised to pay for retirements do.

Securitization

Securitization occurs when a hotel groups together assets or receivables and sells them in units to the market through a trust. Any asset with a cashflow can be securitized. The cash flows from these receivables are used to pay the holders of these units. Companies often do this in order to remove these assets from their balance sheets and monetize an asset. Although these assets are "removed" from the balance sheet and are supposed to be the responsibility of the trust, that does not end the hotel's involvement. Often the hotel maintains a special interest in the trust which is called an "interest only strip" or "first loss piece". Any payments from the trust must be made to regular investors in precedence to this interest. This protects investors from a degree of risk, making the securitization more attractive. The aforementioned brings into question whether the assets are truly off balance sheet given the hotel's exposure to losses on this interest.

Debt, Inflation and the Exchange rate

As noted above, debt is normally denominated in a particular monetary currency, and so changes in the valuation of that currency can change the effective size of the debt. This can happen due to inflation or deflation, so it can happen even though the borrower and the lender are using the same currency. Thus it is important to agree on standards of deferred payment in advance, so that a degree of fluctuation will also be agreed as acceptable. It is for instance common to agree to "US dollar denominated" debt.

The form of debt involved in banking accounts for a large proportion of the money in most industrialised nations. There is therefore a complex relationship between inflation, deflation, the money supply, and debt. The store of value represented by the entire economy of the industrialized nation itself, and the state's ability to levy tax on it, acts to the foreign holder of debt as a guarantee of repayment, since industrial goods are in high demand in many places worldwide.

Inflation Indexed Debt

Borrowing and repayment arrangements linked to inflation-indexed units of account are possible and are used in some countries. For example, the US government issues two types of inflation-indexed bonds, Treasury Inflation-Protected Securities (TIPS) and I-bonds. These are one of the safest forms of investment available, since the only major source of risk – that of inflation – is eliminated. A number of other governments issue similar bonds, and some did so for many years before the US government. In countries with consistently high inflation, ordinary borrowings at banks may also be inflation indexed.

Debt Ratings, Risk and Cancellation

Lendings to stable financial entities such as large companies or governments are often termed "risk free" or "low risk" and made at a so-called "risk-free interest rate". This is because the debt and interest are highly unlikely to be defaulted. A good example of such risk-free interest is a US Treasury security - it yields the minimum return available in economics, but investors have the comfort of the (almost) certain expectation that the US Treasury will not default on its debt instruments. A risk-free rate is also commonly used in setting floating interest rates, which are usually calculated as the risk-free interest rate plus a bonus to the creditor based on the creditworthiness of the debtor (in other words, the risk of him defaulting and the creditor losing the debt). In reality, no lending is truly risk free, but borrowers at the "risk free" rate are considered the least likely to default.

However, if the real value of a currency changes during the term of the debt, the purchasing power of the money repaid may vary considerably from that which was expected at the commencement of the loan. So from a practical investment point of view, there is still considerable risk attached to "risk free" or "low risk" lendings. The real value of the money may have changed due to inflation, or, in the case of a foreign investment, due to exchange rate fluctuations.

Ratings and Creditworthiness

Specific bond debts owed by both governments and private corporations is rated by rating agencies, such as Moody's, A.M. Best and Standard and Poor's. The government or hotel itself will also be given its own separate rating. These agencies assess the ability of the debtor to honor his obligations and accordingly give him a credit rating.

A change in ratings can strongly affect a hotel, since its cost of refinancing depends on its creditworthiness. Bonds below Baa/BBB (Moody's/S&P) are considered junk- or high risk bonds. Their high risk of default (approximately 1.6% for Ba) is compensated by higher interest payments. Bad Debt is a loan that can not (partially or fully) be repaid by the debtor. The debtor is said to default on his debt. These types of debt are frequently repackaged and sold below face value. Buying junk bonds is seen as a risky but potentially profitable form of investment.

Cancellation

Short of bankruptcy, very often debts are wholly or partially forgiven. Traditions in some cultures demand that this be done on a regular (often annual) basis, in order to prevent systemic inequities between groups in society, or anyone becoming a specialist in holding debt and coercing repayment. Under English law, when the creditor is deceived into forgoing payment, this is a crime. International Third World debt has reached the scale that many economists are convinced that debt cancellation is the only way to restore global equity in relations with the developing nations.

Effects of Debt

Debt allows people and organizations to do things that they otherwise wouldn't be able or allowed to. Commonly, people in industrialised nations use it to purchase houses, cars and many other things too expensive to buy with cash on hand. Companies also use debt in many ways to leverage the investment made in their private equity. This leverage, the proportion of debt to equity, is considered important in determining the riskiness of an investment; the more debt per equity, the riskier.

Debt as a whole is a sign that a society is optimistic, that it believes in its future earnings capacity, arguably that it lacks a strong work ethic (though the money must be repaid), and perhaps that it is postponing the solution to present problems (for example, it may compensate a fall in revenues that is perceived as short term by an increase in debt).

Excesses in debt accumulation have been blamed for exacerbating economic problems. For example, prior to the beginning of the Great Depression debt/GDP ratio was very high. Economic agents were heavily indebted. This excess in debt, equivalent to excessive expectations on future returns, accompanied asset bubbles on the stock markets. When expectations corrected, deflation and credit crunch followed. Deflation effectively made debt more expansive and, as Fisher explained, this reinforced deflation again, because, in order to reduce their debt level, economic agents reduced their consumption and investment. The reduction in demand reduced business activity and caused further unemployment. In a more direct sense, more bankruptcies also occurred due both to increased debt cost caused by deflation and to the reduced demand.

It is possible for some organizations to enter into alternative types of borrowing and repayment arrangements which will not result in bankruptcy. For example, companies can sometimes convert debt that they owe into equity in themselves. In this case, the creditor hopes to regain something equivalent to the debt and interest in the form of dividends and capital gains of the borrower. The "repayments" are therefore proportional to what the borrower earns and so can not in themselves cause bankruptcy. Once debt is converted in this way, it is no longer known as debt.

Arguments Against Debt

Some argue against debt as an instrument and institution, on a personal, family, social, corporate and governmental level.

Economics criticism focuses on debt fostering inequality. Islam forbids lending with interest, as the Catholic church long did, and the Torah states that all debts should be erased every 7 years and every 50 years. Debt from a religious view point is condemned because, by tying past and future, it cuts from the present where God is to be found.

Feminism concentrates on the perceived coercive nature of debt contracts. Environmental critics point out the disparity between the material use of resources from economic growth and the limited resources of natural production. Examples would be the low ecological yield of natural resources and the limited usable energy from the sun. Debt will increase through time if it is not repaid faster than it grows through interest. In some systems of economics this effect is termed usury, in others, the term "usury" refers only to an excessive rate of interest, in excess of a reasonable profit for the risk accepted.

DEFICIT

A budget deficit occurs when an entity (often a government) spends more money than it takes in. The opposite is a budget surplus. The size of a governmental budget deficit is often an important political issue as well as one of economic policy. Fiscal conservatives denounce deficit spending and advocate balanced budgets. Keynesians argue that under some circumstances, deficit spending is justified. "Starve-the-beast" strategies usually lead to high budget deficits.

An accumulated deficit over several years (or centuries) is referred to as the government debt. Often, a certain part of spending is dedicated to paying of debt with certain maturity, which can be refinanced by issuing new government bonds. That is, a fiscal deficit leads to an increase in an entity's debt to others. A deficit is a flow. And a debt is a stock. Debt is essentially an accumulated flow of deficits.

Any deficit must, ultimately, be repaid, either through taxation, or seignorage. The Ricardian equivalence hypothesis states that this means a public deficit is *exactly the same* as a tax rise. The existence of a deficit has in some cases led to the existence of a capital market and been a great benefit to economic activity.

A formula to calculate debt is:

$$Debt = RB_{t-1} + (r-g)G_t - T_t$$

R = real interest rate.

B_{t-1} = Debt of last year.

r = Interest Rate

g = growth rate

G_t = Government Spending

T_t = Tax Revenue.

Early Deficits

Before the invention of bonds, the deficit could only be financed with loans from private investors or other countries. A prominent example of this was the Rothschild dynasty in the late 18th and 19th century, though there were many earlier examples. These loans became popular when private financiers had amassed enough capital to provide them, and when governments were no longer able to simply print money, with consequent inflation, to finance their spending.

However, large, long-term loans had a high element of risk for the lender and consequently gave high interest rates. Governments later tried to marketize their debts by issuing bonds that were payable to the bearer, rather than the original purchaser. This meant that someone who lent the state money could sell on the debt to someone else, reducing the risks involved and reducing the overall interest rates. Examples of this are British Consols and American Treasury bill bonds.

Structural and Cyclical Deficits

At the lowest point in the business cycle, there is a high level of unemployment. This means that tax revenues are low and expenditure (e.g. on social security) high. Conversely, at the peak of the cycle, unemployment is low, increasing tax revenue and decreasing social security spending. The need to borrow money at the low point of the cycle is a cyclical deficit. A cyclical deficit will be entirely repaid by a cycical surplus at the peak of the cycle.

A structural deficit is the deficit that remains across the business cycle, because general tax levels are too low for the general level of government spending. The observed total budget deficit is equal to the sum of the structural deficit with the cyclical deficit or surplus. The idea of cyclical vs. structural deficits has come under criticism by those economists who believe that the business cycle is too difficult to measure to make cyclical analysis worthwhile.

Inflation and Crowding Out

Government deficits are *not* inherently inflationary. Historically, however, large government deficits have resulted in large and prolonged periods of inflation due to the monetization of government debt (monetary creation). As long as deficits are financed by the sale of government bonds (borrowing), they *do not* result in monetary creation, the principal cause of inflation. The theoretical causal link between the money supply and the price level is described by the quantity theory of money and most strongly advocated by Nobel prize winning macroeconomist Milton Friedman.

Deficits *can* lead to inflation if governments choose to finance deficits through monetary creation rather than borrowing. This often occurrs because the large taxes necessary to finance spending are politically infeasible, and there is insufficient demand for government debt, i.e. investors refuse to buy government bonds. In other words, no one will lend the government money. This is often the case in less developed nations whose economies are too small to tax effectively, but whose governments are considered too risky to attract investors willing to lend out of fear of default. Thus, monetary creation is often the only alternative available to finance spending.

Inflationary deficits are not limited to developing nations, however. Significant monetization of debt often occurrs in developed countries as a result of minimal or no independence of a nation's central bank from its treasury. The central bank is a body which determines interest rates and the nation's money supply, while the treasury finances government expenditures through revenue collection (taxation) or borrowing. A central bank subordinate to a nation's treasury forced to borrow presents a conflict of interest that threatens to cause significant monetization of debt, and thus inflation.

The lack of an independent central bank often leads to strong pressure from the treasury on the bank to purchase the treasury's bonds on the open market (essentially creating money) in order to bid up bond prices. This increase in demand (and consequently the price) for government bonds from the central bank leads to a *decrease* in the yield (interest rate) on the bonds. Note the inverse relationship between a bond's price and its yield. The yield on the bonds is essentially the cost of borrowing faced by the government. It is thus easy to see why a nation's treasury has a significant interest in the central bank maintaining low interest rates through monetary creation.

A nation's treasury has a further (but related) interest to pressure the central bank to buy government debt, creating money. As the treasury increasingly borrows (selling bonds), the increase in the supply of bonds leads to a steady decline in the bonds' price. As the price of the bonds falls, their yield *increases,* consequently increasing the government's cost of borrowing. Thus, governments face *progressively increasing* borrowing costs as deficits grow, and therefore have an increasing incentive to pressure the central bank to buy bonds to keep borrowing costs (interest rates) low.

This actually touches on arguably a more significant economic effect of large government deficits, i.e. higher interest rates. The massive sale of government debt raises interest rates *across* the economy, not just rates paid by the government, and draws available capital (economics) away from prospective private investments to the government. This problem is known as crowding out. Crowding out can actually result in lower investment and thus lower national income (GDP), working against any increase in GDP resulting from the increase in government spending. This can be illustrated using Keynesian macroeconomic theory.

The United States is no stranger to pressure exerted on its central bank. During World War I and World War II the U.S. Treasury put significant pressure on the Federal Reserve (America's central bank) to keep rates low. At the time, the Federal Reserve was much less independent from the Treasury than it is today, and massive monetary creation (and thus inflation) resulted in both instances. The inflation in WWII was considered desirable, however, as the Great Depression was plagued by massive *deflation*.

Most Western democratic nations have realized the inherent inflationary bias in a central bank under the treasury, and have taken significant steps to make their central banks much more independent in leadership and appropriations. An independent central bank is universally regarded by macroeconomists to be positive for economic growth and the macroeconomy as a whole, as the bank is more free to set interest rate policy and contract or expand the money supply as it sees fit. Independence insulates the central bank from expansionary pressure from many sources for lower interest rates which in the short term may bring about lower borrowing costs and rapid growth, but in the long run may cause undesirable and economically harmful inflation. In fact, it seems that there is a direct relationship between the level of independence of a nation's central bank and a nation's level of inflation. More independent central banks seem to better control inflation, maintaining a much lower rate of increase in the aggregate price level.

It is unlikely today that the Federal Reserve or the central banks of other Western democracies will monetize debt as they have in the past, as a healthy fear of inflation has taken hold of central bankers and economists of all political persuasions the world over. It is estimated that a small percentage of U.S. government debt is monetized each year, though the effect of this on inflation is minimal. Less developed and democratic nations however still struggle with large government deficits, monetary creation, and high inflation.

Common Stock

Common stock, also referred to as common or ordinary shares, are, as the name implies, the most usual and commonly held form of stock in a corporation. The other type of shares that the public can hold in a corporation is known as preferred stock. Common stock that has been re-purchased by the corporation is known as treasury stock and is available for a variety of corporate uses.

Common stock typically has voting rights in corporate decision matters, though perhaps different rights from preferred stock. In order of priority in a liquidation of a corporation, the owners of common stock are near the last. Dividends paid to the stockholders must be paid to preferred shares before being paid to common stock shareholders.

COMPREHENSIVE INCOME

Comprehensive income is defined by the Financial Accounting Standards Board, or FASB, as "the change in equity [net assets] of a business enterprise during a period from transactions and other events and circumstances from nonowner sources. It includes all changes in equity during a period except those resulting from investments by owners and distributions to owners."

Comprehensive income is the sum of net income and other items that must bypass the income statement because they have not been realized, including items like an unrealized holding gain or loss from available for sale securities and foreign currency translation gains or losses. These items are not part of net income, yet are important enough to be included in comprehensive income, giving the user a bigger, more comprehensive picture of the organization as a whole.

Items included in comprehensive income, but not net income are reported under the accumulated other comprehensive income section of shareholder's equity.

COST ACCOUNTING

Cost accounting is the process of tracking, recording and analyzing costs associated with the products or activities of an organization. In modern accounting, costs are measured in accordance with the Generally Accepted Accounting Principles (GAAP). GAAP reporting records historical events and assigns a monetary value to each event that has taken place. Costs are measured in units of currency by convention. Cost accounting could also be defined as a kind of management accounting that translates the Supply Chain (the series of events in the production process that, in concert, result in a product) into financial values. Managers use cost accounting to support decision making to reduce a hotel's costs and improve its profitability.

There are at least four approaches:

- Standard Cost Accounting
- Activity-based Costing
- Throughput Accounting
- Marginal Costing

Cost accounting has long been used to help managers understand the costs of running a business. Modern cost accounting originated during the industrial revolution, when the complexities of running a large scale business led to the development of systems for recording and tracking costs to help business owners and managers make decisions. In the early industrial age, most of the costs incurred by a business were what modern accountants call "variable costs" because they varied directly with the amount of production. Money was spent on Labour, raw materials, power to run a factory, etc. in direct proportion to production. Managers could simply total the variable costs for a product and use this as a rough guide for decision-making.

Some costs tend to remain the same even during busy periods, unlike variable costs which rise and fall with volume of work. Over time, the importance of these "fixed costs" has become more important to managers. Examples of fixed costs include the depreciation of plant and equipment, and the cost of departments such as maintenance, tooling, production control, purchasing, quality control, storage and handling, plant supervision and engineering. In the early twentieth century, these costs were of little importance to most businesses. However, in the twenty-first century, these costs are often more important than the variable cost of a product, and allocating them to a broad range of products can lead to bad decision making. Managers must understand fixed costs in order to make decisions about products and pricing.

For example: A hotel produced railway coaches and had only one product. To make each coach, the hotel needed to purchase $60 of raw materials and components, and pay 6 laborers $40 each. Therefore, total variable cost for each coach was $300. Knowing that making a coach required spending $300, managers knew they couldn't sell below that price without losing money on each coach. Any price above $300 became a contribution to the fixed costs of the hotel. If the fixed costs were, say, $1000 per month for rent, insurance and owner's salary, the hotel could therefore sell 5 coaches per month for a total of $3000 (priced at $600 each), or 10 coaches for a total of $4500 (priced at $450 each), and make a profit of $500 in both cases.

Standard Cost Accounting

In modern cost accounting, the concept of recording historical costs was taken further, by allocating the hotel's fixed costs over a given period of time to the items produced during that period, and recording the result as the total cost of production. This allowed the *full cost* of products that were not sold in the period they were produced to be recorded in inventory using a variety of complex accounting methods, which was consistent with the principles of Generally Accepted Accounting Principles (GAAP) as established by the Financial Accounting Standards Board for reporting results of publicly owned companies. It also enabled managers to effectively ignore the fixed costs, and look at the results of each period in relation to the "standard cost" for any given product.

For example: if the railway coach hotel normally produced 40 coaches per month, and the fixed costs were still $1000/month, then each coach could be said to incur an overhead of $25 ($1000/40). Adding this to the variable costs of $300 per coach produced a full cost of $325 per coach.

This method tended to slightly distort the resulting unit cost, but in mass-production industries that made one product line, and where the fixed costs were relatively low, the distortion was very minor.

For example: if the railway coach hotel made 100 coaches one month, then the unit cost would become $310 per coach ($300 + ($1000/100)). If the next month the hotel made 50 coaches, then the unit cost = $320 per coach ($300 + ($1000/50)), a relatively minor difference.

An important part of standard cost accounting is a variance analysis which breaks down the variation between actual cost and standard costs into various components (volume variation, material cost variation, Labour cost variation, etc.) so managers can understand *why costs were different than planned* and take appropriate action to correct the situation.

Weaknesses of Standard Cost Accounting for Management Decision Making

As time went on, standard cost accounting lost its usefulness for management decision making due to a variety of reasons:

- The practice of paying workers on a 'set-piece' basis changed in favour of paying on an hourly rate.
- Modern companies tend to have relatively low truly variable costs (primarily raw material, commissions or casual workers) and very high fixed costs (worker salaries, engineering costs, quality control, etc.).
- Equipment has become more complex and specialized and may be a very significant proportion of total costs.

- Changes in the level of full cost inventory create swings in profitability that are difficult to explain or understand. An increase in inventory can "absorb" costs of production and increase profits, while a decrease in inventory level will decrease profits.
- Organizations with a wide range of products or services have processes which are common to several finished items, making cost allocation irrelevant or misleading.

As a result of the above, using standard cost accounting to analyze management decisions can distort the unit cost figures in ways that can lead managers to make decisions that do not reduce costs or maximize profits. For this reason, managers often use the terms "direct costs" and "indirect costs" to replace the standard costing, to better reflect the way allocation of overhead is actually calculated. Indirect costs (often large) are usually allocated in proportion to either labour cost, other direct costs, or some physical resource utilization.

For example: If the railway coach hotel now paid its workforce a fixed monthly rate of $8,000 (total) and its other fixed costs had risen to $2,600/month, the total fixed costs would then be $10,600/month. The unit cost to make 40 coaches per month would still be $325 per coach ($60 material + ($10,600/40)), but producing 100 coaches would result in a unit cost of $166 per coach ($60 + ($10, 600/100)), provided the hotel had the capacity to increase production to that level.

Managers using the standard cost for 40 coaches per month would likely reject an order for 100 coaches (to be produced in one month) if the selling price was only $300 per unit, seeing that it would result in a loss of $25 per unit. If they analyzed the fixed vs. variable cost distinction, they would see clearly that filling this order would result in a contribution to fixed costs of $240 per coach ($300 selling price less $60 materials) and would result in a net profit for the month of $13,400 (($240 x 100) - 10,600).

The Development of Throughput Accounting

As companies have become more complex and begun producing a variety of products, the use of cost accounting to make decisions to maximize profitability has come under question. Managers learned in the 1980's about the theory of constraints and began to understand that *every production process has a limiting factor* somewhere in the chain of production. As managers learned to identify the constraints, they learned to use throughput accounting to manage them and *maximize the throughput dollars* from each unit of constrained resource.

For example: The railway coach hotel was offered a contract to make 15 open-topped streetcars each month, using a design which included ornate brass foundry work, but very little of the metalwork needed to produce a covered railway coach. The buyer offered to pay $280 per streetcar. The hotel had a firm order for 40 railway coaches each month for $350 per unit.

The hotel accountant determined that the cost of operating the foundry vs. the metalwork shop each month was as follows:

Overhead Cost by Department	*Total Cost*	*Hours Available per month*	*Cost per hour*
Foundry	$ 7,300.00	160	$45.63
Metalshop	$ 3,300.00	160	$20.63
Total	$10,600.00	320	$33.13

The hotel was at full capacity making 40 railway coaches each month. And since the foundry was expensive to operate, and purchasing brass as a raw material for the streetcars was expensive, the accountant determined that the hotel would lose money on any streetcars it built. He showed an analysis of the estimated product costs based on standard cost accounting and recommended that the hotel decline to build any streetcars.

Standard Cost Accounting Analysis	*Streetcars*	*Railway Coach*
Monthly Demand	15	40
Price	$280	$350
Foundry Time (hrs)	3.0	2.0
Metalwork Time (hrs)	1.5	4.0
Total Time	4.5	6.0
Foundry Cost	$136.88	$ 91.25
Metalwork Cost	$ 30.94	$ 82.50
Raw Material Cost	$120.00	$ 60.00
Total Cost	$287.81	$233.75
Profit per Unit	$ (7.81)	$116.25

However, the operations manager had just made improvements in the foundry equipment, and she knew there was idle time for the workers making coaches there. The constraint was the metalwork shop. She made an analysis of profit and loss if the hotel took the contract using throughput accounting to determine the profitability of products by maximizing "throughput" (revenue less variable cost) in the metal shop.

Throughput Cost Accounting Analysis	*Decline Contract*	*Take Contract*
Coaches Produced	40	34
Streetcars Produced	0	15
Foundry Hours	80	113
Metalshop Hours	160	159
Coach Revenue	$14,000	$11,900
Streetcar Revenue	$ 0	$ 4,200
Coach Raw Material Cost	$(2,400)	$(2,040)
Streetcar Raw Material Cost	$ 0	$(1,800)
Throughput Value	$11,600	$12,260
Overhead Expense	$(10,600)	$(10,600)
Profit	$1,000	$1,660

The president saw that the metalshop capacity was limiting the hotel's profitability. They could make only 40 railway coaches per month. But by taking the contract for the streetcars, the hotel could make nearly all the railway coaches ordered, and also meet all the demand for streetcars. The result would increase throughput in the metal shop from $6.25 to $10.38 per hour of available time, and increase profitability by 66 percent.

Activity-based Costing

Activity-based costing (ABC) is a system for assigning costs to products based on the activities they require. In this case, activities are those regular actions performed inside a hotel. "Talking with customer regarding invoice questions" is an example of an activity performed inside most companies.

Accountants assign 100% of each employee's time to the different activities performed inside a hotel (many will use surveys to have the workers themselves assign their time to the different activities). The accountant then can determine the total cost spent on each activity by summing up the percentage of each worker's salary spent on that activity.

Each product or service is produced and delivered via the activities performed in the hotel. The accountant can then assign the different activities to the different products using an appropriate allocation method.

A hotel can use the resulting activity cost data to determine where to focus their operational improvement efforts. For example, a job based manufacturer may find that a high percentage of their workers are spending their time trying to figure out a hastily written customer order. Via ABC, the accountants now have a currency amount that will be associated with the activity of "Researching Customer Work Order Specifications". Senior management can now decide how much focus or money to budget for the resolutions of this process deficiency. Activity-based management includes (but is not restricted to) the use of activity-based costing to manage a business.

Marginal Costing

This method is used particularly for short-term decision-making. Its principal tenets are:

- *Revenue (per product)*—Variable Costs (per product) = Contribution (per product)
- *Total Contribution*—Total Fixed Costs = Total Profit or (Total Loss)

Thus it does not attempt to allocate fixed costs in an arbitrary manner to different products. The short-term objective is to maximise contribution per unit. If constraints exist on resources, then Managerial Accounting dictates that marginal cost analysis be employed to maximise contribution per unit of the constrained resource.

Other costing Methods

More varieties of costing methods have been proposed in order to tailor for different aspects of the business. Some of the uprising ones include inventory costing method, process costing method, average costing method, target costing method. Still, the standard methods and normal costing methods are the most established methods in the world of public accounting. For management accountants in private industry, throughput accounting is rapidly becoming the standard for use in decision making in a fast-paced business environment.

Chapter 5

Depreciation and Double-entry Bookkeeping System

Depreciation is a term used in accounting, economics and finance with reference to the fact that assets with finite lives lose value over time. (There is also a separate use in international finance to refer to a reduction in the exchange rate of a currency). In accounting, depreciation is a term used to describe any method of attributing the cost of an asset across the useful life of the asset, roughly corresponding to normal wear and tear. Depreciation is an example of applying the matching principle as per generally accepted accounting principles. Depreciation in accounting is often mistakenly seen as a basis for recognizing impairment of an asset, but unexpected changes in value, where seen as significant enough to account for, are handled through write-downs or similar techniques which adjust the book value of the asset to reflect its current value. The use of depreciation affects the financial statements and in some countries the taxes of companies and individuals. Depreciation reported for accounting and tax purposes may differ substantially.

Depreciation and its related concept, amortization (generally, the depreciation of intangible assets), are non-cash expenses. Neither depreciation nor amortization will directly affect the cash flow of a hotel, as both are accounting representations of expenses attributable to a given period. In accounting statements, depreciation may either not figure in the cash flow statement, or may be "added back" to net income (along with other items) to derive the operating cash flow. Depreciation recognized for tax purposes will, however, affect the cash flow of the hotel, as tax depreciation will reduce taxable profits; there is generally no requirement that treatment of depreciation for tax and accounting purposes be identical. Where depreciation is shown on accounting statements, the figure usually does not relate to depreciation for tax purposes.

In economics depreciation is the decrease in the economic value of the capital stock of a firm, nation or other entity, either through physical depreciation, obsolescence or changes in the demand for the services of the capital in question. If capital stock is C_0 at the beginning of a period, investment is I and depreciation D, the capital stock at the end of the period, C_1, is $C_0 + I - D$.

Accounting

A hotel needs to report depreciation accurately in its financial statements in order to achieve two main objectives. First, to match its expenses with the income generated by means of those expenses. Second, to ensure that the asset values in the balance sheet are not overstated. An asset acquired in Year 1 is unlikely to be worth the same amount in Year 5.

Depreciation is an average or expected view of the decline in value of an asset. For example, an entity may depreciate its equipment by 15% per year. This rate should be reasonable in aggregate (such as when a manufacturing hotel is looking at all of its machinery), but there is no expectation that each individual item declines in value by the same amount.

Accounting standards bodies have detailed rules on which methods of depreciation are acceptable, and auditors will express a view if they believe the assumptions underlying the estimates do not give a true and fair view.

Recording Depreciation

For historical cost purposes, assets are recorded on the balance sheet at their original cost; this is called the book value. Depreciation is not taken out of these assets directly. It is instead recorded in a contra asset account: an asset account with a normal credit balance, typically called "accumulated depreciation". Balancing an asset account with its corresponding accumulated depreciation account will result in the net book value. The net book value will never fall below the salvage value, meaning that once an asset is fully depreciated, no further expenses will be taken during its life. Companies have no obligation to dispose of depreciated assets, of course, and many depreciated assets continue to generate income.

Recording a depreciation expense will involve a credit to an accumulated depreciation account. The corresponding debit will involve either an expense account or an asset account which represents a future expense, such as work in process. Depreciation is recorded as an adjusting journal entry. A write-down is a form of depreciation that involves a partial write off. Part of the value of the asset is removed from the balance sheet. The reason may be that the book value (accounted value) of the fixed asset has diverged from the market value. An example of this would be a removal of goodwill from an acquisition that went bad.

METHODS OF DEPRECIATION

There are several methods for calculating depreciation, generally based on either the passage of time or the level of activity (or use) of the asset.

Straight-line Depreciation

Straight-line depreciation is the simplest and most often used technique, in which the hotel estimates the "salvage value" of the asset after the length of time over which it is depreciated, and assumes the drop in the asset's value is in equal, constant yearly increments over that amount of time.

The salvage value is an estimate of the value of the asset at the time it will be sold or disposed of; it may be zero. For example, a vehicle that depreciates over 5 years, is purchased at a cost of US$17,000, and will have a "salvage value" of US$2000 will depreciate at US$3,000 per year. ($17,000 " (5 x $3000)) = $2000. In other words it is the cost of the assets divided by number of year of its useful life. If the vehicle were to be sold and the sales price exceeded the depreciated value (net book value) then the excess depreciation would be considered as income by the tax office (capital gains). If the sales price is less than the book value, the resulting capital loss is tax deductible.

If a hotel chooses to depreciate an asset at a different rate from that used by the tax office then this generates a timing difference in the income statement due to the difference (at a point in time) between the taxation department's and hotel's view of the profit.

Sinking fund Method

A method of depreciation under which the depreciation expense is an amount of an Annuity so that the amount of the annuity at the end of the useful life would equal the Acquisition Cost of the asset. Theoretically, the depreciation charge should include interest on accumulated depreciation at the beginning of the period. This method is rarely used in practice. The sinking fund method allocates more depreciation to the later years.

The depreciation for the first year equals the annual deposit needed for a sinking fund to accumulate at the given rate to an amount that equals the depreciation base. Then for each consecutive year, the annual depreciation equals the annual sinking fund deposit plus the interest earned on the fund up to that year.

Declining-balance Depreciation

As declining-balance method is a type of accelerated depreciation, because it recognizes a higher depreciation cost earlier in an asset's lifetime. This may be a more realistic reflection of an asset's actual resale value, as well as the expected benefit from the use of the asset: many assets are most useful when they are new. In the U.S., a form of declining-balance depreciation, MACRS, is used for tax purposes and is based on time.

In declining-balance depreciation, each period's depreciation is based on the previous year's net book value, the estimated useful life, and a factor. The factor is commonly two; this is known as double declining-balance. Each period we calculate depreciation:

$$\text{Depreciation expense} = \text{Previous period NBV} \times \frac{\text{factor}}{N}$$

For the double-declining balance method, using the vehicle example from above, we compute the depreciation after the first year:

$$\text{Previous Period NBV} \times \frac{\text{factor}}{N} = \$17000 \times \frac{2}{5} = \$6800$$

We subtract $6800 from our previous year's net book value to obtain our new net book value: NBV_1 = $17000 × $ 6800 = $10200. For the second year, we use this new value to calculate depreciation. Notice that it is significantly lower than the first year:

$$\$10200 \times \frac{2}{5} = \$4080$$

This process continues until we reach the salvage value or the end of the asset's useful life. Since declining-balance depreciation doesn't always depreciate an asset fully by its end of life, some methods also compute a straight-line depreciation each year, and apply the greater of the two. This has the effect of converting from declining-balance depreciation to straight-line depreciation at a midpoint in the asset's life. It should also be noted that the book value of the asset being depreciated is never brought below its salvage value, regardless of the method used.

Activity Depreciation

Activity depreciation methods are not based on time, but on a level of activity. This could be miles driven for a vehicle, or a cycle count for a machine. When the asset is acquired, we estimate its life in terms of this level of activity. Assume the vehicle above is estimated to go 50,000 miles in its lifetime. We calculate a per-mile depreciation rate: ($17,000 cost – $2,000 salvage) / 50,000 miles = $0.30 per mile. Each year, we then calculate the depreciation expense by multiplying the rate by the actual activity level..

Sum of years Digits Depreciation

Sum of Years Digits is a historical depreciation method that results in a more accelerated write off than straight line, but less than declining balance or later methods. Salvage value is counted in the method. There are no property classes of later methods.

1. Given;
   - N = Depreciable life of asset
   - B = Cost basis
   - S = Salvage value
   - $D(t)$ = Depreciation charge for year t
   - $\text{Sum}=\dfrac{N(N+1)}{2}$
   - $D(t) = (N - t + 1) \times \dfrac{(B-S)}{\text{sum}}$

Example: If an asset costs $1000, has a depreciable life of 5 years and a salvage value of $90, compute its depreciation schedule.

Year	*D(t)*	*Sum of D(t)*	*Remaining Book Value*
1	$303	$303	$697
2	$242	$546	$454
3	$182	$728	$272
4	$121	$849	$151
5	$61	$910	$90

The equation for year 1 would look like this:

$$D(t) = (5 - 1 + 1) \times \frac{(1000-90)}{\frac{5(5+1)}{2}} = 303.33$$

Note: Most depreciation schedules round to the nearest dollar.

Units of Production Depreciation

Units of Production depreciation is used in the U.S. in cases where MACRS is inappropriate, and the value to depreciate is based in the asset, such as a mine or natural resources. The method calculates the depreciation based on the units of the asset place in service as compared to the total units of the asset.

Units of time Depreciation

Units of Time Depreciation is similar to units of production, and is used for depreciation equipment used in mine or natural resource exploration, or cases where the amount the asset is used is not linear year to year.

Taxes

When an hotel spends money for a service or anything else that is short-lived, this expenditure is usually immediately tax deductible, and the hotel enjoys an immediate tax benefit. However, when a hotel buys an asset that will last longer than one year, like a computer, car, or building, the hotel cannot immediately deduct the cost and enjoy an immediate tax benefit. Instead, the hotel must *depreciate* the cost over the useful life of the asset, taking a tax deduction for a part of the cost each year. Eventually the hotel does get to deduct the full cost of the asset, but this happens over several years; the number of years depends on an estimate of how long it typically takes that type of asset to become effectively useless, and require a replacement.

A computer may depreciate completely over five years; a factory building, over 30 years. The maximum allowable useful life estimate under U.S. income tax regulations is 40 years. Other countries have other systems, many of which remove the choice of depreciation rate and method from the hotel altogether. In these jurisdictions accounting depreciation and tax depreciation are almost always significantly different numbers, as in many instances a form of "accelerated depreciation" can be used for tax purposes to lower (taxable) net income in a given period (or, in some instances, a fixed asset may be allowed to be expensed for tax purposes; Section 179 of the Internal Revenue Code allows for this treatment in some circumstances). Technically, these are not considered "tax reductions" but tax deferrals: lowering taxable income now by increasing expenses should increase future taxable income (and taxes) at a later date.

Economics

In economics, the value of a capital asset is equal to the present value of the flow of services the asset will generate in future, appropriately adjusted for uncertainty. Economic depreciation over a given period is the reduction in the remaining value of future services. Under certain circumstances, such as an unanticipated increase in the price of the services generated by an asset, its value may increase rather than declining. Depreciation is then negative.

National Accounts

In national accounts, depreciation represents the decline in the aggregate capital stock arising from the use of capital in production, also referred to as consumption of fixed capital. Hence, depreciation is equal to the difference between aggregate (gross) investment and net investment or between Gross National Product and Net National Product. Unlike depreciation in business accounting, depreciation in national accounts is, in principle, not a method of allocating the costs of past expenditures on fixed assets over subsequent accounting periods. Rather, fixed assets at a given moment in time are valued according to the remaining benefits derived from their use.

Diluted EPS

Diluted EPS is a hotel's EPS figure as calculated using fully diluted shares outstanding (i.e. including the impact of stock option grants and convertible bonds). This is important in showing the users of the income statement a "worst-case" scenario if everyone that could have received stock without purchasing it directly for the full market value, decreasing the "worst-case" EPS.

To find diluted EPS, basic EPS is calculated for each of the categories on the income statement first. Then each of the dilutive securities are ranked based on their effects, from most dilutive to least dilutive and anti-dilutive. Then the basic EPS number is diluted one by one by applying each one, skipping any instruments that have an anti-dilutive effect.

DOUBLE-ENTRY BOOKKEEPING SYSTEM

In hotel accountancy, the double-entry bookkeeping (or double-entry accounting) system is the basis of the standard system used by hotel businesses and other organizations to record financial transactions. Its premise is that a business's (or other organization's) financial condition and results of operations are best represented by several variables, called accounts, each of which reflects a particular aspect of the business as a monetary value.

Every transaction is recorded by entries in at least two accounts. The total of the debit values must equal the total value of the credit values. The premise for this is that any monetary transaction must logically affect two aspects of a hotel. For example, if an item is purchased (Debit Inventory), then it must also be paid for (Credit Bank Account). Alternatively, if an item is sold (Credit Inventory), then the hotel must also be paid for it (Debit Bank Account). Most transactions consist of two entries, but can have three or more entries e.g. Supplier Invoice Total = Net value + taxes. This system is called double entry because all transactions must "balance" - the debit and credit sides must equal the same amount.

Historically, debit entries have been recorded on the left hand side and credit values on the right hand side of a general ledger account. The ledger accounts are set up as T accounts so called because they resemble the letter T when the account is empty.

The origins of a primitive double-entry system have been traced as far back as the 12th century. Some sources suggest that Giovanni di Bicci de' Medici first introduced this method for the Medici bank. The earliest extant records that follow the modern double-entry form are those of Amatino Manucci, a Florentine merchant at the beginning of the 14th century. By the end of the 15th century, the merchant venturers of Venice used this system widely. Luca Pacioli, a monk and collaborator of Leonardo da Vinci, first codified the system in a 1494 mathematics textbook. Pacioli is often called the "father of accounting" because he was the first to publish a detailed description of the double-entry system, which enabled others to study and use it.

THE BOOKKEEPING AND ACCOUNTING PROCESS

In the normal course of hotel business, a document is produced each time a transaction occurs. Sales and purchases usually have invoices or receipts. Deposit slips are produced when lodgements (deposits) are made to a bank account. Cheques are written to pay money out of the account. Bookkeeping involves recording the details of all of these source documents into a journal (also known as a book of first entry or daybook). In the single entry system, each transaction is recorded only once. Most individuals who balance their cheque-book each month are using such a system, and most personal finance software follows this approach.

Businesses, however, usually use a more complex double-entry system, where each document is recorded as multiple journal entries, the totals of which always have to balance. For example, when a business receives a shipment of 100 widgets at a cost of $10 each from a supplier, the amount of inventory increases by $1000. However, the business's debt (the amount of money owed to creditors) also increases by $1000. When the supplier's invoice is paid, the debt (creditors' account) is decreased by $1000, and the bank account balance is also decreased by $1000.

This allows a business to know much more information about its current financial position than is possible using a single entry system. The double-entry journal permits the business to determine at any time the amount of funds the business has on deposit in the bank, as well as how much it owes it suppliers, how much customers owe it, how much tax is due, etc.

These journal entries are then transferred to their own accounts in the ledger, or book of accounts. The ledger contains the individual accounts that will appear on a trial balance. Posting is the process of transferring the values to a ledger. Once the journal entries have all been posted, the ledger accounts are added up in a process called balancing. Each account will now have a total value.

A working document called an unadjusted trial balance is created which lists all the balances from all the accounts in the ledger. Note that the balance on each account is not posted to the unadjusted trial balance. The amounts are copied to a two column list with debit balance amounts recorded in the left column and credit balance amounts recorded in the right column. This list contains each accounts value at the date of the Trial Balance e.g month end date and each account is listed to ensure that the total of all the debit account balances (left column) equals the total of all the credit account balances (right column). The two columns must have the same total, if not then double-entry has failed somewhere in the process and the difference must be found before further adjustments can be made.

At this point, the accountant produces a number of adjustments which ensure that the values comply with accounting principles. These values are then passed through the accounting system resulting in an adjusted trial balance.

This process continues until the accountant is satisfied that the resulting figures are correct and can be used to produce financial statements.

Finally financial statements are drawn from the trial balance, which may include:

- The income statement, also known as a statement of financial results, profit and loss statement, or simply P&L
- The balance sheet
- The cash flow statement
- The Statement of retained earnings

Short Examples

Buying an asset (such as a new machine):

1. The amount of fixed assets in the business increases.
2. The amount of cash (a current asset) is reduced.

Selling merchandise on credit:

1. The amount of receivables (an asset) for the business increases.
2. The sales revenue for the business increases (eventually this will become part of equity).

Upon payment, the receivables account decreases while the cash account increases. Should the receivable be "written off" as uncollectible debt, the receivable account decreases and the bad debt is added to expenses (which also becomes part of equity when netted against income and cost of goods sold). In larger firms, a portion of the receivable account is written off beforehand as expected to be uncollectible.

Paying a creditor:

1. The amount of payables (a liability) for the business decreases.
2. The amount of cash in the business is reduced.

An Explanation of Debits and Credits

Double-entry bookkeeping is governed by the accounting equation. At any point in time, the following equation must be true:

assets = liabilities + equity

For a particular time period, the equation becomes:

assets = liabilities + equity + (revenue " expenses)

Finally, this equation may be rearranged algebraically as follows:

assets + expenses = liabilities + equity + revenue

This equation must be true, for any time period. If it is, then the accounts are said to be in balance. If the accounts are not in balance, an error has occurred.

For the accounts to remain in balance, a change in one account must be matched with a change in another account. These changes are known as debits and credits. Note that the usage of these terms in accounting is not identical to their everyday usage. Whether one uses a debit or credit to increase or decrease an account depends on the normal balance of the account. Asset and expense accounts (on the left side of the equation) have a normal balance of *debit*. Liability, equity, and revenue accounts (on the right side of the equation) have a normal balance of *credit*. On a general ledger, debits are recorded on the left side and credits on the right side for each account. Since the accounts must always balance, for each transaction there will be a debit and a matching credit, and the sum of all debits for all accounts must equal the sum of all credits.

Debits and credits are then defined as follows:

- *Debit*: an *increase* in one of the accounts with a normal balance osnts = Gains (income) and Liabilities (also credit money paid out of bank accounts)

The following accounts have a normal balance of debit:

- Assets
- *Accounts receivable*: debts promised by other entities but not yet paid
- Drawings by the owners on equity
- Expenses
- Losses (that is, when expenses exceed revenue)

The following accounts have a normal balance of credit:

- Liabilities
- Accounts payable and taxes, notes or loans payable: debts promised to outsiders but not yet paid
- Revenue
- Profit (that is, when revenue exceeds expenses)

Examples of debits and credits:

Purchase of a Computer

Debit = Computer A/c (Fixed *Asset* A/c)

Credit = Creditors A/c (*Liability* A/c)

Paying supplier for the computer

Debit: Creditors A/c (*Liability* A/c) You are redu`ing a Liability A/c

Credit: Bank A/c (*Asset* A/c) Money going Out, you are reducing an asset account

Credit and debit items are summarised at the end of a recording period in a trial balance which is a list of all the debit and credit balances. The trial balance acts as a self checking mechanism for the correctness of entries in the individual accounts and also as a starting point for the preparation of the Final Account which is made up of the balance sheet and the trading, profit and loss account.

The following table summarizes the basic accounts. A "+" indicates an increase; a """ indicates a decrease.

Debit/credit

Account	*Debit*	*Credit*
Assets	+	"
Liabilities	" o	+
Shareholder Equity	"	+
Revenue	(")	+
Expenses	+	(")

An Explanation of a T account

A T account is called such because it looks like the letter "T" when drawn like so:

Debits	Credits

Debit entries are made on the left side of the middle line and credit entries are made on on the right side of the middle line.

Double-entry working examples

Example 1

In this example the following will be used: Books of first entry (a.k.a. Books of prime entry)

- Sales Invoice Daybook (records customer Invoice Daybook)
- Bank Receipts Daybook (records customer and non customer receipts)
- Purchase Invoice Daybook (records supplier Invoice Daybook)
- Bank Payments Daybook (records supplier and non supplier payments)

Ledger Cards

- Customer Ledger Cards
- Supplier Ledger Cards

General Ledger (Nominal Ledger)
Bank Account Ledger
Trade Creditors Ledger
Trade Debtors Ledger

From the above we will create:

- Trial Balance
- Profit and Loss Statement (Dr and Cr Formating, classic format)
- Profit and Loss Statement (List Format, Modern version used today)
- Balance Sheet (Dr and Cr Formatting, classic format)
- Balance Sheet (List Format, Modern version used today)

Purchases/Creditors

Purchase Invoice Daybook

Purchase Invoice Daybook

Date	*Supplier Name*	*Reference*	*Amount*	*Electricity*	*Widgets*
10 Jul 2006	Electricity Hotel	PI1	1000	1000	
12 Jul 2006	Widget Hotel	PI2	1600		1600
		Total	2600	1000	1600
		Credit	Debit	Debit	
		Trade Creditors	*Profit and loss*	*Profit and loss*	
		control a/c	control a/c	control a/c	

Each individual line is posted as follows:

The amount value is posted as a credit to the individual supplier's ledger a/c

The analysis amount is posted a debit to the relevant general ledger a/c

From example above:

Line 1—Amount value 1000 is posted as a credit to the *Supplier's* ledger a/c ELE01-Electricity Hotel

Line 1—Electricty value 1000 is posted as a debit to the *Electricity* general ledger a/c code

Double-entry has been observed Dr = 1000 Cr = 1000

Line 2—Amount value 1600 is posted as a credit to the *Supplier's* ledger a/c WID01-Widget Hotel

Line 2—Widget value 1600 is posted as a debit to the *Widget* general ledger a/c code

Double-entry has been observed Dr = 1600 Cr = 1600

The totals of each column are posted as follows:

Amount total value 2600 posted as a credit to the *Trade creditors control a/c*

Electricity total value 1000 posted as a debit to the *Profit and loss control a/c*

Widget total value 1600 posted as a debit to the *Profit and loss control a/c*

Double-entry has been observed Dr = 2600 Cr = 2600

Bank Payments Daybook

Bank Payments Daybook

Date	*Supplier Name*	*Reference*	*Amount*	*Trade Creditors*	*Other*
17 Jul 2006	Electricity Hotel	BP701	1000	1000	
19 Jul 2006	Widget Hotel	BP702	900	900	
28 Jul 2006	Owner's Wages	BP703	400		400
		Total	2300	1900	400
		Credit *Profit and loss* control a/c	Debit *Trade Creditors* control a/c	Debit *Wages* control a/c	

Keys: PI = Purchase Invoice, BP = Bank Payment

Each indivdual line is posted as follows: The amount value is posted as a debit to the individual supplier's ledger a/c

The analysis amount is posted as a credit to the relevant general ledger a/c

From example above:

Line 1 - Amount value 1000 is posted as a debit to the *Supplier's* ledger a/c ELE01-Electricity Hotel

Line 1 - *Trade creditors* value 1000 is posted as a credit to the *Bank* general ledger a/c code

Double-entry has been observed Dr = 1000 Cr = 1000

Line 2 - *Amount* value 900 is posted as a debit to the *Supplier's* ledger a/c WID01-Widget Hotel

Line 2 - *Trade creditors* value 900 is posted as a credit to the *Bank* general ledger a/c code

Double-entry has been observed Dr = 900 Cr = 900

Line 3 - *Amount* value 400 is posted as a debit to the *Wages* general ledger a/c code

Line 3 - *Trade creditors* value 400 is posted as a credit to the *Bank* general ledger a/c code

Double-entry has been observed Dr = 400 Cr = 400

The totals' of each column are posted as follows:

Amount total value 2300 posted as a debit to the *Trade creditors control a/c*

Electricity total value 1900 posted as a credit to the *Profit and loss control a/c*

Widget total value 400 posted as a credit to the *Profit and loss control a/c*

Double-entry has been observed Dr = 2300 Cr = 2300

The daybooks are the key documents (books) to the double entry system. From these daybooks we create the ledger accounts. Each transaction will be recorded in at least two ledger accounts.

Supplier Ledger Cards

Supplier ledger cards

A/c Code: ELE01 - Electricity Hotel

Date	*Details*	*Reference*	*Amount*	*Date*	*Details*	*Reference*	*Amount*
17 Jul 2006	*Bank Payments* Daybook	BP701	1000	10 Jul 2006	Invoice	PI1	1000
31 Jul 2006	Balance c/f		0				
			1000				1000
				01 Aug 2006	Balance b/f		0

A/c Code: WID01 - Widget Hotel

Date	*Details*	*Reference*	*Amount*	*Date*	*Details*	*Reference*	*Amount*
19 Jul 2006	*Bank Payments* Daybook	BP702	900	12 Jul 2006	Invoice	PI2	1600
31 Jul 2006	Balance c/f		700				
			1600				1600
				01 Aug 2006	Balance b/f		700

Sales/Customers

Sales daybook

Sales Invoice Daybook

Date	*Customer Name*	*Reference*	*Amount*	*Parts*	*Service*
02 Jul 2006	JJ Manufacuring	SI1	2500	2500	
29 Jul 2006	JJ Manufacturing	SI2	3200		3200
		Total	5700	2500	3200
			Debit *Trade debtors* control a/c	Credit *Profit and loss* control a/c	Credit *Profit and loss* control a/c

Each indivdual line is posted as follows:

The amount value is posted as a debit to the individual customer's ledger a/c

The analysis amount is posted a credit to the relevant general ledger a/c

From example above:

Line 1 - *Amount* value 2500 is posted as a debit to the *Customer's* ledger a/c JJM01-JJ Manufacturing

Line 1 - *Electricty* value 2500 is posted as a credit to the *Sales-parts* general ledger a/c code

Double-entry has been observed Dr = 2500 Cr = 2500

Line 2 - *Amount* value 3200 is posted as a credit to the *Customer's* ledger a/c JJM01-JJ Manufacturing

Line 2 - *Electricty* value 3200 is posted as a debit to the *Sales-service* general ledger a/c code

Double-entry has been observed Dr = 3200 Cr = 3200

The totals' of each column are posted as follows:

Amount total value 5700 posted as a debit to the *Trade debtors control a/c*

Sales-parts total value 2500 posted as a credit to the *Profit and loss control a/c*

Sales-service total value 3200 posted as a credit to the *Profit and loss control a/c*

Double-entry has been observed Dr = 5700 Cr = 5700

Bank Receipts daybook

Bank Receipts Daybook

Date	*Customer Name*	*Reference*	*Amount*	*Customers*	*Others*
20 Jul 2006	JJ Manufacturing	BR1	2500	2500	0
		Total	2500	2500	0
			Debit *Bank a/c* control	Credit *Trade* control	Credit *Other* control

Keys: SI = Sales Invoice, BR = Bank Receipt

Each indivdual line is posted as follows: The amount value is posted as a credit to the individual customer's ledger a/c

The analysis amount is posted as a debit to the relevantgeneral ledger a/c

From example above:

Line 1 - *Amount* value 2500 is posted as a credit to the *Customer's* ledger a/c JJM01 - JJ Manufacturing

Line 1 - *Customers* value 2500 is posted as a debit to the *Bank* general ledger a/c code

Double-entry has been observed Dr = 2500 Cr = 2500

The totals' of each column are posted as follows:

Amount total value 2500 posted as a credit to the *Trade debtors control a/c*

Customers total value 2500 posted as a debit to the *Profit and loss control a/c*

Double-entry has been observed Dr = 2500 Cr = 2500

The daybooks are the key documents (books) to the double entry system. From these daybooks we create the ledger accounts. Each transaction will be recorded in at least two ledger accounts.

Customer Ledger Cards

Customer ledger cards

A/c Code: JJM01 - JJ Manufacturing

Date	*DetailsReference*	*Amount*	*Date*	*Details*	*Reference*	*Amount*
02 Jul 2006	Sales invoice SI1 daybook	2500	20 Jul 2006	Bank receipts daybook	BR1	2500
02 Jul 2006	Sales invoice SI2 daybook	3200	31 Jul 2006	balance c/f		3200
		5700				5700
01 Aug 2006	Balance b/f	3200				

General Ledger

General Ledger

Sales parts

Date	*Details*	*Reference*	*Amount*	*Date*	*Details*	*Reference*	*Amount*
31 Jul 2006	Balance c/f b/f		2500 2500	02 Jul 2006	Sales invoice Daybook	SI1	2500

Sales service

Date	*Details*	*Reference*	*Amount*	*Date*	*Details*	*Reference*	*Amount*
31 Jul 2006	Balance c/f		3200	29 Jul 2006	Sales invoice daybook	SI2	3200
			3200				3200
				01 Aug	Balance b/f		3200

Electricity

Date	*Details*	*Reference*	*Amount*	*Date*	*Details*	*Reference*	*Amount*
10 Jul 2006	Electricity Co.	PI1	1000	31 Jul 2006	Balance c/f		1000
			1000				1000
01 Aug 2006	Balance b/f		1000				

Widgets

Date	*Details*	*Reference*	*Amount*	*Date*	*Details*	*Reference*	*Amount*
12 Jul 2006	Widget Co.	PI2	1600	31 Jul 2006	Balance c/f		1600
			1600				1600
01 Aug 2006	Balance b/f		1600				

Other a/c

Date	*Details*	*Reference*	*Amount*	*Date*	*Details*	*Reference*	*Amount*
28 Jul 2006	Owner's Wages	BP703	400	31 Jul 2006	Balance c/f		400

Date	Details	Reference	Amount	Date	Details	Reference	Amount
			400				400
01 Aug 2006	Balance b/f		400				

Bank Control A/c

Date	Details	Reference	Amount	Date	Details	Reference	Amount
31 Jul 2006	Bank receipts daybook	BR-Jul	2500	31 Jul 2006	Bank payments daybook	BP-Jul	2300
				31 Jul 2006	Balance c/f		200
			2500				2500
01 Aug 2006	Balance b/f		200				

Trade Debtors Control A/c

Date	Details	Reference	Amount	Date	Details	Reference	Amount
01 Jul 2006	Balance b/f		0	31 Jul 2006	Bank receipts daybook	BR-Jul	2500
31 Jul 2006	Sales Invoice Daybook	SI-Jul	5700	31 Jul 2006	Balance c/f		3200
			5700				5700
01 Aug 2006	Balance b/f		3200				

Trade Creditors Control A/c

Date	Details	Reference	Amount	Date	Details	Reference	Amount
31 Jul 2006	Bank Payments Daybook	BP-Jul	1900	01 Jul 2006	Balance b/f		0
31 Jul 2006	Balance c/f		700	31 Jul 2006	Purchase Daybook	PI-Jul	2600
			2600				2600
				01 Aug 2006	Balance b/f		700

Profit and loss control A/c							
Date	*Details*	*Reference*	*Amount*	*Date*	*Details*	*Reference*	*Amount*
31 Jul 2006	Purchase invoice daybook	PI-Jul	2600	31 Jul 2006	Sales invoice daybook	SI-Jul	5700
31 Jul 2006	Bank payments daybook	BP-Jul	400				
31 Jul 2006	Balance c/f		2700				
			5700				5700
				01 Aug 2006	Balance b/f		2700

The customers ledger cards shows the breakdown of how the trade debtors control a/c is made up. The trade debtors control a/c is the total of outstanding debtors and the customer ledger cards shows the amount due for each individual customer. The total of each individual customer account added together should equal the total in the trade debtors control a/c.

The supplier ledger cards shows the breakdown of how the trade creditors control a/c is made up. The trade creditors control a/c is the total of outstanding creditors and the suppliers ledger cards shows the amount due for each individual supplier. The total of each individual supplier account added together should equal the total in the trade creditors control a/c.

Each Bank a/c shows all the money in and out through a bank. If you have more than one bank account for your hotel you will have to maintain separate bank account ledger in order to complete bank reconcilliation statements and be able to see how much is left in each account.

The Bank control a/c keeps the total for all bank accounts. The balance of each individual bank acount, when added together, must equal the balance in the bank control a/c.

Bank Account

Bank A/c

Date	*Details*	*Reference*	*Amount*	*Date*	*Details*	*Reference*	*Amount*
01 Jul 2006	Balance b/f		0	17 Jul 2006	Bank Payments Daybook	BP701	1000
20 Jul 2006	Bank Receipts Daybook	BR1	2500	19 Jul 2006	Bank Payments Daybook	BP702	900
				28 Jul 2006	Bank Payments Daybook	BP703	400
				31 Jul 2006	Balance c/f		200
			2500				2500
01 Aug 2006		Balance b/f	200				

Unadjusted Trial balance

Trial balance as at 31st July 2006

A/c description	*Debit*	*Credit*
Sales-parts		2500
Sales-sevice		3200
Widgets	1600	
Electricity	1000	
Other	400	
Bank Control A/c	200	
Trade Debtors Control A/c	3200	
Trade Creditors Control A/c		700
	6400	6400

Both sides must have the same overall total

Debits = Credits.

The individual customer accounts are not to be listed in the trial balance, as the Trade debtors control a/c is the summary of each individual customer a/c.

The individual supplier accounts are not to be listed in the trial balance, as the Trade creditors control a/c is the summary of each individual supplier a/c.

The individual bank accounts are not to be listed in the trial balance, as the Bank control account is the summary of each individual bank a/c.

The profit and loss control account is not to be listed in the trial balance, as thr profit and loss control account is a summary of the trial balance.

Important notes:

1. This example is designed to show double entry. There are methods of creating a trial balance that significantly reduce the time it takes to record entries in the general ledger and trial balance.
2. In practice it is the norm to list each bank account in the trial balance. This allows you to distinguish between bank accounts which are overdrawn or not and which bank accounts are loans or savings accounts.

Journal Entries

Depreciation Wages Stock Accurals Prepayments

Adjusted Trial balance

Trial balance as at 31st July 2006

A/c description Debit Credit

Profit and Loss Statement and Balance Sheet

Classic Format (Debits and Credits)

Profit and loss statement
for the month ending 31st July 2006

		Dr		Cr
x	Cost of Sales		Sales	
x	Widgets	1600	Sales-parts 2500	
x		——	Sales-service 3200	
x		1600		——
x	Gross Profit	4100		5700
x	Less expenses			
x	Electricity	1000		
x	Other	400		
x		——		

x		1400	
x	Net Profit	2700	
x			
x		5700	5700
x			

Balance sheet as at 31st July 2006

		Dr		Cr
x	Current Assets		Current Liabilities	
x	Bank A/c	200	Trade Creditors	700
x	Trade Debtors	3200	Capital and Reserves	
x			Revenue Reserves a/c	2700
x				
x		3400		3400
x				

Modern Format (List method)

Profit and loss statement
for the month ending 31st July 2006

		Dr
x	Sales	
x	Sales-parts	2500
x	Sales-service	3200
x		
x		5700
x	Widgets	1600
x		
x	Gross Profit	4100
x	Less expenses	
x	Electricity	1000
x	Other	400
x		
x		1400
x		
x	Net Profit	2700
x		

Balance sheet as at 31st July 2006

		Dr
x	Current Assets	
x	Bank A/c	200
x	Trade Debtors	3200

x		
x		3400
x	Current Liabilities	
x	Trade Creditors	700
x		
x		700
x		
x	Net Current Assets	2700
x		
x	Capital and Reserves	
x	Revenue Reserves a/c	2700
x		
x		2700
x		

Example 2

Transactions

XYZ Hotel is closing its books for the end of the month. Each of the daily journals has been summarized and the amounts are ready to be transferred to the general ledger. The amounts to be transferred are:

- Purchase raw materials by using line of credit: $500,000
- Pay workers from cash in bank to make goods: $1,500.000
- Pay sales force from cash in bank to sell goods: $1,000,000
- Sell goods for cash: $3,500,000

To close the books for the month, we will adjust expenses and revenue to be zero by appropriately crediting and debiting the income summary and then closing the income summary to retained earnings (part of equity).

These items are entered in the ledger below; each matching credit and debit have been numbered to make finding them in the ledger easier.

Ledgers

General Ledger (in 000s)

Transaction	*Debit*	*Credit*	*Balance*
	Expenses		
Balance forward			-0-
1 Raw materials	$ 500		$ 500
2 Labour	$ 1500		$ 2000
3 Sales costs	$ 1000		$ 3000
5 Income summary		($ 3000)	-0-
Total	$ 3000	$ 3000	
	Revenue		
Balance forward			-0-
4 Revenue from sales		$ 3500	$ 3500
6 Income summary	($ 3500)		-0-
Total	$ 3500	$ 3500	
	Cash		
Balance forward			$11000
2 Labour		$ 1500	$ 9500
3 Sales costs		$ 1000	$ 8500
4 Revenue from sales	$ 3500		$12000
Total	$ 3500	$ 2500	
	Accounts Payable		
Balance forward			$ 1000
1 Raw materials		$ 500	$ 1500
Total	-0-	$ 500	
	Income summary		
Balance forward			-0-
5 Expense	$ 3000		"$ 3000
6 Revenue		$ 3500	$ 500
7 Retained earnings	$ 500		-0-
Total	$ 3500	$ 3500	
	Retained earnings		
Balance forward			$10000
7 Income summary		$ 500	$10500
Total	-0-	$ 500	
Total all accounts:	$13500	$13500	

The amount in equity (in the form of retained earnings) has changed with a net credit of $500,000. Since equity has a normal balance of credit, this means there is now $500,000 *more* in equity than at the beginning of the month.

SINGLE-ENTRY ACCOUNTING SYSTEM

Single-entry accounting system is a one sided accounting entry to maintain financial information. Most businesses maintain a record of all transactions based on the double-entry accounting system. However, many small, simple businesses maintain only a single-entry system that records the "bare-essentials." In some cases only records of cash, accounts receivable, accounts payable and taxes paid may be maintained. Records of assets, inventory, expenses, revenues and other elements usually considered essential in an accounting system may not be kept, except in memorandum form. Single-entry systems are usually inadequate except where operations are especially simple and the volume of activity is low.

This type of accounting system with additional information can typically be compiled into an income statement and balance sheet by a professional accountant.

Advantages

Single-entry systems are used in the interest of simplicity. They are usually less expensive to maintain than double-entry systems because they do not require the services of a trained person.

Disadvantages

1. Data may not be available to management for effectively planning and controlling the business.
2. Lack of systematic and precise bookkeeping may lead to inefficient administration and reduced control over the affairs of the business.
3. Single-entry records do not provide a check against clerical error, as does a double-entry system. This is one of the most serious defects of single-entry systems.

4. Single-entry records seldom make provision for recording all transactions. In addition, many internal transactions, such as adjusting entries are often not recorded.
5. Because no accounts are provided for many of the items appearing in both the Income Statement and Balance Sheet, omission of important data is possible.
6. In the absence of detailed records of all assets, lax administration of those assets may occur.
7. Theft and other losses are less likely to be detected.

Chapter 6

Corporate Accounting

TAXATION

Unlike India, in the U.S. Internal Revenue Code, the growth of the annuity value during the accumulation phase is tax deferred, that is, not subject to current income tax for annuities owned by individuals. The tax deferred status of deferred annuities has led to their common usage in the United States. Under the US tax code, the benefits from annuity contracts do not always have to be taken in the form of a fixed stream of payments (annuitization), and many of the contracts are bought primarily for the tax benefits rather than to get a fixed stream of income. If an annuity was used in a qualified pension plan or an IRA funding vehicle, then 100% of the annuity payment is taxable as current income upon distribution. If the annuity contract is purchased with after-tax dollars, then the contract holder upon annuitization recovers his basis pro-rata in the ratio of basis divided by the expected value according to the IRS regulations from Section 1.72-5. After the taxpayer has recovered all his basis, then 100% of the payments thereafter are subject to ordinary income tax.

EARNINGS BEFORE INTEREST AND TAXES

Earnings before interest and taxes (EBIT), also known as operating income and operating profit, is a term used to describe a hotel's earnings. A professional investor contemplating a change to the capital structure of a firm (e.g., through a leveraged buyout) first evaluates a firm's fundamental earnings potential (reflected by EBITDA and EBIT), and then determines the optimal use of debt vs. equity. To calculate EBIT, basic expenses (e.g., the cost of goods sold, selling and administrative expenses) are subtracted from revenues. Profit is later obtained by subtracting interest and taxes from the result.

Earnings before Interest, Taxes, Depreciation, and Amortization

EBITDA *«ee-bit-dah»* or *«ee-bit-dee-eh»* is an acronym for Earnings before Interest, Taxes, Depreciation, and Amortization. The same calculation can be arrived at from "operating income before depreciation and amortization" (OIBDA). It is one measure of 'operating cash flow'.

It differs from the cash flow from operations found in the Statement of Cash Flow primarily by ignoring payments for taxes or interest. EBITDA does not add back many of the other non-cash operating expenses, like the Statement of Cash Flow does. EBITDA also differs from free cash flow because of the difference above, and also because it does not recognize the cash requirements for replacing capital assets. Although there are different POVs regarding the use of this metric by equity owners, most everyone agrees to its validity when used by debtholders, or to evaluate a business's ability to handle debt.

Use by debt holders

The holder of debt is concerned with the business's ability to pay the interest and to repay the principal when due. Since interest is paid before income tax is calculated, he has no interest in taxes. The debtholder is not interested in whether the business can replace its assets when they wear out, so he can ignore both capital expenditures and their amortization. EBITDA measures the cash earnings that he can expect to be applied to interest and debt retirement.

There are two EBITDA metrics used.

1. The interest coverage ratio is used to determine a firm's ability to pay interest on outstanding debt. It is calculated : EBITDA / Interest Expense. The greater the year-to-year variance in EBITDA, the greater the multiple should be.
2. The measure of the pay-back period for a debt is : Debt/EBITDA. The longer the payback period, the greater the risk.

The ratios can be customized by reducing Debt by any cash on the balance sheet or by deducting maintenance capx from EBITDA to form a measure closer to free cash flow.

Use by Equity Owners -pro

A hotel's Net Income is distorted by decisions that the hotel made in previous years. This is because of the differences between accrual accounting and cash basis accounting. Some purchases are depreciated or amortized over 20 years or more, with a negative impact on the Net Income long after the actual financial effects of the purchases have ceased. The EBITDA does not suffer this distortion, so investors can get a better idea of how profitable the hotel really is

Depreciation of capital expenditures is a particularly strong factor. For example, if a hotel spends $99 million in new desktop computers for all its employees, the hotel will often decide to depreciate the purchase over their expected lifetime of three years. This way, in the first year, when the hotel calculates its "income" number, it pretends that it has only spent $33 million that year on desktop computers. The hotel's income number paints a more rosy and optimistic picture than actually occurred that year. In each of the second and third years, the hotel also pretends that it has spent $33 million per year on desktop computers. Hence, the hotel's financial picture was probably healthier than indicated by the income number, since the $33 million had actually already been paid out.

Capital expenditures typically vary from year to year. Accrual accounting accounts for this by spreading the expense of capital investments over the years in which they will be generating value for the hotel. EBITDA removes this effect. Investors can use EBITDA to approximate the fundamental earning power of the hotel's operations while separately factoring in the projected capital expenditures needed to maintain those operations. This is valuable because of the time value of money principle. (An expenditure is less costly if it is to be made several years into the future, because during the interim period the firm can use the cash for that expenditure to generate income in other ways.)

Because EBITDA is measured before interest (which vary with the amount of debt financing), it approximates the hotel's earnings potential as if financed with zero debt. It corrects for the differences between hotels' valuations due to their capital structure. If the investor can change the capital structure of a firm (e.g., through a leveraged buyout) he first evaluates a firm's fundamental earnings potential (reflected by EBITDA or EBIT), and then determines the optimal use of debt vs. equity.

Use by equity owners-con

In layman's terms, EBITDA is called "Earnings, before all the bad stuff". Warren Buffett famously asked, "Does management think the tooth fairy pays for capital expenditures?" People who understand the how's and why's of accounting think that Net Income is a better measure of a business' performance than EBITDA.

The basic debate over the value of accrual vs. cash accounting comes down to the question. "When you bought your Christmas presents in December 2001, did you consider them to be a 2001 expense? Or did you consider them to only show up in 2002 when you made the January credit card payment? Most people acknowledge the costs in 2001, even though there was no cash transaction.

Depreciation

The same argument applies to the purchase of long-life capital assets. You can consider depreciation to be either:

1. The allocation of the original cost, at a later date, when the asset was used to generate revenue. The time-value-of-money (same argument used above) means that the depreciation UNDERSTATES the cost.
2. The amount of cash required to be retained in order to finance the eventual replacement asset. Since inflations is the basis for time-value-of-money, the amounts set aside today must be invested and grow in value in order to pay the inflated price in the future. Or
3. The decrease in value of the balance sheet asset since the last reporting period. Assets wear out with use. A hotel with old assets is not worth as much as a hotel with new ones.

No matter which POV you choose, non-cash expenses are 'real' costs. This amount of cash received from sales is only a return of capital. No matter that the proponents of EBITDA claim to separately consider the future requirements for capital asset replacements, none due in public. When management is free to create their own estimate, their numbers are never justified with details and always low-balled beyond belief. Depreciation is not an exact measure, but it is beyond management manipulation, and supported by disclosed math calculations.

Interest

The only reason to ignore interest and financing expenses is if the investor CAN in fact create his own personal leverage that will equalize the leverage between different investments. No investors can. In the big picture, investors lever their portfolio, not individual stock positions. Even if long-term leverage could be equalized, most businesses use extensive short term debt to finance 1-2-3 month cash requirements.

The investor can never replicate these cash flows. If the investor separately measures the hotel's leverage and combines this metric with EBITDA, it would be valid. But leverage rates are rarely quoted in the media. Even sophisticated investors do not know how to weigh the trade-offs between the two metrics.

Taxes

There is no excuse for ignoring taxes. Management is payed to manage taxes, just like other expenses. This is why they incorporate in tax havens. The less money going to taxes, the more is left for equity owners.

Manipulation

The major argument for EBITDA is that is beyond management manipulation. Yet once management is told this is the metric they will be judged by, they immediately find ways to manipulate it.

Unprofitable Businesses

When comparing businesses with no profits, their potential to make profit is more important than their Net Loss. Since taxes on losses will be misleading in this context, taxes can be ignored. Capital expenditures and their related debt result in fixed costs. These are of less importance than the variable costs that can be expected to grow with increasing sales volume, in oder to cover the fixed costs. So depreciation and interest costs are of less importance. It is likely than an unprofitable business is burning cash (has a negative cash flow), so investors are most concerned with "how long the cash will last before the business must get more financing" (resulting in debt or equity dilution). For these reasons EBITDA is the metric most appropriate.

Be clear that EBITDA is not used as a valuation metric in these circumstances. It is a starting point on which future growth is applied and future profitability discounted back to the present. Equity owners only benefit from net profits, after all the expenses are paid.

During the dot com bubble companies promoted their stock by emphasizing either EBITDA or pro forma earnings in their financial reports, and explaining away the (often poor) "income" number. This would involve ignoring one-time write-offs, asset impairments and other costs deemed to be non-recurring. Because EBITDA (and its variations) are not measures generally accepted under U.S. GAAP, the U.S. Securities and Exchange Commission requires that companies registering securities with it (and when filing its periodic reports) reconcile EBITDA to net income in order to avoid misleading investors. A negative EBITDA figure is not meaningful when consideration valuation multiples (namely Enterprise Value/EBITDA).

STOCK

In financial markets, stock is the capital raised by a corporation through the issuance and distribution of shares. A person or organisation which holds at least a partial share of stocks is called a shareholder. The aggregate value of a corporation's issued shares is its market capitalization. In the United Kingdom and Australia, the term *share* is used the same way, but *stocks* there refer to either a completely different financial instrument, the bond, or more widely to all kinds of marketable securities.

Type of stock

There are several types of stock.

Common Stock

Common stock, also referred to as common shares or ordinary shares, are, as the name implies, the most usual and commonly held form of stock in a corporation. Shareholders of common stock have voting rights in corporate decision matters. It is the residual corporate interest that bears the ultimate risks of loss and receives the benefits of success.

Preferred Stock

Preferred stock, sometimes called preference shares, have priority over common stock in the distribution of dividends and assets. Most preferred shares provide no voting rights in corporate decision matters. However, some preferred shares have special voting rights to approve certain extraordinary events (such as the issuance of new shares, or the approval of the acquisition of the hotel), or to elect directors.

Dual Class Stock

Dual class stock is shares issued for a single hotel with varying classes indicating different rights on voting and dividend payments. Each kind of shares has its own class of shareholders entitling different rights.

Treasury stock

Treasury stock is shares that have been bought back from the public. Treasury Stock is considered issued, but not outstanding.

STOCK DERIVATIVES

A stock derivative is any financial claim which has a value that is dependent on the price of the underlying stock. Futures and options are the main types of derivatives on stocks. The underlying security may be a stock index or an individual firm's stock, e.g. single-stock futures. Stock futures are contracts where the buyer, or long, takes on the obligation to buy on the contract maturity date, and the seller, or short takes on the obligation to sell. Stock index futures are generally not delivered in the usual manner, but by cash settlement.

A stock option is a class of option. Specifically, a call option is the right (*not* obligation) to buy stock in the future at a fixed price and a put option is the right (*not* obligation) to sell stock in the future at a fixed price. Thus, the value of a stock option changes in reaction to the underlying stock of which it is a derivative. The most popular method of valuing stock options is the Black Scholes model.

Apart from call options granted to employees, most stock options are transferable. The first hotel to issue shares of stock was the Dutch East India Hotel, in 1602. The innovation of joint ownership made a great deal of Europe's economic growth possible following the Middle Ages. The technique of pooling capital to finance the building of ships, for example, made the Netherlands a maritime superpower. Before adoption of the joint-stock corporation, an expensive venture such as the building of a merchant ship could be undertaken only by governments or by very wealthy individuals or families.

SHAREHOLDER

A shareholder or *stockholder* is an individual or hotel (including a corporation) that legally owns one or more shares of stock in a joint stock hotel. Companies listed at the stock market strive to enhance shareholder value. Stockholders are granted special privileges depending on the class of stock, including the right to vote (usually one vote per share owned) on matters such as elections to the board of directors, the right to share in distributions of the hotel's income, the right to purchase new shares issued by the hotel, and the right to a hotel's assets during a liquidation of the hotel. However, stockholder's rights to a hotel's assets are subordinate to the rights of the hotel's creditors. This means that stockholders typically receive nothing if a hotel is liquidated after bankruptcy (if the hotel had had enough to pay its creditors, it would not have entered bankruptcy), although a stock may have value after a bankruptcy if there is the possibility that the debts of the hotel will be restructured.

Stockholders or shareholders are considered by some to be a partial subset of stakeholders, which may include anyone who has a direct or indirect equity interest in the business entity or someone with even a non-pecuniary interest in a non-profit organization. Thus it might be common to call volunteer contributors to an association stakeholders, even though they are not shareholders.

Although directors and officers of a hotel are bound by fiduciary duties to act in the best interest of the shareholders, the shareholders themselves normally do not have such duties towards each other. However, in a few unusual cases, some courts have been willing to imply such a duty between shareholders. For example, in California, majority shareholders of closely held corporations have a duty to not destroy the value of the shares held by minority shareholders. The largest shareholders (in terms of percentages of companies owned) are often mutual funds, and especially passively managed exchange-traded funds.

Application

The owners of a hotel may want additional capital to invest in new projects within the hotel. They may also simply wish to reduce their holding, freeing up capital for their own private use. By selling shares they can sell part or all of the hotel to many part-owners. The purchase of one share entitles the owner of that share to literally share in the ownership of the hotel a fraction of the decision-making power, and potentially a fraction of the profits, which the hotel may issue as dividends.

In the common case of a publicly traded corporation, where there may be thousands of shareholders, it is impractical to have all of them making the daily decisions required to run a hotel. Thus, the shareholders will use their shares as votes in the election of members of the board of directors of the hotel.

In a typical case, each share constitutes one vote (except in a co-operative society where every member gets one vote regardless of the number of shares he holds). Corporations may, however, issue different classes of shares, which may have different voting rights. Owning the majority of the shares allows other shareholders to be out-voted - effective control rests with the majority shareholder (or shareholders acting in concert). In this way the original owners of the hotel often still have control of the hotel.

Shareholder Rights

Although ownership of 51% of shares does result in 51% ownership of a hotel, it does not give the shareholder the right to use a hotel's building, equipment, materials, or other property. This is because the hotel is considered a legal person, thus it owns all its assets itself. This is important in areas such as insurance, which must be in the name of the hotel and not the main shareholder.

In most countries, including the United States, boards of directors and hotel managers have a fiduciary responsibility to run the hotel in the interests of its stockholders. Nonetheless, as Martin Whitman writes:

> *"...it can safely be stated that there does not exist any publicly traded hotel where management works exclusively in the best interests of OPMI [Outside Passive Minority Investor] stockholders. Instead, there are both "communities of interest" and "conflicts of interest" between stockholders (principal) and management (agent). This conflict is referred to as the principal/agent problem. It would be naive to think that any management would forego management compensation, and management entrenchment, just because some of these management privileges might be perceived as giving rise to a conflict of interest with OPMIs."*

Even though the board of directors runs the hotel, the shareholder has some impact on the hotel's policy, as the shareholders elect the board of directors. Each shareholder typically has a percentage of votes equal to the percentage of shares he or she owns. So as long as the shareholders agree that the management (agent) are performing poorly they can elect a new board of directors which can then hire a new management team. In practice, however, genuinely contested board elections are rare. Board candidates are usually nominated by insiders or by the board of the directors themselves, and a considerable amount of stock is held and voted by insiders.

Owning shares does not mean responsibility for liabilities. If a hotel goes broke and has to default on loans, the shareholders are not liable in any way. However, all money obtained by converting assets into cash will be used to repay loans and other debts first, so that shareholders cannot receive any money unless and until creditors have been paid (most often the shareholders end up with nothing).

Means of Financing

Financing a hotel through the sale of stock in a hotel is known as equity financing. Alternatively, debt financing (for example issuing bonds) can be done to avoid giving up shares of ownership of the hotel. Unofficial financing known as trade financing usually provides the major part of a hotel's working capital (day-to-day operational needs). Trade financing is provided by vendors and suppliers who sell their products to the hotel at short-term, unsecured credit terms, usually 30 days. Equity and debt financing are usually used for longer-term investment projects such as investments in a new factory or a new foreign market. Customer provided financing exists when a customer pays for services before they are delivered, e.g. subscriptions and insurance.

TRADING

A stock exchange is an organization that provides a marketplace (either physical or virtual) for trading shares, where investors (represented by stock brokers) may buy and sell shares in a wide range of companies. A given hotel will usually list its shares by meeting and maintaining the listing requirements of a particular stock exchange. In the United States, through the inter-market quotation system, stocks listed on one exchange can also be bought or sold on several other exchanges, including relatively new internet-only exchanges. Stocks are broadly grouped into NYSE-listed and NASDAQ-listed stocks. Exchanges where NYSE-listed stocks may be bought are generally not the same group as the exchanges where NASDAQ-listed stocks may be bought. Many large foreign companies choose to list on a U.S. exchange as well as an exchange in their home country in order to broaden their investor base. These shares are called American Depository Receipts (ADRs) – or, in the case of companies such as UBS and Daimler Chrysler – "foreign ordinary shares."

The most common way to trade stock options is trading standardized options contracts that are listed by various futures and options exchanges – there are currently six exchanges in the United States that list standardized options contracts based on underlying stocks – The Philadelphia Stock Exchange (PHLX), American Stock Exchange (AMEX) and NYSE Arca in New York City, and the Chicago Board Options Exchange (CBOE) which are all open-outcry marketplaces, and the International Securities Exchange (ISE) and Boston Options Exchange (BOX) are electronic marketplaces. However, even for the non-electronic exchanges, competition and the introduction of automated execution (AutoEx) has led, by late 2006, to hybridization where all but the largest trades are executed electronically. In Europe the main exchanges where stock options are traded are Euronext.liffe and Eurex.

There are also over-the-counter options contracts that are traded not on exchanges, but between two independent parties. At least one of those parties is usually a large financial institution with a balance sheet big enough to underwrite such a contract. Large U.S. companies also list in foreign exchanges for the same reason. Although it makes sense for some companies to raise capital by offering stock on more than one exchange, in today's era of electronic trading, there is limited opportunity for private investors to make profit on pricing discrepancies between one stock exchange and another. As such, arbitrage opportunities disappear quickly due to the efficient nature of the market.

Buying

There are various methods of buying and financing stocks. The most common means is through a stock broker. Whether they are a full service or discount broker, they arrange the transfer of stock from a seller to a buyer. Most trades are actually done through brokers listed with a stock exchange, such as the New York Stock Exchange.

There are many different stock brokers from which to choose, such as full service brokers or discount brokers. The full service brokers usually charge more per trade, but give investment advice or more personal service; the discount brokers offer little or no investment advice but charge less for trades. Another type of broker would be a bank or credit union that may have a deal set up with either a full service or discount broker.

There are other ways of buying stock besides through a broker. One way is directly from the hotel itself. If at least one share is owned, most companies will allow the purchase of shares directly from the hotel through their investor relations departments. However, the initial share of stock in the hotel will have to be obtained through a regular stock broker. Another way to buy stock in companies is through Direct Public Offerings which are usually sold by the hotel itself. A direct public offering is an initial public offering in which the stock is purchased directly from the hotel, usually without the aid of brokers.

When it comes to financing a purchase of stocks there are two ways: purchasing stock with money that is currently in the buyers ownership, or by buying stock on margin. Buying stock on margin means buying stock with money borrowed against the stocks in the same account. These stocks, or collateral, guarantee that the buyer can repay the loan; otherwise, the stockbroker has the right to sell the stock (collateral) to repay the borrowed money. He can sell if the share price drops below the margin requirement, at least 50% of the value of the stocks in the account. Buying on margin works the same way as borrowing money to buy a car or a house, using the car or house as collateral. Moreover, borrowing is not free; the broker usually charges 8-10% interest.

Selling

Selling stock is procedurally similar to buying stock. Generally, the investor wants to buy low and sell high, if not in that order (short selling); although a number of reasons may induce an investor to sell at a loss.

As with buying a stock, there is a transaction fee for the broker's efforts in arranging the transfer of stock from a seller to a buyer. This fee can be high or low depending on which type of brokerage, discount or full service, handles the transaction.

After the transaction has been made, the seller is then entitled to all of the money. An important part of selling is keeping track of the earnings. Importantly, on selling the stock, in jurisdictions that have them, capital gains taxes will have to be paid on the additional proceeds, if any, that are in excess of the cost basis.

Stock Price Fluctuation

The price of a stock fluctuates fundamentally due to the theory of supply and demand. Like all commodities in the market, the price of a stock is directly proportional to the demand. However, there are many factors on basis of which the demand for a particular stock may increase or decrease. These factors are studied using methods of fundamental analysis and technical analysis to predict the changes in the stock price.

Technology's Influence on Trading

Stock trading has evolved tremendously. Since the very first Initial Public Offering (IPO) in the 13th century owning shares of a hotel has been a very attractive incentive. Even though the origins of stock trading go back to the 13th century, the market as we know it today did not catch on strongly until the late 1800s.

Co-production between technology and society has led the push for effective and efficient ways of trading. Technology has allowed the stock market to grow tremendously, and society has encouraged the growth. Within seconds of an order for a stock, the transaction can now take place. Most recent advancements with trading have been due to the Internet. The Internet has allowed online trading. In contrast to the past where only those who could afford expensive stockbrokers, anyone who wishes to be active in the stock market can now do so at a very low cost per transaction. Trading can even be done through Computer-Mediated Communication (CMC) use of mobile devices such as handheld computers and cellular phones. These advances in technology have made day trading possible.

Option Naming Conventions

Stock option names are written in the following format: SYMBOL+MONTH+STRIKE

SYMBOL = Option Root Symbol

MONTH = Month the option expires

STRIKE = Strike price

Expiration Month Codes

Month	Call	Put
January	A	M
February	B	N
March	C	O
April	D	P
May	E	Q
June	F	R
July	G	S
August	H	T
September	I	U
October	J	V
November	K	W
December	L	X

Strike Price Codes

Code	Strike Prices						Code	Strike Prices					
A	5	105	205	305	405	505	N	70	170	270	370	470	570
B	10	110	210	310	410	510	O	75	175	275	375	475	575
C	15	115	215	315	415	515	P	80	180	280	380	480	580
D	20	120	220	320	420	520	Q	85	185	285	385	485	585
E	25	125	225	325	425	525	R	90	190	290	390	490	590
F	30	130	230	330	430	530	S	95	195	295	395	495	595
G	35	135	235	335	435	535	T	100	200	300	400	500	600
H	40	140	240	340	440	540	U	7.5	37.5	67.5	97.5	127.5	157.5
I	45	145	245	345	445	545	V	12.5	42.5	72.5	102.5	132.5	162.5
J	50	150	250	350	450	550	W	17.5	47.5	77.5	107.5	137.5	167.5
K	55	155	255	355	455	555	X	22.5	52.5	82.5	112.5	142.5	172.5
L	60	160	260	360	460	560	Y	27.5	57.5	87.5	117.5	147.5	177.5
M	65	165	265	365	465	565	Z	32.5	62.5	92.5	122.5	152.5	182.5

The basic Trades or Traded Stock Options

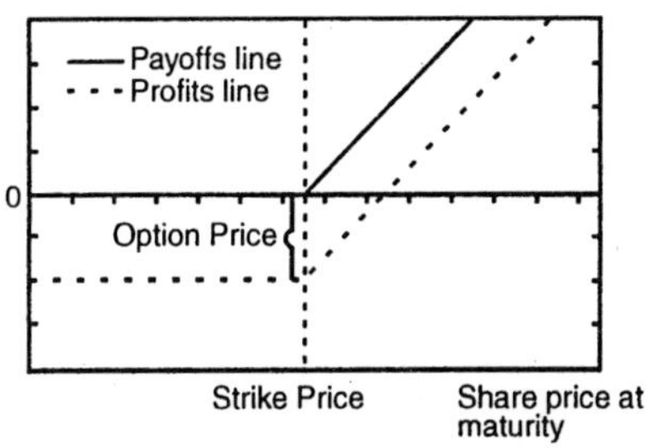

Payoffs and profits from a long call.

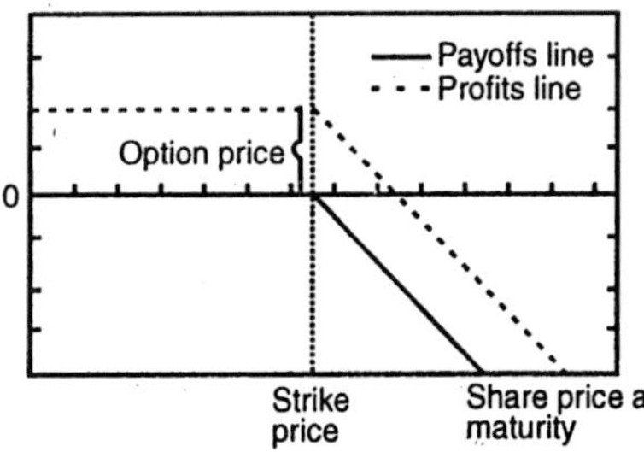

Payoffs and profits from a short call.

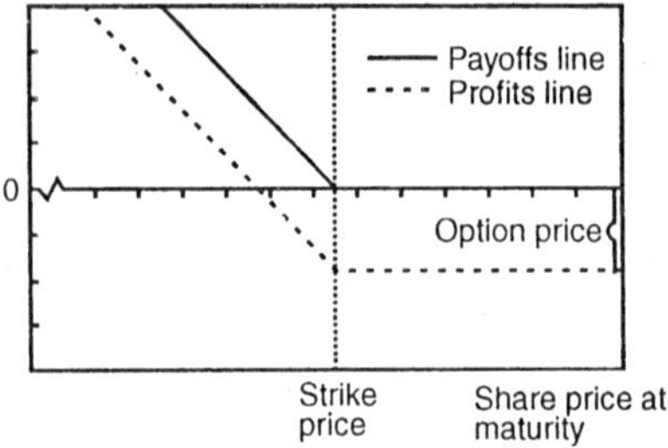

Payoffs and profits from a long put.

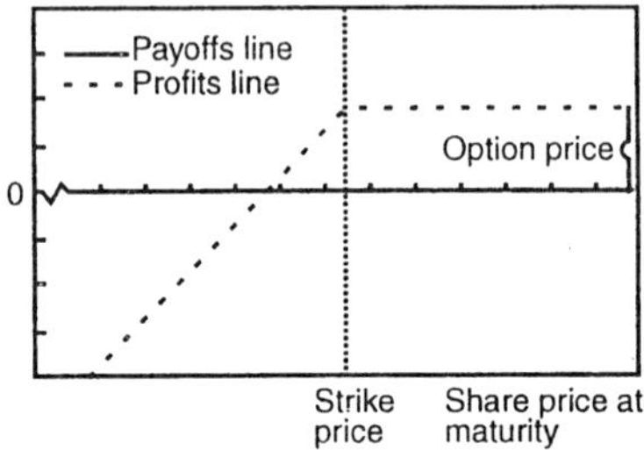

Payoffs and profits from a short put.

These trades are described from the point of view of a speculator. If they are combined with other positions, they can also be used in hedging.

Long Call

A trader who believes that a stock's price will increase may buy the right to purchase the stock (a call option) rather than just buy the stock. He would have no obligation to buy the stock, only the right to do so until the expiry date. If the stock price increases over the exercise price by more than the premium paid, he will profit. If the stock price decreases, he will let the call contract expire worthless, and only lose the amount of the premium. A trader might buy the option instead of shares, because for the same amount of money, he can obtain a larger number of options than shares. If the stock rises, he will thus realize a larger gain than if he had purchased shares. This is an example of the principle of leverage.

Short Call (Naked short call)

A trader who believes that a stock's price will decrease can short sell the stock or instead sell a call. Both tactics are generally considered inappropriate for small investors. The trader selling a call has an obligation to sell the stock to the call buyer at the buyer's option. If the stock price decreases, the short call position will make a profit in the amount of the premium. If the stock price increases over the exercise price by more than the amount of the premium, the short will lose money. Unless a trader already owns the shares which he may be required to provide, the potential loss is unlimited. However, such a trader who sells a call option for those shares he already owns has sold a covered call.

Long Put

A trader who believes that a stock's price will decrease can buy the right to sell the stock at a fixed price. He will be under no obligation to sell the stock, but has the right to do so until the expiry date. If the stock price decreases below the exercise price by more than the premium paid, he will profit. If the stock price increases, he will just let the put contract expire worthless and only lose his premium paid.

Short Put (Naked put)

A trader who believes that a stock's price will increase can sell the right to sell the stock at a fixed price. The trader now has the obligation to purchase the stock at a fixed price. The trader has sold insurance to the buyer of the put requiring the trader to insure the stockholder below the fixed price. This trade is generally considered inappropriate for a small investor. If the stock price increases, the short put position will make a profit in the amount of the premium. If the stock price decreases below the exercise price by more than the premium, the short position will lose money.

Introduction to Option Strategies

Combining any of the four basic kinds of option trades (possibly with different exercise prices) and the two basic kinds of stock trades (long and short) allows a variety of options strategies. Simple strategies usually combine only a few trades, while more complicated strategies can combine several.

Covered call – Long the stock, short a call. This has essentially the same payoff as a short put.

Straddle – Long a call and long a put with the same exercise prices (a long straddle), or short a call and short a put with the same exercise prices (a short straddle).

Strangle – Long a call and long a put with different exercise prices (a long strangle), or short a call and short a put with different exercise prices (a short strangle).

Bull spread – Long a call with a low exercise price and short a call with a higher exercise price, or long a put with a low exercise price and short a put with a higher exercise price.

Bear spread – Short a call with a low exercise price and long a call with a higher exercise price, or short a put with a low exercise price and long a put with a higher exercise price.

Butterfly – Butterflies require trading options with 3 different exercise prices. Assume exercise prices X1 < X2 < X3 and that (X1 + X3) /2 = X2

Long butterfly – long 1 call with exercise price X1, short 2 calls with exercise price X2, and long 1 call with exercise price X3. Alternatively, long 1 put with exercise price X1, short 2 puts with exercise price X2, and long 1 put with exercise price X3.

Short butterfly – short 1 call with exercise price X1, long 2 calls with exercise price X2, and short 1 call with exercise price X3. Alternatively, short 1 put with exercise price X1, long 2 puts with exercise price X2, and short 1 put with exercise price X3.

Box spreads – Any combination of options that has a constant payoff at expiration. For example combining a long butterfly made with calls, with a short butterfly made with puts will have a constant payoff of zero, and in equilibrium will cost zero. In practice any profit from these spreads will be eaten up by commissions (hence the name "alligator spreads").

Uses of Options

Contracts similar to options are believed to have been used since ancient times. In the real estate market, call options have long been used to assemble large parcels of land from separate owners, *e.g.* a developer pays for the right to buy several adjacent plots, but is not obligated to buy these plots and might not unless he can buy all the plots in the entire parcel. Film or theatrical producers often buy the right – but not the obligation – to dramatize a specific book or script. Lines of credit give the potential borrower the right – but not the obligation – to borrow within a specified time period.

Many choices, or embedded options, have traditionally been included in bond contracts. For example many bonds are convertible into common stock at the buyer's option, or may be called (bought back) at specified prices at the issuer's option. Mortgage borrowers have long had the option to repay the loan early.

Privileges were options sold over the counter in nineteenth century America, with both puts and calls on shares offered by specialized dealers. Their exercise price was fixed at a rounded-off market price on the day or week that the option was bought, and the expiry date was generally three months after purchase. They were not traded in secondary markets.

TREASURY STOCK

In the United Kingdom, treasury stocks refer to government bonds or gilts. The British equivalent of *treasury stock* as used in the United States is treasury share. In the United States, a treasury stock or reacquired stock is stock which is bought back by the issuing hotel. It reduces the number of outstanding stocks on the open market ("open market" including insiders' holdings). On the balance sheet, treasury stock is listed under shareholder equity as a negative number. Stock repurchases are often used as a tax-efficient method to put cash into shareholders' hands, rather than pay dividends. Sometimes, companies do this when they feel that their stock is undervalued on the open market. Other times, companies do this to provide a "bonus" or incentive compensation plan for employees. Rather than receive cash, recipients receive an asset that might appreciate in value faster than cash saved in a bank account.

Limitations of treasury stock include:

Treasury stock does not pay a dividend

Treasury stock has no voting rights

Total treasury stock can not exceed the maximum proportion of total capitalization specified by law in the relevant country

After buyback, the hotel can either retire the shares (however, retired shares are not listed as treasury stock on the hotel's financial statements) or hold the shares for later resale. Buying back stocks reduces the number of outstanding shares. However, the smaller number of shares outstanding is not the reason why stock prices usually increase after announcements of buybacks. To see this, note that achoteling the decrease in the number of shares outstanding is a reduction in hotel assets, in particular, cash assets, which are used to buy back shares. The correct reason for the price jump is that by buying back its own shares, the hotel, who supposedly knows more about the true value of its stock than investors, sends a signal to investors that the stock is currently undervalued. The stock price increases as a response to this positive signal.

One way of accounting for treasury stock is with the cost method. In this method, the paid-in capital account is reduced in the balance sheet when the treasury stock is bought. When the treasury stock is sold back on the open market, the paid-in capital is either debited or credited if it is sold for more or less than the initial cost respectively. Another common way for accounting for treasury stock is the par value method. In the par value method, when the stock is purchased back from the market the books will reflect the action as a retirement of the shares. Therefore, common stock is debited and treasury stock is credited. However, when the treasury stock is resold back to the market the entry in the books will be the same as the cost method.

In either method, any transaction involving treasury stock cannot increase the amount of retained earnings. If the treasury stock is sold for more than cost, then the paid-in capital treasury stock is the account that is increased not retained earnings. In auditing financial statements, there is a common practice to check for this error to detect possible attempts to "cook the books".

If you believe in efficient market theory, a hotel buying back its stock should have no effect at all on its stock price. If the market fairly prices a hotel's shares at $50/share, if a hotel buys back 100 shares for $5000, it now has $5000 less cash but there are 100 fewer shares outstanding; the net effect should be that the value per share is unchanged. However, buying back shares does improve certain per-share ratios, such as price/earnings (earnings per share is increased due to fewer shares outstanding), but that is only because valuing a hotel's shares according to those ratios is not accurate when a hotel is holding a lot of cash. If a hotel's shares are underpriced, then a hotel can benefit its other shareholders by buying back shares. If a hotel's shares are overpriced, then a hotel is actually hurting its remaining shareholders by buying back stock.

One other reason for a hotel to buy back its own stock is to reward holders of stock options. Option holders are not rewarded by dividends, if issued, since holders of options have not invested any capital into the hotel. Option holders are often employees and executives of the hotel that benefit from the rise in stock. If you believe that share buyback programs increase the share value, at least temporarily, the option holder is the benficiary if she/he sells the options.

EARNINGS PER SHARE

Earnings per share (EPS) are the earnings returned on the initial investment amount. The FASB requires companies' income statements to report EPS for each of the major categories of the income statement: continuing operations, discontinued operations, extraordinary items, and net income. The EPS formula does not include preferred dividends for categories outside of continuing operations and net income as shown here. This formula also shows the most basic formula for earnings per share.

$$\text{Earnings per Share} = \frac{\text{Profit}}{\text{Weighted Average Common Shares}}$$

The EPS formula is shown here for Net Income and Continuing Operations (substitute income from continuing operations for net income).

$$\text{Earnings per Share} = \frac{\text{Net Income-preferred Dividends}}{\text{Weighted Average Common Shares}}$$

Note: Only dividends actually declared in the current year are subtracted. The exception is when preferred shares are cumulative, in which case annual dividends are deducted regardless of whether they have been declared or not. Dividends in arrears are not relevant when calculating EPS.

Earnings per share for continuing operations and net income are more complicated in that any preferred dividends are removed from net income before calculating EPS. Remember that preferred stock rights have precedence over common stock. If preferred dividends total $100,000, then that is money not available to distribute to each share of common stock. The value used for hotel earnings can either be the last twelve months' Net income (referred to as trailing twelve months, or ttm), or analysts' predictions for the next twelve months' net income (referred to as forward).

The number of shares used for the calculation can either be basic (only shares that are currently outstanding) or diluted (includes all shares that could potentially enter the market). Companies often use a weighted average of shares outstanding over the reporting term. (The weight refers to the time period covered by each share level) EPS can be calculated for the previous year ("trailing EPS"), for the current year ("current EPS"), or for the coming year ("forward EPS"). Note that last year's EPS would be actual, while current year and forward year EPS would be estimates.

PREFERRED STOCK

A preferred stock, also known as a preferred share or simply a preferred, is a share of stock carrying additional rights above and beyond those conferred by common stock. Unlike common stock, preferred stock usually has several rights attached to it:

- The core right is that of preference in dividends. Before a dividend can be declared on the common shares, any dividend obligation to the preferred shares must be satisfied.
- The dividend rights are often cumulative, such that if the dividend is not paid it accumulates in arrears.
- Preferred stock has a par value or liquidation value associated with it. This represents the amount of capital that was contributed to the corporation when the shares were first issued.
- Preferred stock has a claim on liquidation proceeds of a stock corporation, equivalent to its par or liquidation value. This claim is senior to that of common stock, which has only a residual claim.
- Almost all preferred shares have a fixed dividend amount. The dividend is usually specified as a percentage of the par value or as a fixed amount. For example Pacific Gas and Electric 6% Series A preferred. Unlike debt securities, however, a hotel is not legally required to pay preferred dividends and will not be in default for missing a preferred dividend payment.
- Variable preferreds are rare exceptions; their changing dividends depend on prevailing interest rates, or varying as a percentage of net income.
- Some preferred shares have special voting rights to approve certain extraordinary events (such as the issuance of new shares or the approval of the

acquisition of the hotel) or to elect directors, but most preferred shares provide no voting rights associated with them. Some preferred shares only gain voting rights when the preferred dividends are in arrears.

- Usually preferred shares contain protective provisions which prevent the issuance of new preferred shares with a senior claim. Individual series of preferred shares may have a senior, pari-passu or junior relationship with other series issued by the same corporation.

The above list, although including several customary rights, is far from comprehensive. Preferred shares, like other legal arrangements, may specify nearly any right conceivable. Preferred shares normally carry a call provision, enabling the issuing corporation to repurchase the share at its (usually limited) discretion. Some corporations contain provisions in their charters authorising the issuance of preferred stock whose terms and conditions may be determined by the board of directors when issued. These "blank check" preferred shares are often used as takeover defense. These shares may be assigned very high liquidation value that must be redeemed in the event of a change of control or may have enormous supervoting powers.

Users

Preferred shares are more common in private companies, where it is more useful to distinguish between the control of and the economic interest in the hotel. Also, government regulations and the rules of stock exchanges discourage the issuance of publicly traded preferred shares. For example the Tel Aviv Stock Exchange prohibits listed companies from having more than one class of capital stock.

A single hotel may issue several classes of preferred stock. For example, a hotel may undergo several rounds of financing, with each round receiving separate rights and having a separate class of preferred stock; such a hotel might have "Series A Preferred", "Series B Preferred", "Series C Preferred" and common stock.

Canada

Preferred shares represent a significant portion of Canadian capital markets, with over CAD 5-billion in preferred share issues in 2005.

Canadian issuers

Many issuers are financial organizations that may count capital raised in the preferred share market as Tier 1 capital, provided that the shares issued are perpetual. Another class of issuer are "Split Share Corporations".

Canadian investors

Investors in Canadian preferred shares are generally those who wish to hold fixed-income investments in a taxable portfolio. Preferential tax treatment of dividend income, as opposed to interest income, may in many cases result in a greater after-tax return than might be achieved with bonds.

United Kingdom issuers

Perpetual non-cumulative preference shares may be included as Tier 1 capital. Perpetual cumulative preferred shares are Upper Tier 2 capital. Dated preferred shares (normally having an original maturity of at least five years) may be included in Lower Tier 2 capital.

United States

In the United States issuance of publicly listed preferred stock is generally limited to financial institutions, REITs and public utilities. Because in the US dividends on preferred stock are not tax deductible (like interest expense), the effective cost of capital raised by preferred stock is 35% greater than issuing the equivalent amount of debt at the same interest rate. This has lead to the development of TRuPS (Trust-preferred security) which are essentially debt instruments with the same properties as preferred stock.

However, with a dividend tax of 15% and a top marginal tax rate of 35%, one dollar of dividend income taxed at these rates provides the same after-tax income as approximately $1.30 in interest. The size of the preferred stock market in the United States has been estimated as USD 200-billion, as of August, 2006, compared to USD 16-trillion for equities and USD 5-trillion for bonds.

Common types

There are various types of preferred stocks that are common to many corporations:

- *Cumulative Preferred Stock*—If the dividend is not paid, it will accumulate for future payment.
- *Non-cumulative Preferred Stock*—Dividend for this type of preferred stock will not accumulate if it is unpaid. This type is very rare, because the payment of dividends is always at the discretion of the board of directors.
- *Convertible Preferred Stock*—This type of preferred stock carries the option to convert into a common stock at a prescribed price.
- *Exchangable Preferred Stock*—This type of preferred stock carries the option to be exchanged for some other security upon certain conditions.
- *Participating Preferred Stock*—This type of preferred stock allows the possibility of additional dividend above the stated amount under certain conditions.
- *Perpetual Preferred Stock*—This type of preferred stock has no fixed date on which invested capital will be returned to the shareholder, although there will always be redemption privileges held by the corporation. Most preferred stock is issued without a set redemption date.
- *Puttable Preferred Stock*—These issues have a "put" privilege whereby the holder may, upon certain conditions, force the issuer to redeem shares.

P/E RATIO

The P/E ratio of a stock (also called its "earnings multiple", or simply "multiple", "P/E", or "PE") is used to measure how cheap or expensive its share prices is. The lower the P/E, the less you have to pay for the stock, relative to what you can expect to earn from it. It is a valuation ratio included in other financial ratios.

$$\text{P/E ratio} = \frac{\text{Price per Share}}{\text{Earnings per Share}}$$

The price per share (numerator) is the market price of a single share of the stock. The earnings per share (denominator) is the net income of the hotel for the most recent 12 month period, divided by number of shares outstanding. The EPS used can also be the "diluted EPS" or the "comprehensive EPS"

For example, if stock A is trading at $24 and the Earnings per share for the most recent 12 month period is $3, then the P/E ratio is 24/3=8. Stock A said to have a P/E of 8 (or a multiple of 8). Put another way, you are paying $8 for every one dollar of earnings.

It is probably the single most consistent red flag to excessive optimism and over-investment. It also serves, regularly, as a marker of business problems and opportunities. By relating price and earnings per share for a hotel, one can analyze the market's valuation of a hotel's shares relative to the wealth the hotel is actually creating.

One reason to calculate P/Es is for investors to compare the value of stocks, one stock with another. If one stock has a P/E twice that of another stock, it is *probably* a less attractive investment. But comparisons between industries, between countries, and between time periods may be dangerous. To have faith in a comparison of P/E ratios, one should compare comparable stocks.

DETERMINING SHARE PRICES

Share prices in a publicly traded hotel are determined by market supply and demand, and thus depend upon the expectations of buyers and sellers. Among these are:

- The hotel's future and recent performance
- New product lines
- Prospects for companies of this type, the "market sector"
- Prevailing moods and fashions.

By dividing the price of one share in a hotel by the profits earned by the hotel per share, you arrive at the P/E ratio. If earnings move up in line with share prices (or vice versa) the ratio stays the same. But if stock prices gain in value and earnings remain the same or go down, the P/E rises. For example, if a stock price was $70 per share and it got $2 in earnings, the P/E is 35, historically high.

The price used to calculate a P/E ratio is usually the most recent price. The earnings figure used is the most recently available, but this figure is often a year old and does not necessarily reflect the current position of the hotel. Many times, you will hear this referred to as a trailing P/E, because it involves taking earnings from the last four quarters.

It is possible, however, to use the earnings estimate for the next four quarters. When doing so, the ratio is referred to as a projected or forward P/E.

Interpretation

The average U.S. equity P/E ratio from 1900 to 2005 is 14 (or 16, depending on whether the geometric mean or the arithmetic mean is used to average), meaning it takes about 14 years for a hotel you purchase to earn back your full purchase price for you. Normally, stocks with high earning growth are traded at higher P/E values. Say, stock A may earn $6 per share the next year. Then the future P/E ratio is $24/6 = 4. So, you are paying $4 for every one dollar of earnings, which makes the stock more attractive than it was the previous year.

Various interpretations of a particular P/E ratio are possible, and the historical table below is just indicative and cannot be a guide, as current P/E ratios have, obviously, to be compared to current - inflation-corrected - interest rates :

N/A A hotel with no earnings has an undefined P/E ratio.

0-10 Either the stock is undervalued or the hotel's earnings are thought to be in decline.

10-17 For many companies a P/E ratio in this range may be considered fair value.

17-25 Either the stock is overvalued or the hotel's earnings have increased since the last earnings figure was published.

25+ A hotel whose shares have a very high P/E either really does have an exceptionally rosy future or the stock may be the subject of a speculative bubble.

It is usually not enough to look at the P/E ratio of one hotel and determine its status. Usually, an analyst will look at a hotel's P/E ratio compared to the industry the hotel is in, the sector the hotel is in, as well as the overall market (usually the S&P 500). Sites such as Reuters offer these comparisons in one table. Example of RHAT Oftentimes, comparisons will also be made between quarterly and annual data. Only after a comparison with the industry, sector, and market can an analyst determine whether a P/E ratio is high or low with the above mentioned distinctions (i.e., undervaluation, over valuation, fair valuation, etc).

The Market P/E

To calculate the P/E ratio of a market index such as the S&P500, it is not accurate to take the "simple average" of the P/Es of all stock constituents. The preferred and accurate method is to calculate the weighted average. In this case, each stock's underlying market cap (price multiplied by number of shares in issue) is summed to give the total value in terms of market capitalization for the whole market index. The same method is computed for each stock's underlying net earnings (earnings per share multiplied by number of shares in issue). In this case the total of all net earnings is computed and this gives the total earnings for the whole market index. The final stage is to divide the total market capitalization by the total earnings to give the market P/E ratio. The reason for using the weighted average method rather than 'simple' average can best be described by considering a recessionary period of the economic cycle, where a number of stocks would be reporting a loss. For example, a hotel with a share price of $100, may have made a slight loss of say 10 cents giving a P/E ratio of - 1000 (100/0.1). In another case, a hotel with a share price of $1 may have made a serious loss of 50 cents giving a P/E ratio of - 2 (1/0.5). This mathematical anomaly would create a misrepresentation of the underlying hotel losses on the overall market index.

The P/E and Inflation

There is evidence that the P/E of the market has more to do with changes in consumer prices than any other factor. From 1900 to 2005, the highest average P/E occurred when the average change in consumer prices was 2.6%. In general, the P/E ratio is inversely proportional to the absolute value of the change in prices, in other words, the higher the price change, the lower the P/E.

Some claim that the P/E ratio is mostly dictated by interest rates, but the level of correlation of P/E ratios to interest rates is much lower versus that to the magnitude of price change.

An example An easy and perhaps intuitive way to understand the concept is with an analogy:

Let's say, I offer you a privilege to collect a dollar every year from me forever. How much are you willing to pay for that privilege now? Let's say, you are only willing to pay me 50 cents, because you may think that paying for that privilege coming from me could be risky. On the other hand, suppose that the offer came from Bill Gates, how much would you be willing to pay him? Perhaps, your answer would be at least more than 50 cents, let's say, $20. Well, the price earnings ratio or sometimes known as earnings multiple is nothing more than the number of dollars the market is willing to pay for a privilege to be able to earn a dollar forever in perpetuity. Bill Gates's P/E ratio is 20 and my P/E ratio is 0.5.

Now view it this way: The P/E ratio also tells you how long it will take before you can recover your investment (ignoring of course the time value of money). Had you invested in Bill Gates, it would have taken you at least 20 years, while investing in me could have taken you less than a year, i.e. only 6 months.

If a stock has a relatively high P/E ratio, let's say, 100 (which Google exceeded during the summer of 2005), what does this tell you? The answer is that it depends. A few reasons a stock might have a high P/E ratio are:

The market expects the earnings to rise rapidly in the future. For example a gold mining hotel which has just begun to mine may not have made any money yet but next quarter it will most likely find the gold and make a lot of money. The same applies to pharmaceutical companies – often a large amount of their revenue comes from their best few patented products, so when a promising new product is approved, investors may buy up the stock.

The hotel was previously making a lot of money, but in the last year or quarter it had a special one time expense (called a "charge"), which lowered the earnings significantly. Stockholders, understanding (possibly incorrectly) that this was a one time issue, will still buy stock at the same price as before, and only sell at at least that same price.

Hype for the stock has caused people to buy the stock for a higher price than they normally would. This is called a bubble. One of the most important uses for the P/E metric is to decide whether a stock is undergoing a bubble or an anti-bubble by comparing its P/E to other similar companies. Historically, bubbles have been followed by crashes. As such, prudent investors try to stay out of them.

The hotel has some sort of business advantage which seems to ensure that it will continue making money for a long time with very little risk. Thus investors are willing to buy the stock even at a high price for the peace of mind that they will not lose their money.

A large amount of money has been inserted into the stock market, out of proportion with the growth of companies across the same time period. Since there are only a limited amount of stocks to buy, supply and demand dictate that the prices of stocks must go up. This factor can make comparing P/E ratios over time difficult.

Likewise, a specific stock may have a temporarily high price when, for whatever reason, there has been high demand for it. This demand may have nothing to do with the hotel itself, but may rather relate to, for example, an institutional investor trying to diversify out risk.

Inputs

Accuracy and context

In practice, decisions must be made as to exactly how to specify the inputs used in the calculations.

Does the current market price accurately value the organization?

How is income to be calculated and for what periods? How do we calculate total capitalization?

Can these values be trusted?

What are the revenue and earnings growth prospects over the time frame one is investing in?

Was there special one time charges which artificially lowered (or artificially raised) the earnings used in the calculation, and did those charges cause a drop in stock price or were they ignored?

Were these charges truly one-time, or is the hotel trying to manipulate us into thinking so?

What kind of P/E ratios is the market giving to similar companies, and also the P/E ratio of the entire market?

Historical vs Projected Earnings

A distinction has to be made between the *fundamental (or intrinsic) P/E* and the way we actually compute P/Es. The fundamental or intrinsic P/E examines earnings forecasts. That is what was done in the analogy above. In reality, we actually compute P/Es using the latest 12 month corporate earnings. Using past earnings introduces a temporal mismatch, but it is felt that having this mismatch is better than using future earnings, since future earnings estimates are notoriously inaccurate and susceptible to deliberate manipulation.

On the other hand, merely because a stock is trading at a low fundamental P/E is not an indicator that the stock is undervalued. A stock may be trading at a low P/E because the investors are less optimistic about the future earnings from the stock. Thus, one way to get a fair comparison between stocks is to use their *primary P/E.* This primary P/E is based on the earnings projections made for the next years to which a discount calculation is applied.

THE P/E CONCEPT IN BUSINESS CULTURE

The P/E ratio of a hotel is a significant focus for management in many companies and industries. This is because management is primarily paid with their hotel's stock (a form of payment that is supposed to align the interests of management with the interests of other stock holders), in order to increase the stock price. The stock price can increase in one of two ways: either through improved earnings or through an improved multiple that the market assigns to those earnings. As mentioned earlier, a higher P/E ratio is the result of a sustainable advantage that allows a hotel to grow earnings over time (ie, investors are paying for their peace of mind). Efforts by management to convince investors that their companies do have a sustainable advantage have had profound effects on business:

1. The primary motivation for building conglomerates is to diversify earnings so that they go up steadily over time.
2. The choice of businesses which are enhanced or closed down or sold within these conglomerates is often made based on their perceived volatility, regardless of the absolute level of profits or profit margins.

3. One of the main genres of financial fraud, "slush fund accounting" (hiding excess earnings in good years to cover for losses in lean years), is designed to create the image that the hotel always slowly but steadily increases profits, with the goal to increase the P/E ratio.
4. These and many other actions used by companies to structure themselves to be perceived as commanding a higher P/E ratio can seem counterintuitive to some, because while they may decrease the absolute level of profits they are designed to increase the stock price. Thus in this situation maximizing the stock price acts as a perverse incentive.

DIVIDEND

When a hotel earns a profit, some of it is reinvested in the business and called retained earnings, and some of it can be paid to its shareholders as a dividend. The frequency of these varies by country. In the United States dividends are usually declared quarterly by the board of directors. In some other countries dividends are paid biannually, as an interim dividend shortly after the hotel announces its interim results and a final dividend typically following its annual general meeting. In other countries, the board of directors will propose the payment of a dividend to shareholders at the annual meeting who will then vote on the proposal.

In the United States, decisions regarding the amount and frequency of dividends is solely at the discretion of the board of directors. Shareholders are explicitly forbidden from introducing shareholder resolutions involving specific amounts of dividends. Where a hotel makes a loss during a year, it may opt to continue paying dividends from the retained earnings from previous years or to suspend the dividend. Where a hotel receives a one-off gain, e.g. from the sale of some assets, and has no plans to reinvest the proceeds, the money is often returned to shareholders in the form of a *special* dividend.

DIVIDEND YIELD

Publicly traded companies often make periodic quarterly or yearly cash payments to their owners, the shareholders, in direct proportion to the number of shares held. According to US law, such payments can only be made out of current earnings or out of reserves (earnings retained from previous years). The hotel decides on the total payment and this is divided by the number of shares. The resulting dividend is an amount of cash per share. The dividend yield is the dividend paid in the last accounting year divided by the current share price.

If a stock paid out $5 per share in cash dividends to its shareholders last year and its price is currently $50, then it has a dividend yield of 10%. Historically, at severely high P/E ratios (such as over 100x), a stock has NO (0.0%) or negligible dividend yield. With a P/E ratio over 100x, and supposing a portion of earnings is paid as dividend, it would take *over a century* to earn back the purchase price. Such stocks are extremely overvalued, unless a huge growth of earnings in the next years is expected.

The P/E is calculated primarily for common shares, not for preferred shares. The appropriate calculation for preferreds is the preferred dividend coverage ratio. A related concept is the "PEG ratio". This is the P/E ratio adjusted by a growth coefficient. It is sometimes used in high growth industries and new ventures. Its use is controversial.

Another practice, which is not mainstream, based on behavioral finance, is to take market behaviour parameters, among which the stock image, as factors playing a part in the level and evolution of the P/E. The P/E can be applied not only to shares, but to other assets also. Thus the P/E, comparing Price to Rental Incoming for housing, is an important measure in determining the existence or absence of Property bubbles.

Forms of Payment

Cash

Cash dividends (most common) are those paid out in form of "real cash". Such dividends are a form of investment interest/income and are taxable to the recipient in the year they are paid. This is the most common method of sharing corporate profits.

Stock

Stock or scrip dividends (common) are those paid out in form of additional stock shares of the issuing corporation, or other corporation (e.g., its subsidiary corporation). They are usually issued in proportion to shares owned (e.g., for every 100 shares of stock owned, 5% stock dividend will yield 5 extra shares). This is very similar to a stock split in that it increases the total number of shares while lowering the price of each share and does not change the market capitalization or the total value of the shares held.

Property

Property dividends or dividends *in specie* (Latin for "in kind") (rare) are those paid out in form of assets from the issuing corporation or another corporation, such as a subsidiary corporation. Property dividends are usually paid in the form of products or services provided by the corporation. When paying property dividends, the corporation will often use securities of other companies owned by the issuer.

Dates

Dividends must be "declared" (approved) by a hotel's Board of Directors each time they are paid. There are four important dates to remember regarding dividends.

Declaration date

The declaration date is the day the Board of Director's announces their intention to pay a dividend. On this day, the hotel creates a liability on its books; it now owes the money to the stockholders. On the declaration date, the Board will also announce a date of record and a payment date.

Date of record

Shareholders who properly registered their ownership on or before the date of record will receive the dividend. Shareholders who are not registered as of this date will not receive the dividend. Registration in most countries is essentially automatic for shares purchased before the ex-dividend date.

Ex dividend date

The "ex dividend" date is set by the exchange where the stock is traded, several days (usually two) before the date of record, so that all trades made on previous dates can be properly settled and the shareholder list on the date of record will accurately reflect the current owners. Purchasers buying before the ex-dividend date will receive the dividend. The stock is said to trade "cum dividend" (meaning "with dividend") on these dates. Purchasers buying on or after the ex-dividend date will not receive the dividend. The stock trades ex-dividend on these dates.

Payment date

The payment date is the day when the dividend cheques will actually be mailed to the shareholders of a hotel or credited to brokerage accounts.

Dividend-reinvestment plans

Some companies have dividend reinvestment plans, or DRIPs. These plans allow shareholders to use dividends to systematically buy small amounts of stock, usually with no commission and sometimes at a slight discount. In some cases the shareholder might not need to pay taxes on these re-invested dividends, but in most cases they do.

Shareholders like dividends because...

- Shareholders have their own personal cash needs and self-select the companies whose dividends satisfy these.

- Preferred shareholders like common share dividends because it creates a cushion that must be cut before their own dividends are.
- Shareholders feel the risk of returns from reinvested earnings at a later date, is higher than the risk of cash received today.
- Benjamin Graham and David Dodd, in the 1934 book Security Analysis, suggest that retaining earnings is, in effect, management dictating to owners how to invest their money.

Reasons Companies don't pay Dividends

- Management and the board may believe that the money is best re-invested into the hotel: research and development, capital investment, expansion, etc. Proponents suggest that a management eager to return profits to shareholders may have run out of good ideas for the future of the hotel.
- When dividends are paid, shareholders in many countries suffer from double taxation of those dividends: the hotel pays income tax to the government when it earns any income, and then when the dividend is paid, the individual shareholder pays income tax on the dividend payment. This is often used as justification for retaining earnings, or for performing a stock buyback, in which the hotel buys back stock, thereby increasing the value of the stock left outstanding. The shareholder will pay a tax on capital gains (which is often taxed at a lower rate than ordinary income) only when the shareholder chooses to sell the stock. If a holder of the stock chooses to not participate in the buyback, the price of the holder's shares should rise, but the tax on these gains is delayed until the actual sale of the shares. Certain types of specialized investment companies (such as a REIT in the U.S.) allow the shareholder to partially or fully avoid double taxation of dividends.

- Shareholders in companies which pay little or no cash dividends can reap the benefit of the hotel's profits when they sell their shareholding, or when a hotel is wound down and all assets liquidated and distributed amongst shareholders.

Franking Credits

In Australia and New Zealand, companies also forward franking credits to shareholders along with dividends. These franking credits represent the tax paid by the hotel upon its pre-tax profits. One dollar of hotel tax paid generates one franking credit. Companies can forward any proportion of franking up to a maximum amount that is calculated from the prevailing hotel tax rate: for each dollar of dividend paid, the maximum level of franking is the hotel tax rate divided by (1 - hotel tax rate). At the current 30% rate, this works out at 0.30 of a credit per 70 cents of dividend, or 42.857 cents per dollar of dividend. The shareholders who are able to use them offset these credits against their income tax bills at a rate of a dollar per credit, thereby effectively eliminating the double taxation of hotel profits. This system is called dividend imputation. The UK's taxation system operates along similar lines: dividends come with an attached tax credit which ensures that double taxation does not take place.

Dividends from trusts

In real estate investment trusts and royalty trusts, the distributions paid often will be consistently greater than the hotel earnings. This can be sustainable because the accounting earnings do not recognize any increasing value of real estate holdings and resource reserves. If there is no economic increase in the value of the hotel's assets then the excess distribution (or dividend) will be a return of capital and the book value of the hotel will have shrunk by an equal amount. This may result in capital gains which may be taxed differently than dividends representing distribution of earnings.

Reliability of Dividends

To determine the long run reliability of dividends, use either of two metrics that show the hotel's ability to pay.

Dividend Cover

Divide the hotel's Earnings per share by the Dividend. A Dividend Cover of less than 1 means the hotel is paying out more in dividends for the year than it earned.

Payout Ratio

Divide the hotel's Cash Flow from Operations by the Dividend. This ratio is used by analysts of Income Trusts in Canada.

Etymology

The word "dividend" ultimately comes from the Latin word "*dividendum*" meaning "the thing which is to be divided".

In the United States, credit unions generally use the term "dividends" to refer to interest payments they make to depositors. These are not dividends in the normal sense and are not taxed as such; they are just interest payments. Credit unions call them dividends since, as credit unions are owned by their members, interest payments are effectively payments to owners. Consumer co-operative societies use the term "dividend" for profit-sharing payments to their members. Unlike joint stock hotel dividends, these payments are made in proportion to a members' spending with the co-operative society, not the number of shares they hold in it.

BOOK VALUE

Book Value is the shareholders' equity of a business (assets - liabilities) as measured by the accounting 'books'. The term is used in the context where the speaker is trying to distinguish between the accounting measures (usually historical cost) and the market value. While it can be used to refer to the business' total equity, it is most used

1. As a 'per share' value': The balance sheet Equity value is divided by the number of shares outstanding at the date of the balance sheet (not the average o/s in the period).
2. As a 'diluted per share value': The Equity is bumped up by the exercise price of the options, warrants or preferred shares. Then it is divided by the number of shares that has been increased by those added.

Uses

1. Book value is used in the financial ratio price/book. It is a valuation metric that sets the floor for stock prices under a worst-case scenario. When a business is liquidated, the book value is what may be left over for the owners after all the debts are paid. Paying only a price/book = 1 means the investor will get all his investment back. Share of capital intensive industries trade at lower price/book ratios becausc they generate lower earnings per dollar of assets. Business depending on human capital will generate higher earnings per dollar of assets, so will trade at higher price/book ratios.
2. Book value per share can be used to generate a measure of comprehensive earnings, when the opening and closing values are reconciled.

Bk/s, beg.of year - Dividends + Sh issue Premium + Comprehensive EPS = Bk/s, end of year

Changes are caused by

The sale of shares/units by the business increases the total book value. Book/sh will increase if the additional shares are issued at a price higher than the pre-existing book/sh.

The purchase of its own shares by the business will decrease total book value. Book/sh will decrease if more is paid for them than was received when originally issued (pre-existing book/sh).

Dividends paid out will decrease book value and book/sh.

Comprehensive earnings/losses will increase/decrease book value and book/sh. Comprehensive earnings, in this case, includes net income from the Income Statement, foreign exchange translation changes to Balance Sheet items, accounting changes applied retroactively, and the opportunity cost of options exercised.

New share Issues do not Dilute Shareholder value

It is a common misperception that the issue of more shares will decrease the value of the current owner. While it is correct that when the number of shares is doubled the EPS will be cut in half, it is too simple to be the full story. It all depends on how much was paid for the new shares and what return the new captital earns once invested.

Net book value of Long term Assets

Book value is often used interchangeably with "net book value", which is the original acquisition cost less accumulated depreciation, depletion or amortization.

Chapter 7

Bonds, Leases and Mortgages

OPTION (FINANCE)

An option contract is an agreement in which the buyer (*holder*) has the right (but not the obligation) to exercise by buying or selling an asset at a set price (strike price) on or before a future date (the exercise date or expiration); and the seller (*writer*) has the obligation to honor the terms of the contract. Since the option gives the buyer a right and the writer an obligation, the buyer pays the option premium to the writer. The buyer is considered to have a long position, and the seller a short position.

Because the contract's value is determined by an underlying asset and other variables, it is classified as a derivative. For every open contract there is a buyer and a seller. Traders in exchange-traded options do not usually interact directly, but through a clearing house such as, in the U.S., the Options Clearing Corporation (OCC). The OCC guarantees that an assigned writer will fulfill his obligation if the option is exercised.

The Contract Specifies

Whether it is a put option or call option. Put options give the holder the right to sell the asset at the strike price. Call options give the holder the right to purchase the asset at the strike price.

The underlying security (e.g. XYZ Co.)

The strike price or exercise price. It can be specified, or based on a reference rate, or measured at agreed-upon intervals during the life of the contract.

The date that will be either the last possible date for exercise (American options) , or the only date for exercise (European options). This date is commonly known as the expiration date.

The quantity of the security included in each contract. This is standard and predetermined by the exchanges for traded options, e.g. common share options have 100 shares in 1 contract.

The ratio of actual settlement price to the price quoted in the market, also known as the 'multiplier'.

Types of Options

Real option (real option) is a choice that an investor has when investing in the real economy (i.e. in the production of goods or services, rather than in financial contracts). This option may be something as simple as the opportunity to expand production, or to change production inputs. Real options are an increasingly influential tool in corporate finance. They are typically difficult or impossible to trade, and lack the liquidity of exchange-traded options.

Traded options (also called "Exchange-Traded Options" or "Listed Options") is a class of Exchange traded derivatives. As for other classes of exchange traded derivatives, trade options have standardized contracts, quick systematic pricing, and are settled through a clearing house (ensuring fulfillment). Trade options include:

Stock options,

Commodity options,

Bond options,

Interest rate options

Index (equity) options,

Currency cross rate options, and

Swaption.

Vanilla options are 'simple', well understood, and traded options; Exotic options are more complex, or less easily understood. Asian options, lookback options, barrier options are considered to be exotic, especially if the underlying instrument is more complex than simple equity or debt.

Employee stock options (employee stock option) are issued by a hotel to its employees as compensation.

BOND

In finance, a bond is a debt security, in which the issuer owes the holders a debt and is obliged to repay the principal and interest (the coupon) at a later date, termed maturity. Other stipulations may also be attached to the bond issue, such as the obligation for the issuer to provide certain information to the bond holder, or limitations on the behaviour of the issuer. Bonds are generally issued for a fixed term (the maturity) longer than ten year. U.S Treasury securities issued debt with life of ten years or more is a bond. New debt between one year and ten years is a note, and new debt less than a year-bill. A bond is mostly just a loan, but in the form of a security, although terminology used is rather different. The *issuer* is equivalent to the *borrower*, the *bond holder* to the *lender*, and the *coupon* to the *interest*. Bonds enable the issuer to finance long-term investments with external funds. Debt securities with a maturity shorter than one year are typically *bills*. Certificates of deposit (CDs) or commercial paper are considered money market instruments.

Traditionally, the U.S. Treasury uses the word *bond* only for their issues with a maturity longer than ten years, and calls issues between one and ten year notes. Elsewhere in the market this distinction has disappeared, and both *bonds* and *notes* are used irrespective of the maturity. Market participants normally use *bonds* for large issues offered to a wide public, and *notes* rather for smaller issues originally sold to a limited number of investors. There are no clear demarcations. There are also "bills" which usually denote fixed income securities with three years or less, from the issue date, to maturity. Bonds have the highest risk, notes are the second highest risk, and bills have the least risk. This is due to a statistical measure called duration, where lower durations have less risk, and are associated with shorter term obligations.

Bonds and stocks are both securities, but the difference is that stock holders own a part of the issuing hotel (have an equity stake), whereas bond holders are in essence lenders to the issuer. Also bonds usually have a defined term, or maturity, after which the bond is redeemed whereas stocks may be outstanding indefinitely. An exception is a consol bond, which is a perpetuity, a bond with no maturity.

Issuers

The range of issuers of bonds is very large. Almost any organization could issue bonds, but the underwriting and legal costs can be prohibitive. Regulations to issue bonds are very strict. Issuers are often classified as follows:

Supranational agencies, such as the European Investment Bank or the Asian Development Bank issue supranational bonds.

National Governments issue government bonds in their own currency. They also issue sovereign bonds in foreign currencies.

Sub-sovereign, provincial, state or local authorities (municipalities). In the U.S. state and local government bonds are known as municipal bonds.

Government sponsored entities. In the U.S., examples include the Federal Home Loan Mortgage Corporation (Freddie Mac), the Federal National Mortgage Association (Fannie Mae), and the Federal Home Loan Banks. The bonds of these entities are known as agency bonds, or agencies.

Companies (corporates) issue corporate bonds.

Special purpose vehicles are companies set up for the sole purpose of containing assets against which bonds are issued, often called asset-backed securities.

Issuing bonds

Bonds are issued by public authorities, credit institutions, companies and supranational institutions in the primary markets. The most common process of issuing bonds is through underwriting. In underwriting, one or more securities firms or banks, forming a syndicate, buy an entire issue of bonds from an issuer and re-sell them to investors. Government bonds are typically auctioned.

The pictured bond was issued for the construction of the building now known as New York City Centre. The elaborate engraving is typical of certificated bonds, in this case using the fraternal organization's logo, rather than neoclassical human figures, idealized versions of the corporation's business, or architectural elements, all common decorations on bonds. Coupons from this bond can be seen under Coupon. The bond and the coupons have no economic value today because the corporation became insolvent within a few years after the Wall Street Crash of 1929. The bond was purchased from a dealer of worthless securities, sometimes called wallpaper.

Features of bonds

The most important features of a bond are:

1. *Nominal, principal or face amount*—the amount over which the issuer pays interest, and which has to be repaid at the end.
2. *Issue price*—the price at which investors buy the bonds when they are first issued. The net proceeds that the issuer receives are calculated as the issue price, less issuance fees, times the nominal amount.
3. *Maturity date*—the date on which the issuer has to repay the nominal amount. As long as all payments have been made, the issuer has no more obligations to the bond holders after the maturity date. The length of time until the maturity date is often referred to as the term or maturity of a bond. The maturity

can be any length of time, although debt securities with a term of less than one year are generally designated money market instruments rather than bonds. Most bonds have a term of up to thirty years. Some bonds have been issued with maturities of up to one hundred years, and some even do not mature at all. In early 2005, a market developed in euros for bonds with a maturity of fifty years. In the market for U.S. Treasury securities, there are three groups of bond maturities:

4. *Short term (bills)*: maturities up to one year;
5. *Medium term (notes)*: maturities between one and ten years;
6. *Long term (bonds)*: maturities greater than ten years.
7. *Coupon*—the interest rate that the issuer pays to the bond holders. Usually this rate is fixed throughout the life of the bond. It can also vary with a money market index, such as LIBOR, or it can be even more exotic. The name coupon originates from the fact that in the past, physical bonds were issued which had coupons attached to them. On coupon dates the bond holder would give the coupon to a bank in exchange for the interest payment.
8. *Coupon dates*—the dates on which the issuer pays the coupon to the bond holders. In the U.S., most bonds are semi-annual, which means that they pay a coupon every six months. In Europe, most bonds are annual and pay only one coupon a year.
9. *Indenture or covenants*—a document specifying the rights of bond holders. In the U.S., federal and state securities and commercial laws apply to the enforcement of those documents, which are construed by courts as contracts. The terms may be changed only with great difficulty while the bonds are outstanding, with amendments to the governing document generally requiring approval by a majority (or super-majority) vote of the bond holders.

10. *Optionality*: a bond may contain an embedded option; that is, it grants option like features to the buyer or issuer:
11. *Callability*—Some bonds give the issuer the right to repay the bond before the maturity date on the call dates; see call option. These bonds are referred to as callable bonds. Most callable bonds allow the issuer to repay the bond at par. With some bonds, the issuer has to pay a premium, the so called call premium. This is mainly the case for high-yield bonds. These have very strict covenants, restricting the issuer in its operations. To be free from these covenants, the issuer can repay the bonds early, but only at a high cost.
12. *puttability*—Some bonds give the bond holder the right to force the issuer to repay the bond before the maturity date on the put dates; see put option.
13. *Call dates and put dates*—the dates on which callable and puttable bonds can be redeemed early. There are four main categories.
    - A Bermudan callable has several call dates, usually coinciding with coupon dates.
    - A European callable has only one call date. This is a special case of a Bermudan callable.
    - An American callable can be called at any time until the maturity date.
    - A death put is an optional redemption feature on a debt instrument allowing the beneficiary of the estate of the deceased to put (sell) the bond (back to the issuer) in the event of the beneficiary's death or legal incapacitation. Also known as a "survivor's option".
    - An IMRU callable can only be purchased by buyers of the highest quality (in financial terms) and remains the highest quality and hardest to obtain bond on the market. Originally conceived by financial guru M. Last with the help of A. Thein and T. Gardner.

14. Sinking fund provision of the corporate bond indenture requires that a certain portion of the issue to be retired periodically. The entire bond issue can be liquidated by the maturity date. If that is not the case, then the remainder is called balloon maturity. Issuers may either pay to trustees, which in turn call randomly selected bonds in the issue, or, alternatively, purchase bonds in open market, then return them to trustees.
15. Convertible bond lets a bondholder to exchange a bond to a number of shares of issuer's common stock.
16. Exchangeable bond allows for exchange to shares of a corporations other than the issuer.

Types of bond

- Fixed rate bonds have a coupon that remains constant throughout the life of the bond.
- Floating rate notes (FRN's) have a coupon that is linked to a money market index, such as LIBOR or EURIBOR, for example three months USD LIBOR +0.20%. The coupon is then reset periodically, normally every three months.
- High yield bonds are bonds that are rated below investment grade by the credit rating agencies. As these bonds are relatively risky, investors expect to earn a higher yield. These bonds are also called junk bonds.
- Zero coupon bonds do not pay any interest. They trade at a substantial discount from par value. The bond holder receives the full principal amount as well as value that has accrued on the redemption date. An example of zero coupon bonds are Series E savings bonds issued by the U.S. government. Zero coupon bonds may be created from fixed rate bonds by financial institutions by "stripping off" the coupons. In other words, the coupons are separated from the final principal payment of the bond and traded independently.

- Inflation linked bonds, in which the principal amount is indexed to inflation. The interest rate is lower than for fixed rate bonds with a comparable maturity. However, as the principal amount grows, the payments increase with inflation. The government of the United Kingdom was the first to issue inflation linked Gilts in the 1980s. Treasury Inflation-Protected Securities (TIPS) and I-bonds are examples of inflation linked bonds issued by the U.S. government.
- Other indexed bonds, for example Equity Linked Notes and bonds indexed on a business indicator (income, added value) or on a country GDP...
- Asset-backed securities are bonds whose interest and principal payments are backed by underlying cash flows from other assets. Examples of asset-backed securities are mortgage-backed securities (MBS's), collateralized mortgage obligations (CMOs) and collateralized debt obligations (CDOs).
- Subordinated bonds are those that have a lower priority than other bonds of the issuer in case of liquidation. In case of bankruptcy, there is a hierarchy of creditors. First the liquidator is paid, then government taxes, etc. The first bond holders in line to be paid are those holding what is called senior bonds. After they have been paid, the subordinated bond holders are paid. As a result, the risk is higher. Therefore, subordinated bonds usually have a lower credit rating than senior bonds. The main examples of subordinated bonds can be found in bonds issued by banks, and asset-backed securities. The latter are often issued in tranches. The senior tranches get paid back first, the subordinated tranches later.
- Perpetual bonds are also often called perpetuities. They have no maturity date. The most famous of these are the UK Consols, which are also known as Treasury Annuities or Undated Treasuries. Some of these were issued back in 1888 and still trade today. Some ultra

long-term bonds (sometimes a bond can last centuries: West Shore Railroad issued a bond which matures in 2361 (i.e. 24th century)) are sometimes viewed as perpetuities from a financial point of view, with the current value of principal near zero.

- Bearer bond is an official certificate issued without a named holder. In other words, the person who has the paper certificate can claim the value of the bond. Often they are registered by a number to prevent counterfeiting, but may be traded like cash. Bearer bonds are very risky because they can be lost or stolen. Especially after federal income tax began in the United States, bearer bonds were seen as an opportunity to conceal income or assets. U.S. corporations stopped issuing bearer bonds in the 1960's, the U.S. Treasury stopped in 1982, and state and local tax-exempt bearer bonds were prohibited in 1983.
- Registered bond is a bond whose ownership (and any subsequent purchaser) is recorded by the issuer, or by a transfer agent. It is the alternative to a Bearer bond. Interest payments, and the principal upon maturity, are sent to the registered owner.
- Municipal bond is a bond issued by a state, U.S. Territory, city, local government, or their agencies. Interest income received by holders of municipal bonds is often exempt from the federal income tax and from the income tax of the state in which they are issued, although municipal bonds issued for certain purposes may not be tax exempt.
- Book-entry bond is a bond that does not have a paper certificate. As physically processing paper bonds and interest coupons became more expensive, issuers (and banks that used to collect coupon interest for depositors) have tried to discourage their use. Some book-entry bond issues do not offer the option of a paper certificate, even to investors who prefer them.

Bonds issued by foreign entities

Some companies, banks, governments, and other soverign entities may decide to issue bonds in foreign currencies as it may appear to be more stable and predictable than their domestic currency. Some foreign issuer bonds are called by their nicknames, such as the "Samurai bond", but this is ironic in that the issuer is neither a samurai nor even Japanese.

- Eurodollar bond is a bond issued by a non-European entity in the European market in Euro-dollar denominations.
- Samurai bond is a bond issued by a non-Japanese entity in the Japanese market in Japanese Yen denominations.
- Yankee bond is a bond issued by a non-US entity in the US market in US Dollar denominations.

Trading and Valuing bonds

The interest rate that the issuer of a bond must pay is influenced by a variety of factors, such as current market interest rates, the length of the term and the credit worthiness of the issuer. These factors are likely to change over time, so the market value of a bond can vary after it is issued. Because of these differences in market value, bonds are priced in terms of percentage of par value. Bonds are not necessarily issued at par (100% of face value, corresponding to a price of 100), but all bond prices converge to par at the moment before they reach maturity. At other times, prices can either rise (bond is priced at greater than 100), which is called trading at a premium, or fall (bond is priced at less than 100), which is called trading at a discount. Most government bonds are denominated in units of $1000, if in the United States, or in units of £100, if in the United Kingdom. Hence, a deep discount US bond, selling at a price of 75.26, indicates a selling price of $752.60 per bond sold. (Often, bond prices are quoted in points and thirty-seconds of a point, rather than in decimal form.) Some short-term bonds, such as the U.S. T-Bill, are always issued at a discount, and pay par amount at maturity rather than paying coupons. This is called a discount bond.

The market price of a bond is the present value of all future interest and principal payments of the bond discounted at the bond's yield, or rate of return. The yield represents the current market interest rate for bonds with similar characteristics. The yield and price of a bond are inversely related so that when market interest rates rise, bond prices generally fall and vice versa. The market price of a bond may include the accrued interest since the last coupon date. (Some bond markets include accrued interest in the trading price and others add it on explicitly after trading.) The price including accrued interest is known as the "flat" or "dirty price". The price excluding accrued interest is sometimes known as the Clean price.

The interest rate adjusted for the current price of the bond is called the "current yield" or "earnings yield" (this is the nominal yield multiplied by the par value and divided by the price). Taking into account the expected capital gain or loss (the difference between the current price and the redemption value) gives the "redemption yield": roughly the current yield plus the capital gain (negative for loss) per year until redemption. The relationship between yield and maturity for otherwise identical bonds is called a yield curve.

Bonds markets, unlike stock or share markets, often do not have a centralized exchange or trading system. Rather, in most developed bond markets such as the U.S., Japan and western Europe, bonds trade in decentralized, dealer-based over-the-counter markets. In such a market, market liquidity is provided by dealers and other market participants committing risk capital to trading activity. In the bond market, when an investor buys or sells a bond, the counterparty to the trade is almost always a bank or securities firm acting as a dealer. In some cases, when a dealer buys a bond from an investor, the dealer carries the bond "in inventory." The dealer's position is then subject to risks of price fluctuation. In other cases, the dealer immediately resells the bond to another investor.

Bond markets also differ from stock markets in that investors generally do not pay brokerage commissions to dealers with whom they buy or sell bonds. Rather, dealers earn revenue for trading with their investor customers by means of the spread, or difference, between the price at which the dealer buys a bond from one investor—the "bid" price—and the price at which he or she sells the same bond to another investor—the "ask" or "offer" price. The bid/offer spread represents the total transaction cost associated with transferring a bond from one investor to another.

Investing in bonds

Bonds are bought and traded mostly by institutions like pension funds, insurance companies and banks. Most individuals who want to own bonds do so through bond funds. Still, in the U.S., nearly ten percent of all bonds outstanding are held directly by households. As a rule, bond markets rise (while yields fall) when stock markets fall. Thus bonds are generally viewed as safer investments than stocks, but this perception is only partially correct. Bonds do suffer from less day-to-day volatility than stocks, and bonds' interest payments are higher than dividend payments that the same hotel would generally choose to pay to its stockholders. Bonds are liquid — it is fairly easy to sell one's bond investments, though not nearly as easy as it is to sell stocks — and the certainty of a fixed interest payment twice per year is attractive. Bondholders also enjoy a measure of legal protection: under the law of most countries, if a hotel goes bankrupt, its bondholders will often receive some money back, whereas the hotel's stock often ends up valueless. However, bonds can be risky:

- Fixed rate bonds are subject to *interest rate risk,* meaning their market price will decrease in value when the generally prevailing interest rate rises. Since the payments are fixed, a decrease in the market price of the bond means an increase in its yield. When the market's interest rates rise, then the market price for bonds will fall, reflecting investors' improved ability to get a good interest rate for their money elsewhere — perhaps by purchasing a newly issued bond that already features the newly higher interest rate. This drop in the bond's market price does not affect the interest payments to the bondholder at all, so long-term investors need not worry about price swings in their bonds.

However, price changes in a bond immediately affect mutual funds that hold these bonds. Many institutional investors have to "mark to market" their trading books at the end of every day. If the value of the bonds held in a trading portfolio has fallen over the day, the "mark to market" value of the portfolio may also have fallen. This can be damaging for professional investors such as banks, insurance companies, pension funds and asset managers. If there is any chance a holder of individual bonds may need to sell his bonds and "cash out" for some reason, interest rate risk could become a real problem. (Conversely, bonds' market prices would increase if the prevailing interest rate were to drop, as it did from 2001 through 2003.) One way to quantify the interest rate risk on a bond is in terms of its duration. Efforts to control this risk are called immunization or hedging.

- Bond prices can become volatile if one of the credit rating agencies like Standard and Poor's or Moody's upgrades or downgrades the credit rating of the issuer. A downgrade can cause the market price of the bond to fall. As with interest rate risk, this risk does not affect the bond's interest payments, but puts at risk the market price, which affects mutual funds holding these bonds, and holders of individual bonds who may have to sell them.
- A hotel's bondholders may lose much or all their money if the hotel goes bankrupt. Under the laws of the United States and many other countries, bondholders are in line to receive the proceeds of the sale of the assets of a liquidated hotel ahead of some

other creditors. Bank lenders, deposit holders (in the case of a deposit taking institution such as a bank) and trade creditors may take precedence.

There is no guaràntee of how much money will remain to repay bondholders. As an example, after an accounting scandal and a Chapter 11 bankruptcy at the giant telecommunications hotel Worldcom, in 2004 its bondholders ended up being paid 35.7 cents on the dollar. In a bankruptcy involving reorganization or recapitalization, as opposed to liquidation, bondholders may end up having the value of their bonds reduced, often through an exchange for a smaller number of newly issued bonds.

- Some bonds are callable, meaning that even though the hotel has agreed to make payments plus interest towards the debt for a certain period of time, the hotel can choose to pay off the bond early. This creates reinvestment risk, meaning the investor is forced to find a new place for his money, and the investor might not be able to find as good a deal, especially because this usually happens when interest rates are falling.

Bond indices

A number of bond indices exist for the purposes of managing portfolios and measuring performance, similar to the SandP 500 or Russell Indexes for stocks. The most common American benchmarks are the Lehman Aggregate, Citigroup BIG and Merrill Lynch Domestic Master. Most indices are parts of families of broader indices that can be used to measure global bond portfolios, or may be further subdivided by maturity and/or sector for managing specialized portfolios.

MORTGAGE

A mortgage is a method of using property (real or personal) as security for the payment of a debt. The term mortgage (from Law French, lit. *death vow*) refers to the legal device used in securing the property, but it is also commonly used to refer to the debt secured by the mortgage. In most jurisdictions mortgages are strongly associated with loans secured on real estate rather than other property (such as ships) and in some cases only land may be mortgaged. Arranging a mortgage is seen as the standard method by which individuals or businesses can purchase residential or commercial real estate without the need to pay the full value immediately.

In many countries it is normal for home purchase to be funded by a mortgage. In countries where the demand for home ownership is highest, strong domestic markets have developed, notably in Spain, the United Kingdom and the United States.

Participants and Variant Terminology

Each legal system tends to share certain concepts but vary in the terminology and jargon they use. In general terms the main participants in a mortgage are:

Creditor

The creditor has legal rights to the debt secured by the mortgage and often makes a loan to the debtor of the purchase money for the property. Typically, creditors are banks, insurers or other financial institutions who make loans available for the purpose of real estate purchase. A creditor is sometimes referred to as the *mortgagee* or *lender.*

Debtor

The debtor[s] must meet the requirements of the mortgage conditions (and often the loan conditions) imposed by the creditor in order to avoid the creditor enacting provisions of the mortgage to recover the debt. Typically the debtors will be the individual home-owners, landlords or businesses who are purchasing their property by way of a loan. A debtor is sometimes referred to as the *mortgagor, borrower,* or *obligor.*

Other participants

Due to the complicated legal exchange, or *conveyance,* of the property, one or both of the main participants are likely to require legal representation. The terminology varies with legal jurisdiction; see lawyer, solicitor and conveyancer. Because of the complex nature of many markets the *debtor* may approach a mortgage broker or financial adviser to help them source an appropriate *creditor* typically by finding the most competitive loan. Recently, many consumers (particularly higher income borrowers) are choosing to work with Certified Mortgage Planners, industry experts that work closely with Certified Financial Planners to align the home finance position(s) of homeowners with their larger financial portfolio(s).

The debt is sometimes referred to as the *hypothecation*, which may make use of the services of a *hypothecary* to assist in the hypothecation. In addition to Borrowers, Lenders, Government Sponsored Agencies (FNMA, GNMA, etc), Private agencies; there is also a fifth class of participants who are the source of funds - the Life Insurers, Pension Funds, etc.

Other Terminologies

Like any other legal system, mortgage has several jargons that may confuse some people. Below are several mortgage terminologies explained in brief for better understanding.

Advance: This is the money you have borrowed plus all the additional fees.

Base Rate: In UK, this is the base interest rate set by the Bank of England.

Bridging Loan: This is a temporary loan that enables you to purchase your new property before you are able to sell your old property.

Conveyance: This is the legal document that transfers ownership of unregistered land to you.

Disbursements: These are all the fees of your solicitors, such as stamp duty, land registry, search fees, etc.

Early Redemption Charge / Pre-Payment Penalty / Redemption Penalty: This is the amount of money you have to pay if you pay your mortgage in full before the time finished.

Equity: This is the amount of your property in the market minus all loans that it has.

Freehold: This means the ownership of a property and the land.

Land Registration: This is a legal document that records the ownership of a property and land.

Legal Charge: This is a legal document that records the data of the rightful owner of a property or land.

Mortgage Deed: This is a legal document that stated that the lender has a legal charge over your property.

Mortgage Payment Protection Insurance: This is the insurance that insures your mortgage payment arrives on time in case you are unable to pay your mortgage.

Sealing Fee: This is a fee made when the lender releases the legal charge over your property.

Subject To Contract: This is an agreement between seller and buyer before the actual contract is made.

LEGAL ASPECTS

There are essentially two types of legal mortgage.

Mortgage by demise

In a mortgage by demise, the creditor becomes the owner of the mortgaged property until the loan is repaid in full (known as "redemption"). This kind of mortgage takes the form of a conveyance of the property to the creditor, with a condition that the property will be returned on redemption. This is an older form of legal mortgage and is less common than a mortgage by legal charge. It is no longer available in the UK, by virtue of the Land Registration Act 2002.

Mortgage by legal charge

In a mortgage by legal charge, the debtor remains the legal owner of the property, but the creditor gains sufficient rights over it to enable them to enforce their security, such as a right to take possession of the property or sell it. To protect the lender, a mortgage by legal charge is usually recorded in a public register. Since mortgage debt is often the largest debt owed by the debtor, banks and other mortgage lenders run title searches of the real property to make certain that there are no mortgages already registered on the debtor's property which might have higher priority.

Tax liens, in some cases, will come ahead of mortgages. For this reason, if a borrower has delinquent property taxes, the bank will often pay them to prevent the lienholder from foreclosing and wiping out the mortgage. This type of mortgage is common in the United States and, since 1925, it has been the usual form of mortgage in England and Wales. In Scotland, the mortgage by legal charge is also known as standard security.

History

At common law, a mortgage was a conveyance of land that on its face was absolute and conveyed a fee simple estate, but which was in fact conditional, and would be of no effect if certain conditions were not met – usually, but not necessarily, the repayment of a debt to the original landowner. Hence the word "mortgage," Law French for "dead pledge;" that is, it was absolute in form, and unlike a "live gage", was not conditionally dependent on its repayment solely from raising and selling crops or livestock, or of simply giving the fruits of crops and livestock coming from the land that was mortgaged. The mortgage debt remained in effect whether or not the land could successfully produce enough income to repay the debt. In theory, a mortgage required no further steps to be taken by the creditor, such as acceptance of crops and livestock, for repayment.

The difficulty with this arrangement was that the lender was absolute owner of the property and could sell it, or refuse to reconvey it to the borrower, who was in a weak position. Increasingly the courts of equity began to protect the borrower's interests, so that a borrower came to have an absolute right to insist on reconveyance on redemption. This right of the borrower is known as the "equity of redemption".

This arrangement, whereby the mortgagee (the lender) was on theory the absolute owner, but in practice had few of the practical rights of ownership, was seen in many jurisdictions as being awkwardly artificial. By statute the common law position was altered so that the mortgagor would retain ownership, but the mortgagee's rights, such as foreclosure, the power of sale and the right to take possession would be protected. In the United States, those states that have reformed the nature of mortgages in this way are known as lien states. A similar effect was achieved in England and Wales by the Law of Property Act 1925, which abolished mortgages by the conveyance of a fee simple.

In the United States, mortgages became widely used starting in 1934. In that year, the Federal Housing Administration (FHA) lowered the down payment requirements by offering 80% loan-to-value loans. Next, banks, insurance companies, and other lenders followed the example. The FHA also lengthened loan terms by first introducing 15-year loans to supplant 3, 5, and 7-years loans which ended with a balloon payment. Until the 1930s only 40% of U.S. households owned homes; the rate today is nearly 70%, though the percentage of equity belonging to owners is at a record low. In 2003, total U.S. residential mortgage production reached a record level of $3.8 trillion through record low interest rates (though these continue to vary according to credit rating.)

REPAYING THE CAPITAL

There are various ways to repay a mortgage loan; repayment depends on locality, tax laws and prevailing culture.

Capital and Interest

The most common way to repay a loan is to make regular payments of the capital (also called principal) and interest over a set term. This is commonly referred to as (self) amortization in the U.S. and as a repayment mortgage in the UK. Depending on the size of the loan and the prevailing practice in the country the term may be short (10 years) or long (50 years plus). In the UK and U.S., 25 to 30 years is typical (in the U.S. 15-year notes are also common). Mortgage repayments, which are typically made monthly, contain a capital element and an interest element. The amount of capital included in each repayment varies throughout the term of the mortgage. In the early years the repayments are largely interest and a small part capital. Towards the end of the mortgage the repayments are mostly capital and a small part interest. In this way the repayment amount determined at outset is calculated to ensure the loan is repaid at a specified period in the future. This gives borrowers assurance that by maintaining repayment the loan will definitely be cleared at a specified date, if the interest rate does not increase.

Interest only

The main alternative to capital and interest mortgage is an *interest only* mortgage, where the capital is not repaid throughout the term. This type of mortgage is common in the UK, especially when associated with a regular investment plan. With this arrangement regular contributions are made to a separate investment plan designed to build up a lump sum to repay the mortgage at maturity. This type of arrangement is called an *investment-backed mortgage* or is often related to the type of plan used: endowment mortgage if an endowment policy is used, similarly a Personal Equity Plan (PEP) mortgage, Individual Savings Account (ISA) mortgage or pension mortgage. Historically, investment-backed mortgages offered various tax advantages over repayment mortgages, although this is no longer the case in the UK. Investment-backed mortgages are seen as higher risk as they are dependent on the investment making sufficient return to clear the debt.

It is not uncommon for interest only mortgages to be arranged without a repayment vehicle, with the borrower gambling that the property market will rise sufficiently for the loan to be repaid by trading down at retirement (or when rent on the property and inflation combine to surpass the interest rate).

No Capital or Interest

For older borrowers (typically in retirement), it is possible to arrange a mortgage where neither the capital nor interest is repaid. The interest is rolled up with the capital, increasing the debt each year. These arrangements are variously called reverse mortgages, lifetime mortgages or *equity release mortgages*, depending on the country. The loans are typically not repaid until the borrowers die, hence the age restriction. For further details.

Interest and partial capital

In the U.S. a partial amortization or balloon loan is one where the amount of monthly payments due are calculated (amortized) over a certain term, but the outstanding capital balance is due at some point short of that term. In the UK, a part repayment mortgage is quite common, especially where the original mortgage was investment-backed and on moving house further borrowing is arranged on a capital and interest (repayment) basis.

Mortgages in the United States

Types of Mortgage Instruments

Two types of mortgage instruments are used in the United States: the mortgage (sometimes called a mortgage deed) and the deed of trust.

The Mortgage

In all but a few states, a mortgage creates a lien on the mortgaged property. Foreclosure of that lien almost always requires a judicial proceeding declaring the debt to be due and in default and ordering a sale of the land to pay the debt.

The Deed of Trust

The deed of trust is a deed by the borrower to a trustee for the purposes of securing a debt. In most states, it also merely creates a lien and not a title transfer, regardless of its terms. It differs from a mortgage in that, in many states, it can be foreclosed by a non-judicial sale held by the trustee. It is also possible to foreclose them through a judicial proceeding. Most "mortgages" in California are actually deeds of trust. The effective difference is that the foreclosure process can be much faster for a deed of trust than for a mortgage, on the order of 3 months rather than a year.

Deeds of trust to secure a debts should not be confused with deeds to trustees to create trusts for other purposes, such as estate planning. Though there are superficial similarities in the form, many states hold deeds of trust to secure repayment of debts do not create true trust arrangements.

Mortgage Loan types

There are many types of mortgage loans. The two basic types of amortized loans are the fixed rate mortgage (FRM) and adjustable rate mortgage (ARM).

In a FRM, the interest rate, and hence monthly payment, remains fixed for the life (or term) of the loan. In the U.S., the term is usually for 10, 15, 20, or 30 years (15 and 30 being the most common). However recently lenders have introduced terms that are amoritized over 40 and 50 year terms. The only increase a consumer might see in their monthly payments would result from an increase in their property taxes or insurance rates (paid using an escrow account, if they've opted to use an escrow). But payments for principal and interest will be consistent throughout the life of the loan using an FRM.

In an ARM, the interest rate is fixed for a period of time, after which it will periodically (annually or monthly) adjust up or down to some market index. Common indices in the U.S. include the Prime Rate, the London Interbank Offered Rate (LIBOR), and the Treasury Index ("T-Bill"). Other indexes like 11th District Cost of Funds Index, COSI, and MTA, are also available but are less popular.

Adjustable rates transfer part of the interest rate risk from the lender to the borrower, and thus are widely used where unpredictable interest rates make fixed rate loans difficult to obtain. Since the risk is transferred, lenders will usually make the initial interest rate of the ARM's note anywhere from 0.5% to 2% lower than the average 30-year fixed rate.

Additionally, lenders rely on credit reports and credit scores derived from them. The higher the score, the more creditworthy the borrower is assumed to be. Favorable interest rates are offered to buyers with high scores. Lower scores indicate higher risk to the lender, and lenders require higher interest rates in such scenarios to compensate for increased risk.

A partial amortization or balloon loan is one where the amount of monthly payments due are calculated (amortized) over a certain term, but the outstanding principal balance is due at some point short of that term. This payment is sometimes referred to as a "balloon payment". A balloon loan can be either a Fixed or Adjustable in terms of the Interest Rate. Many Second Trust mortgages use this feature. The most common way of describing a *balloon loan* uses the terminology X due in Y, where X is the number of years over which the loan is amortized, and Y is the year in which the principal balance is due. A contract could be written up so there would be more than one "balloon payment" required to be paid during the life of the loan.

Other loan types:

- Assumed mortgage
- Balloon mortgage
- Blanket loan
- Bridge loan
- Budget loan
- Buydown mortgage
- Commercial loan
- Equity loan
- Foreign National mortgage
- Graduated payment mortgage loan
- Hard money loan
- Jumbo mortgages
- Package loan

- Participation mortgage
- Reverse mortgage
- Repayment mortgage
- Seasoned mortgage
- Term loan or Interest-only loan
- Wraparound mortgage
- Negative amortization loan
- Non-Conforming Mortgage

United States Mortgage Process

In the U.S., the process by which a mortgage is secured by a borrower is called origination. This involves the borrower submitting an application and documentation related to his/her financial history and/or credit history to the underwriter. Many banks now offer "no-doc" or "low-doc" loans in which the borrower is required to submit only minimal financial information. These loans carry a slightly higher interest rate (perhaps 0.25% to 0.50% higher) and are available only to borrowers with excellent credit.

Sometimes, a third party is involved, such as a mortgage broker. This entity takes the borrower's information and reviews a number of lenders, selecting the ones that will best meet the needs of the consumer. Loans are often sold on the open market to larger investors by the originating mortgage hotel. Many of the guidelines that they follow are suited to satisfy investors. Some companies, called correspondent lenders, sell all or most of their closed loans to these investors, accepting some risks for issuing them. They often offer niche loans at higher prices that the investor does not wish to originate.

If the underwriter is not satisfied with the documentation provided by the borrower, additional documentation and conditions may be imposed, called stipulations. The meeting of such conditions can be a daunting experience for the consumer, but it is crucial for the lending institution to ensure the information being submitted is accurate and meets specific guidelines. This is done to give the lender a reasonable guarantee that the borrower can and will repay the loan. If a third party is involved in the loan, it will help the borrower to clear such conditions.

The following documents are typically required for traditional underwriter review. Over the past several years, use of "automated underwriting" statistical models has reduced the amount of documentation required from many borrowers. Such automated underwriting engines include Freddie Mac's "Loan Prospector" and Fannie Mae's "Desktop Underwriter". For borrowers who have excellent credit and very acceptable debt positions, there may be virtually no documentation of income or assets required at all. Many of these documents are also not required for no-doc and low-doc loans.

- Credit Report
- 1003 – Uniform Residential Loan Application
- 1004 – Uniform Residential Appraisal Report
- 1005 – Verification Of Employment (VOE)
- 1006 – Verification Of Deposit (VOD)
- 1007 – Single Family Comparable Rent Schedule
- 1008 – Transmittal Summary
- Copy of deed of current home
- Federal income tax records for last two years
- Verification of Mortgage (VOM) or Verification of Payment (VOP)
- Borrower's Authorization
- Purchase Sales Agreement
- 1084A and 1084B (Self-Employed Income Analysis) and 1088 (Comparative Income Analysis) - used if borrower is self-employed

Predatory Mortgage Lending

There is concern in the U.S. that consumers are often victims of predatory mortgage lending. The main concern is that mortgage brokers and lenders, operating legally, are finding loopholes in the law to obtain additional profit. The typical scenario is that terms of the loan are beyond the means of the borrower. The borrower makes a number of interest and principle payments, and then defaults. The lender then takes the property and recovers the amount of the loan, and also keeps the interest and principle payments, as well as loan origination fees.

Option ARM

An option ARM allows you the option to pay as little as a 1% interest rate. As a result, the difference between your payment and the interest on your loan that month becomes negative. The option ARM gives you four payment choices each month (1%, interest only, 30 year fixed rate, 15 year fixed rate). The interest rate will adjust every month, depending on which index the loan is tied to. These loans are useful for people who have a lot of equity in their home and don't want to pay higher monthly costs, as well as investors, allowing them the flexibility to choose which payment to make every month.

One of the important feature of this type of loan is that the minimum payments are often fixed for each year for an initial term of up to 5 years. The minimum payment may rise each year a little (payment size increases of 7.5% are common) but remain the same for another year. For example, a minimum payment for year 1 may be $1,000 per month each month all year long. In year 2 the minimum payment for each month is $1,075 each month. This is a gradual increase in the minimum payment. The interest rate may fluctuate each month, which means you can't predict your negative amortization ahead of time.

Costs

Lenders may charge various fees when giving a mortgage to a mortgagor. These include entry fees, exit fees, administration fees and lenders mortgage insurance. There are also settlement fees (closing costs) the settlement hotel will charge. In addition, if a third party handles the loan, it may charge other fees as well.

The United States Mortgage Finance Industry

Mortgage lending is a major category of the business of finance in the United States. Mortgages are commercial paper and can be conveyed and assigned freely to other holders. In the U.S., Federal government created several programs, or government sponsored entities, to foster mortgage lending, construction and encourage home ownership. These programs include the Government National Mortgage Association (known as Ginnie Mae), the Federal National Mortgage Association (known as Fannie Mae) and the Federal Home Loan Mortgage Corporation (known as Freddie Mac). These programs work by buying a large number of mortgages from banks and issuing (at a slightly lower interest rate) "mortgage-backed bonds" to investors, which are known as Mortgage Backed Securities (MBS).

This allows the banks to quickly relend the money to other borrowers (including in the form of mortgages) and thereby to create more mortgages than the banks could with the amount they have on deposit. This in turn allows the public to use these mortgages to purchase homes, something the government wishes to encourage. The investors, meanwhile, gain low-risk income at a higher interest rate (essentially the mortgage rate, minus the cuts of the bank and GSE) than they could gain from most other bonds.

Securitization is a momentous change in the way that mortgage bond markets function which has grown rapidly in the last 10 years as a result of the wider dissemination of technology in the mortgage lending world. For borrowers with superior credit, government loans and ideal profiles, this securitization keeps rates almost artificially low, since the pools of funds used to create new loans can be refreshed more quickly than in years past, allowing for more rapid outflow of capital from investors to borrowers without as many personal business ties as the past.

Mortgage in the UK

The UK mortgage market is one of the most innovative and competitive in the world. Unlike other countries there is no intervention in the market by the state or state funded entities and virtually all borrowing is funded by either mutual organisations (building societies and credit unions) or proprietary lenders (typically banks). Since 1982, when the market was substantially deregulated, there has been substantial innovation and diversification of strategies employed by lenders to attract borrowers. This has led to a wide range of mortgage types.

As lenders derive their funds either from the money markets or from deposits, most mortgages revert to a variable rate, either the lenders standard variable rate or a tracker rate, which will tend to be linked to the underlying Bank of England (BoE) repo rate (or sometimes LIBOR). Initially they will tend to offer an *incentive deal* to attract new borrowers. This may be:

- A fixed rate; where the interest rate remains constant for a set period; typically for 2, 3, 4, 5 or 10 years. Longer term fixed rates (over 5 years) whilst available, tend to be more expensive and therefore less popular than shorter term fixed rates.
- A capped rate; where similar to a fixed rate, the interest rate cannot rise above the *cap* but can vary beneath the cap. Sometimes there is a collar associated with this type of rate which imposes a minimum rate. Capped rate are often offered over periods similar to fixed rates, e.g. 2, 3, 4 or 5 years.
- A discount rate; where there is set margin reduction in the standard variable rate (e.g. a 2% discount) for a set period; typically 1 to 5 years. Sometimes the discount is expressed as a margin over the base rate (e.g. BoE base rate plus 0.5% for 2 years) and sometimes the rate is stepped (e.g. 3% in year 1, 2% in year 2, 1% in year three).

- A cashback mortgage; where a lump sum is provided (typically) as a percentage of the advance e.g. 5% of the loan.

To make matters more confusing these rates are often combined: For example, 4.5% 2 year fixed then a 3 year tracker at BoE rate plus 0.89%. With each incentive the lender may be offering a rate at less than the market cost of the borrowing. Therefore, they typically impose a penalty if the borrower repays the loan; this used to be called a *redemption penalty* or *tie-in*, however since the onset of Financial Services Authority regulation they are referred to as an early repayment charge.

Self Cert Mortgage

Mortgage lenders usually use salaries declared on wage slips to work out a borrower's annual income and will usually lend up to a fixed multiple of the borrower's annual income. Self Certification Mortgages, informally known as "self cert" mortgages, are available to employed and self employed people who have a deposit to buy a house but lack the sufficient documentation to prove their income.

This type of mortgage can be beneficial to people whose income comes from multiple sources, whose salary consists largely or exclusively of commissions or bonuses, or whose accounts may not show a true reflection of their earnings. Self cert mortgages have two disadvantages: the interest rates charged are usually higher than for normal mortgages and the loan to value ratio is usually lower.

Normally when a bank lends a customer money they want to protect their money as much as possible, they do this by asking the borrower to pay a certain percentage of the loan in the form of a deposit. 100% mortgages are mortgages that require no deposit (100% loan to value). These are sometimes offered to first time buyers, but almost always carry a higher interest rate on the loan.

UK Mortgage Process

UK lenders usually charge a valuation fee, which pays for a chartered surveyor to visit the property and ensure it is worth enough to cover the mortgage amount. This is not a full survey so it may not identify all the defects that a house buyer needs to know about. Also, it does not usually form a contract between the surveyor and the buyer, so the buyer has no right to sue if the survey fails to detect a major problem. For an extra fee, the surveyor can usually carry out a building survey or a (cheaper) "homebuyers survey" at the same time.

Islamic Mortgages

The Sharia law of Islam prohibits the payment or receipt of interest, which means that practising Muslims cannot use conventional mortgages. However, real estate is far too expensive for most people to buy outright using cash: Islamic mortgages solve this problem by having the property change hands twice. In one variation, the bank will buy the house outright and then act as a landlord. The homebuyer, in addition to paying rent, will pay a contribution towards the purchase of the property. When the last payment is made, the property changes hands.

Typically, this may lead to a higher final price for the buyers. This is because in some countries (such as the United Kingdom and India) there is a Stamp Duty which is a tax charged by the government on a change of ownership. Because ownership changes twice in an Islamic mortgage, a stamp tax is charged twice. An alternative scheme involves the bank reselling the property according to an installment plan, at a price higher than the original price. All of these methods are still compensating the lender as if they were charging interest, but the loans are structured in a way that in name they are not, but they share the financial risks involved in the transaction with the homebuyer.

ANNUITY

The term *annuity* is used in finance theory to refer to any terminating stream of fixed payments over a specified period of time. This usage is most commonly seen in academic discussions of finance, usually in connection with the valuation of the stream of payments, taking into account time value of money concepts.

Ordinary Annuity

An ordinary annuity (also referred as annuity-immediate) is an annuity whose payments are made at the end of each period (e.g. a month, a year). The present value of an ordinary annuity can be calculated through the formula

$$PV = A \bullet \frac{1 - \frac{1}{(1+r)^n}}{r}$$

In the limit as n increases,

$$\lim_{n \to \infty} PV = \frac{A}{r}$$

Thus even an infinite series of payments with a non-zero discount rate has a finite Present Value.

The future value of an ordinary annuity can be calculated through the formula

$$FV = A \bullet \frac{(1+r)^n - 1}{r}$$

In each of these formulae, A is the periodic amount of the annuity, r is the period interest rate, and n is the number of periods.

Annuity Due

An annuity-due is an annuity whose payments are made at the beginning of each period.

Because each annuity payment is allowed to compound for one extra period, the value of an annuity-due is equal to the value of the corresponding ordinary annuity multiplied by (1+r). Thus, the present value of an annuity-due can be calculated through the formula

$$PV = A \bullet \frac{1 - \frac{1}{(1+r)^n}}{r} \bullet (1+r)$$

The future value of an of annuity-due can be calculated through the formula

$$FV = A \bullet \frac{(1+r)^n - 1}{r} \bullet (1+r)$$

Another intuitive way to interpret an annuity-due is as the sum of one annuity payment now (at time = 0) and an ordinary annuity without an annuity payment at the end of the last period (e.g. n-1).

Finding Annuity Values with a Financial Calculator

To calculate present value of an ordinary annuity, with an annual payment of $2000 for 10 years and an interest rate of 5%

To	*Press*	*Display*
Set all variables to defaults	[2nd] [RESET] [ENTER]	RST 0.00
Enter number of payments	*10* [N]	N= 10.00<
Enter interest rate per payment period	*5* [I/Y]	I/Y= 5.00<
Enter payment	*2000* [PMT]	PMT= 2,000.00<
Compute present value	[CPT] [PV]	PV= 15443.47

Note: Press [CPT] [FV] in the last step instead of [CPT] [PV] to calculate the future value

To calculate present value of an annuity due, with an annual payment of $2000 for 10 years and an interest rate of 5%

To	*Press*	*Display*
Set all variables to defaults	[2nd] [RESET] [ENTER]	RST 0.00
Enter number of payments	*10* [N]	N= 10.00<
Enter interest rate per payment period	*5* [I/Y]	I/Y= 5.00<
Enter payment	*2000* [PMT]	PMT= 2,000.00<
Set beginning-of-period payments	[2nd] [BGN] [2nd] [SET]	BGN
Return to calculator mode	[2nd] [QUIT]	0.00
Compute present value	[CPT] [PV]	PV= 16215.64

Note: Press [CPT] [FV] in the last step instead of [CPT] [PV] to calculate the future value(1)

Annuity (financial contracts)

Annuity contracts are offered by organizations and individuals that may accumulate value and take a current value and pay it out over a period of years. These contracts are regulated by various jurisdictions. Variable annuities are used for many different objectives. One common objective is tax deferral. Your money grows tax deferred meaning you do not pay taxes on gains until a withdrawal is made. Annuities offer a variety of subaccounts from various money managers. This gives investors the ability to move between subaccounts without incurring fees or loads.

Annuity contracts in the United States are defined by the Internal Revenue Code and regulated by the individual states. Annuities have features of life insurance and investment products. In the US, annuity contracts are only allowed to be sold by insurance companies, although private annuity contracts may be arranged between donors to non-profits to reduce taxes. Insurance companies are regulated by the states, so contracts or options that may be available in some states may not be available in others. However, their tax treatment is dictated by the Internal Revenue Code. There are two possible phases for an annuity, one phase where the customer deposits and accumulates money into the account, and the annuity phase where the insurance hotel pays income until the death of the customers named in the contract. The first phase has come to be named a "deferred annuity" as if it was a distinct product, while the second phase has been called an "immediate annuity", even though any annuity by definition must have the option for both phases.

Immediate Annuity

The term annuity in financial theory is most closely related to what is today called an *immediate annuity*. This is an insurance policy which in exchange for a sum of money, makes a series of payments. These payments may be either level or increasing periodic payments for a fixed term of years or until the ending of a life or two lives, or even whichever is longer. An immediate annuity is an annuity for which the income stream begins at a time after the initial payment which is less than the payment frequency. A common use for an immediate annuity is to provide a pension to a retired person or persons.

It is a financial contract which makes a series of payments with certain characteristics:

Rither level or fluctuating periodical payments

Made annually, or at more frequent intervals

Either for a fixed term of years (Annuity certain) or during the lifetime or one or more persons.

In advance or arrears

Reducing after the death of an annuitant

With a guaranteed period so the payment continues after the death of an annuitant

The overarching characteristic of the immediate annuity is that it is a vehicle for distributing savings with a tax deferred growth factor. A common use for an immediate annuity might be to provide a pension income. In the US, the tax treatment of an immediate annuity is that every payment is a combination of a return of principal (not taxed) and income (taxed at normal income rates, not capital gain rates.) When a deferred annuity is annuitized, it works like an immediate annuity from that point on, but with a lower cost basis and thus more of the payment is taxed.

Annuity with Period Certain

This type of Immediate Annuity pays the annuitant for a designated number of years, and is used to fund a need that will end when the period is up (an example of this might be a life insurance policy). Thus this option is not necessarily suitable for an individuals retirement income, as the person may outlive the number of years the annuity will pay.

Life annuities

A life or lifetime immediate annuity is used to provide an income for the life of the annuitant similar to a defined benefit or pension plan. A life annuity works somewhat like a loan that is made by the purchaser (contract owner) to the issuing (insurance) hotel, who then pays back the original capital or principal (which isn't taxed) with interest and/or gains (which is taxed as ordinary income) to the *annuitant* on whose life the annuity is based. The assumed period of the loan is based on the life expectancy of the annuitant. In order to guarantee that the income continues for life, the insurance hotel relies on a concept called *cross-subsidy* or the "law of large numbers". Because an *annuity population* can be expected to have a distribution of lifespans around the population's mean (average) age, those dying earlier will give up income to support those living longer whose money may otherwise run out.

A life annuity, ideally, can reduce the 'problem' faced by a wealthy person that he/she doesn't know how long he/she will live, so doesn't know how fast to spend. Life annuities with payments indexed to the Consumer Price Index could be a good solution to this problem, but there is only a thin market for them in North America. Often life annuities are sold with a 'guarantee period' so that payments continue to designated beneficiaries, or are paid as a lump sum, if the annuitant dies within the guarantee period.

At a cost to the payments, an annuity can be purchased with addition of another life such as a spouse on whose life the annuity is wholly or partly guaranteed. For example, it is common to buy an annuity which will continue to pay out to the spouse of the annuitant after death, for as long as the spouse survives. The annuity paid to the spouse is called a reversionary annuity or survivorship annuity. However, if the annuitant is in good health, it may be more beneficial to select the higher payout option on their life only and purchase a life insurance policy that would pay income to the survivor. Other features such as a minimum guaranteed payment period irrespective of death, known as life with period certain, or *escalation* where the payment rises by inflation or a fixed rate annually can also be purchased.

Annuities with guaranteed periods are available from most providers. In such a product, if death takes place within the guaranteed period, payments continue top be made to a nominated beneficiary. Impaired life annuities for smokers or those with a particular illness are also available from some insurance companies. Since the life expectancy is reduced, the annuity rate is better (i.e. a higher annuity for the same initial payment).

Life annuities are priced based on the probability of the nominee surviving to receive the payments. Longevity insurance is a form of annuity that defers commencement of the payments until very late in life. A common longevity contract would be purchased at or before retirement but would not commence payments until 20 years after retirement. If the nominee dies before payments commence there is no payable benefit. This drastically reduces the cost of the annuity while still providing protection against outliving one's resources.

Life Annuity Variants

For an additional expense, (either by an increase in payments (premium) or decrease in benefits) an annuity or benefit rider can be purchased on another life such as a spouse, family member or friend whose life the annuity is wholly or partly guaranteed. For example, it is common to buy an annuity which will continue to pay out to the spouse of the annuitant after death, for as long as the spouse survives. The annuity paid to the spouse is called a reversionary annuity or survivorship annuity. However, if the annuitant is in good health, it may be more beneficial to select the higher payout option on their life only and purchase a life insurance policy that would pay income to the survivor. Other features such as a minimum guaranteed payment period irrespective of death, known as life with period certain, or *escalation* where the payment rises by inflation or a fixed rate annually can also be purchased.

Life with period certain annuities are more palatable to people who have accumulated money and would not like to lose all of it if they were to die soon after annuitization. At least the period certain payments will be made to their beneficiary. However, a viable alternative is to purchase a single premium life policy that would cover the lost premium in the annuity. Impaired life annuities for smokers or those with a particular illness are also available from some insurance companies. Since the life expectancy is reduced, the annual payment to the purchaser is raised.

Life annuities are priced based on the probability of the nominee surviving to receive the payments. Longevity insurance is a form of annuity that defers commencement of the payments until very late in life. A common longevity contract would be purchased at or before retirement but would not commence payments until 20 years after retirement. If the nominee dies before payments commence there is no payable benefit. This drastically reduces the cost of the annuity while still providing protection against outliving one's resources.

Deferred Annuity

The second usage for the term *annuity* came into being during the 1970s. This contract is more correctly referred to as a *deferred annuity* and is chiefly a vehicle for accumulating savings, and eventually distributing them either in the manner of an immediate annuity or as a lump-sum payment.

All varieties of deferred annuities owned by individuals have one thing in common: any increase in account values is *not* taxed until those gains are withdrawn. This is also known as tax-deferred growth. A deferred annuity which grows by interest rate earnings alone is correctly called a *fixed deferred annuity* (FAs). A deferred annuity that permits allocations to stock or bond funds and for which the account value is not guaranteed to stay above the initial amount invested is correctly called a *variable annuity* (VAs).

A new category of deferred annuities has emerged in 1995, called *equity indexed annuity* (EIA). Equity indexed annuities may have features of both deferred annuities just described. The insurance hotel typically guarantees a minimum return for EIA. An investor can still lose money if he or she cancels (or surrenders) the policy early, before a "break even" period. An over simplified EIA rate of return is equal to the "participation rate" multiplied by a target stock market index's performance excluding dividends. Interest rate caps, or administrative fee may be applicable.

There are two phases to a deferred annuity. The accumulation phase is the time between initial purchase and annuitization. The annuitization phase starts when the annuity is turned into a stream of payments. Before annuitization, the deferred annuity contract may allow the purchase of additional (premium) payments to the contract, increasing the contract's value. It should be noted that less than 1% of deferred annuinties are annuitized by annuitants.

Deferred annuities in the United States have an advantage that all capital gains and income are tax deferred until withdrawn. In theory, this allows more money to be put to work while the savings are accumulating, leading to higher returns. A disadvantage, however, is that when a variable annuity is withdrawn or inherited the interest/gains are treated as ordinary income and are taxed as such.

Features

A wide variety of features and guarantees have been developed by insurance companies in order to make annuity products more attractive. These include death and living benefit options, extra credit options, account balance guarantees, spousal continuation benefits, reduced CDSC (Contingent Deferred Sales Charge) or surrender charges and combinations thereof. Each feature or benefit added to a contract will typically be accompanied by an additional expense either directly (billed to client) or indirectly (inside product).

Deferred annuities are usually divided into two different kinds:

1. Fixed Annuities offer some sort of guaranteed rate of return over the life of the contract. In general these are often positioned to be somewhat like bank CDs, and offer a rate of return competitive to CD's of similar time frames (with different tax treatments as previously mentioned). However, many fixed annuities do not have a completely fixed rate of return over the life of the contract, but rather a

guaranteed minimum rate and a first year "teaser rate". The rate after the first year is often any amount that the insurance hotel wants to pay, but at least the minimum amount (typically 3%). Unlike most CD's, there are usually some clauses in the contract to allow a percentage of the interest and/ or principal to be withdrawn early and without penalty (usually the interest earned in a 12 month period or 10%). Normally, fixed annuities become fully liquid upon death. Most Equity Index Annuities (EIA) also fall into this fixed category (aka Fixed Indexed Annuities - FIA) and their performance is typically tied to a stock market index (usually the SandP 500 or DOW). These products are guaranteed but are not as easy to understand as many think since there are usually caps, spreads, margains and crediting methods that can hender returns. These products also don't pay any of the participating market indices dividends, however the trade-off is you can never earn less than 0% in a negative year.

2. Variable Annuities allow money to be invested in separate accounts (similar to mutual funds) in a tax deferred manner. Overall their primary use is to allow someone to engage in tax deferred investing for retirement at amounts greater than permitted by individual retirement or 401(k) plans. In addition, many variable annuity contracts offer a guaranteed minimum rate of return (either for a future withdrawal and/or in the case of the owners death), even if the underlying separate account investments perform poorly. This can be attractive to people uncomfortable investing in the equity markets without the guarantees. However, an investor will pay for each benefit provided by a variable annuity, since insurance companies in general do not write money losing contracts; look at the charges carefully. These products are often heavily criticized as being sold to the wrong persons, who could have done

better doing something else, since the commissions paid by this product are often very high relative to other investment products.

There are several types of these performance guarantees, and many times one can choose them a la carte, with higher charges for guarantees that are riskier for the insurance companies. There are guaranteed minimum death benefits (GMDBs), which can be received only if the owner of the annuity contract, or the covered annuitant, dies.

These GMDBs come in various flavors, in order of increasing risk to the insurance hotel:

1. Return of premium (a guarantee that you will not have a negative return)
2. Roll-up of premium at a particular rate (a guarantee that you will achieve a minimum rate of return, greater than 0)
3. Maximum anniversary value (looks back at account value on the anniversaries, and guarantees you will get at least as much as the highest values upon death)
4. Greater of maximum anniversary value or particular roll-up

Even riskier for insurance companies are the guaranteed living benefits, which tend to be elective. Unlike death benefits, which the contractholder generally can't time, living benefits have significant risk for the insurance companies as contractholders will likely exercise these benefits when they are worth the most. Annuities with guaranteed living benefits (GLBs) tend to have very high fees.

Some GLB examples, in no particular order:

1. Guaranteed minimum income benefit (a guarantee that one will get a minimum income stream upon annuitization at a particular point in the future.)
2. Guaranteed minimum accumulation benefit (a guarantee that the account value will be at a certain amount at a certain point in the future)

3. Guaranteed minimum withdrawal benefit (a guarantee similar to the income benefit, but one that doesn't require annuitizing)
4. Guaranteed for-life income benefit (a guarantee similar to a withdrawal benefit, but will pay you for as long as you live and does not require annuitization)

Criticisms of Deferred Annuities

Deferred annuities are, generally, sold by financial professionals some might work directly for an insurance hotel. The financial professional who sells annuities do collect a commission from the insurance hotel. This commission will be a percentage of the total premium paid by the investor. This percentage can be as little as 1% and as high as 12%, the commission is usually 6% on average. Since these commissions, on the surface, seem high and there are deferred sales charges on annuities many financial gurus have criticized annuity products.

The investor will, generally, not pay any of this commission directly to the financial professional; the commission is paid by the insurance hotel to the financial professional up front. The insurance hotel will recapture the commission paid to the financial professional through the fees charged to the customer (in a variable or equity index annuity) or the spread in the interest rate market (for a fixed annuity). There are also deferred backend charges that will be applied if the investor closes out their contract before the agreed upon time frame, usually 8 years. These charges can be as little as 1 year or as many as 20 years. These backend charges are of concern to many financial professionals and financial gurus.

There are annuities available that do not have any deferred surrender charges and they do not pay the financial professional commissions. These contracts are called "no-load" variable annuity products and are available, usually, from a fee-based financial planner or a no-load mutual fund hotel. There are, however, still fees that are imposed on these contracts, but they are less than those sold by commissioned brokers.

Variable Annuities are contraversial because many believe the extra fees involved with them will almost certainly reduce the rate of return compared to what the investor could make by investing directly in the market. A big selling point for variable annuities are the guaruntees many have, such as the guaruntee that the customer will not lose their principal. Critics say that these guaruntees are not necessary because over the long term the market has always been positive, while others say that many unsophisticated investors simply will not invest without the guaruntees.

A controversial practice of insurance sales is the selling of insurance contracts within an IRA or 401(k) plan in the US. Since these investment vehicles are already tax deferred, investors do not receive additional tax shelters from the annuities. The benefit of the annuity contract is the guaranteed lifetime income that all annuity contracts must have by state law. However, over 90% of annuitants do not take the life annuity upon retirement but take a lump sum cash out. If you do not intend to take the life income option from an annuity contract at retirement, then consider a low cost deferred annuity. On the other hand, if you need to take lifetime income at retirement, try to buy it when you retire or select a 401(k) plan with an option to buy the annuity just before retirement. Only if you want the security of having a lifetime option guaranteed for you should you take the annuity during the deferral (or savings phase) of your 401(k) planning.

ACTUARIAL CONSIDERATIONS

Actuarial Formulae are used to model annuities and determine their price.

Payment options for Immediate Annuities

In technical language an annuity is said to be payable for an assigned *status*, this being a general word chosen in preference to such words as "time", "term" or "period," because it may include more readily either a term of years certain, or a life or combination of lives. The *magnitude* of the annuity is the sum to be paid (and received) in the course of each year. Thus, if £100 is to be received each year by a person, he is said to have *"an annuity of £100."* If the payments are made half-yearly, it is sometimes said that he has *"a half-yearly annuity of £100"*; but to avoid ambiguity, it is more commonly said he has *an annuity of £100, payable by half-yearly instalments.* An annuity is considered as accruing during each instant of the status for which it is enjoyed, although it is only payable at fixed intervals. If the enjoyment of an annuity is postponed until after the lapse of a certain number of years, the annuity is said to be *deferred.* If an annuity, instead of being payable at the end of each year, half-year, andc., is payable in advance, it is called an *annuity-due.* The holder of an annuity is called an *annuitant,* and the person on whose life the annuity depends is called the *nominee.*

Upon immediate annuitization, a wide variety of options are available in the way the stream of payments is paid. If the annuity is paid over a fixed period independent of any contingency, it is known as an *"annuity with period certain"*, or just *annuity certain;* if it is to continue for ever, it is called a *perpetuity;* and if in the latter case it is not to commence until after a term of years, it is called a *deferred perpetuity.* An annuity depending on the continuance of an assigned life or lives would commonly be called a *life annuity,* but also known as a *life-contingent annuity* or simply *lifetime annuity;* but more commonly the simple term "annuity" is understood to mean a life annuity, unless the contrary is stated. The payments can also be paid over the lifetime of the nominee(s) or for a fixed period, whichever is longer. This is known as *"life with period certain"*.

A hybrid of these is when the payments stop at death, but also after a predetermined number of payments, if this is earlier: known as a *temporary life annuity.* The difference with the period certain annuity is that the period certain annuity will keep paying after the death of the nominee until the period is completed. If not otherwise stated, it is always understood that an annuity is payable yearly, and that the annual payment (or rent, as it is sometimes called) is a single currency unit.

Instances of perpetuities are the dividends upon the public stocks in England, France and some other countries. Thus, although it is usual to speak of £100 consols, the reality is the yearly dividend which the government pays by quarterly instalments. The practice of the French in this is arguably more logical. In speaking of their public funds (*rentes*) they do not mention the ideal capital sum, but speak of the annuity or annual payment that is received by the public creditor. Other instances of perpetuities are the incomes derived from the debenture stocks of railway companies, also the feu-duties commonly payable on house property in Scotland. The number of years' purchase which the perpetual annuities granted by a government or a railway hotel realize in the open market, forms a very simple test of the credit of the various governments or railways.

In the United Kingdom, the income from *Compulsory Purchase Annuities* purchased with pension funds or by an employer immediately on retirement (a *Hancock* annuity) is treated as taxable income. The income from *Purchased Life Annuities*, bought by any other means, has an element which is considered return of capital, and only the excess over this is considered a gain that is subject to income tax. The element considered capital return is based on life expectancy and will therefore increase with age.

Government Incentives

Because of cross-subsidy and the guarantees an annuity can give against running out of income and becoming dependent on state welfare in old age, annuities often have a favourable tax treatment, which may affect how attractive they are relative to other investments.

Immediate annuities are a compulsory feature of certain pension saving schemes in some countries, where the government grants tax deductions, provided that savings are paid into a fund which can only (or mainly) be withdrawn as an annuity. The United Kingdom and the Netherlands have such schemes. From 2003 the tax deduction in the Netherlands is only allowed if, without additional savings, the old age income would be less than 70% of the current income.

In the UK and the Republic of Ireland contributions into pension savings are generally nett of income tax (i.e tax relief is available), up to certain limits. Although a number of different regimes exist, personal pension funds taken out since 1988 must use at least 75% of the fund to purchase an annuity by the 75th birthday of the annuitant. If an annuity is not immediately purchased retirement income up until this age can be drawn from the fund by using *Pension Income Withdrawal* commonly known as *Income Drawdown*. This operates under a strict code of rules and limits according to age and figures said by the Government Actuarial Department to prevent the fund being eroded too fast. Individuals may vary withdrawals between 35% and 100% of a maximum limit, that is reset every three years - known as the *triennial review*. Income Drawdown carries both the investment risk of the invested pension fund and mortality drag that occurs from the loss of cross subsidy and advancing average age expectancy that occurs in the time over which annuity purchase is delayed.

Terminable Annuities

Terminable annuities are employed in the system of British public finance as a means of reducing the National Debt. This result is attained by substituting for a perpetual annual charge (or one lasting until the capital which it represents can be paid off *en bloc*), an annual charge of a larger amount, but lasting for a short term. The latter is so calculated as to pay off, during its existence, the capital which it replaces, with interest at an assumed or agreed rate, and under specified conditions. The practical effect of the substitution of a terminable annuity for an obligation of longer currency is to bind the present generation of citizens to increase its own obligations in the present and near future in order to diminish those of its successors. This end might be attained in other ways; for instance, by setting aside out of revenue a fixed annual sum for the purchase and cancellation of debt (Pitt's method, in intention), or by fixing the annual debt charge at a figure sufficient to provide a margin for reduction of the principal of the debt beyond the amount required for interest (Sir Stafford Northcote's method), or by providing an annual surplus of revenue over expenditure (the "Old Sinking Fund"), available for the same purpose. All these methods have been tried in the course of British financial history, and the second and third of them are still employed; but on the whole the method of terminable annuities has been the one preferred by chancellors of the exchequer and by parliament.

Terminable annuities, as employed by the British government, fall under two heads:—

Those issued to, or held by private persons;

Those held by government departments or by funds under government control.

The important difference between these two classes is that an annuity under (1), once created, cannot be modified except with the holder's consent, *i.e.* is practically unalterable without a breach of public faith; whereas an annuity under (2) can, if necessary, be altered by interdepartmental arrangement under the authority of parliament. Thus annuities of class (1) fulfil most perfectly the object of the system as explained above; while those of class (2) have the advantage that in times of emergency their operation can be suspended without any inconvenience or breach of faith, with the result that the resources of government can on such occasions be materially increased, apart from any additional taxation. For this purpose it is only necessary to retain as a charge on the income of the year a sum equal to the (smaller) perpetual charge which was originally replaced by the (larger) terminable charge, whereupon the difference between the two amounts is temporarily released, while ultimately the increased charge is extended for a period equal to that for which it is suspended.

Annuities of class (1) were first instituted in 1808, but were later regulated by an act of 1829. They may be granted either for a specified life, or two lives, or for an arbitrary term of years; and the consideration for them may take the form either of cash or of government stock, the latter being cancelled when the annuity is set up. Annuities (2) held by government departments date from 1863. They were created in exchange for permanent debt surrendered for cancellation, the principal operations having been effected in 1863, 1867, 1870, 1874, 1883 and 1899. Annuities of this class do not affect the public at all, except of course in their effect on the market for government securities. They are merely financial operations between the government, in its capacity as the banker of savings banks and other funds, and itself, in the capacity of custodian of the national finances. Savings bank depositors are not concerned with the manner in which government invests their money, their rights being confined to the receipt of interest and the repayment of deposits upon specified conditions. The case is, however, different as regards forty millions of consols (included in the above figures), belonging to suitors in chancery, which were cancelled and replaced by a terminable annuity in 1883. As the liability to the suitors in that case was for a specified amount of stock, special arrangements were made to ensure the ultimate replacement of the precise amount of stock cancelled.

ANNUITY CALCULATIONS

The mathematical theory of life annuities is based upon a knowledge of the rate of mortality among mankind in general, or among the particular class of persons on whose lives the annuities depend. It involves a mathematical treatment too complicated to be dealt with fully in this place, and in practice it has been reduced to the form of tables, which vary in different places, but which are easily accessible.

Abraham Demoivre, in his *Annuities on Lives*, put forth a very simple law of mortality which is to the effect that, out of 86 children born alive, 1 will die every year until the last dies between the ages of 85 and 86. This law agreed sufficiently well at the middle ages of life with the mortality deduced from the best observations of his time; but, as observations became more exact, the approximation was found to be not sufficiently close. This was particularly the case when it was desired to obtain the value of joint life, contingent or other complicated benefits. Therefore Demoivre's law is entirely devoid of practical utility. No simple formula has yet been discovered that will represent the rate of mortality with sufficient accuracy. The rate of mortality at each age is, therefore, in practice usually determined by a series of figures deduced from observation; and the value of an annuity at any age is found from these numbers by means of a series of arithmetical calculations.

DE WITT'S PRINCIPLE

The first writer who is known to have attempted to obtain, on correct mathematical principles, the value of a life annuity, was Jan De Witt, grand pensionary of Holland and West Friesland. Our knowledge of his writings on the subject is derived from two papers contributed by Frederick Hendriks to the *Assurance Magazine,* vol. ii. p. 222, and vol. in. p. 93. The former of these contains a translation of De Witt's report upon the value of life annuities, which was prepared in consequence of the resolution passed by the states-general, on the 25th of April 1671, to negotiate funds by life annuities, and which was distributed to the members on the 30th of July 1671. The latter contains the translation of a number of letters addressed by De Witt to Burgomaster Johan Hudde, bearing dates from September 1670 to October 1671. The existence of De Witt's report was well known among his contemporaries, and Hendriks collected a number of extracts from various authors referring to it; but the report is not contained in any collection of his works extant, and had been entirely lost for 180 years, until Hendriks discovered it among the state archives of Holland in hotel with the letters to Hudde. It is a document of extreme interest, and (notwithstanding some inaccuracies in the reasoning) of very great merit, more especially considering that it was the very first document on the subject that was ever written.

It appears that it had long been the practice in Holland for life annuities to be granted to nominees of any age, in the constant proportion of double the rate of interest allowed on stock; that is to say, if the towns were borrowing money at 6%, they would be willing to grant a life annuity at 12%, and so on. De Witt states that "annuities have been sold, even in the present century, first at six years' purchase, then at seven and eight; and that the majority of all life annuities now current at the country's expense were obtained at nine years' purchase"; but that the price had been increased in the course of a few years from eleven years' purchase to twelve, and from twelve to fourteen. He also states that the rate of interest had been successively reduced from 6–¼% to 5%, and then to 4%. The principal object of his report is to prove that, taking interest at 4%, a life annuity was worth at least sixteen years' purchase; and, in fact, that an annuitant purchasing an annuity for the life of a young and healthy nominee at sixteen years' purchase, made an excellent bargain.

It may be mentioned that he argues that it is more to the advantage, both of the country and of the private investor, that the public loans should be raised by way of grant of life annuities rather than perpetual annuities. It appears conclusively from De Witt's correspondence with Hudde, that the rate of mortality assumed as the basis of his calculations was deduced from careful examination of the mortality that had actually prevailed among the nominees on whose lives annuities had been granted in former years. De Witt appears to have come to the conclusion that the probability of death is the same in any half-year from the age of 3 to 53 inclusive; that in the next ten years, from 53 to 63, the probability is greater in the ratio of 3 to 2; that in the next ten years, from 63 to 73, it is greater in the ratio of 2 to 1; and in the next seven years, from 73 to 80, it is greater in the ratio of 3 to 1; and he places the limit of human life at 80. If a mortality table of the usual form is deduced from these suppositions, out of 212 persons alive at the age of 3, 2 will die every year up to 53, 3 in each of the ten years from 53 to 63, 4 in each of the next ten years from 63 to 73, and 6 in each of the next seven years from 73 to 80, when all will be dead.

De Witt calculates the value of an annuity in the following way. Assume that annuities on 10,000 lives each ten years of age, which satisfy the Hm mortality table, have been purchased. Of these nominees 79 will die before attaining the age of 11, and no annuity payment will be made in respect of them; none will die between the ages of 11 and 12, so that annuities will be paid for one year on 9921 lives; 40 attain the age of 12 and die before 13, so that two payments will be made with respect to these lives. Reasoning in this way we see that the annuities on 35 of the nominees will be payable for three years; on 40 for four years, and so on. Proceeding thus to the end of the table, 15 nominees attain the age of 95, 5 of whom die before the age of 96, so that 85 payments will be paid in respect of these 5 lives. Of the survivors all die before attaining the age of 97, so that the annuities on these lives will be payable for 86 years. Having previously calculated a table of the values of annuities certain for every number of years up to 86, the value of all the annuities on the 10,000 nominees will be found by taking 40 times the value of an annuity for 2 years, 35 times the value of an annuity for 3 years, and so on—the last term being the value of 10 annuities for 86 years—and adding them together; and the value of an annuity on one of the nominees will then be found by dividing by 10,000.

De Witt's report being thus of the nature of an unpublished state paper, although it contributed to its author's reputation, did not contribute to advance the exact knowledge of the subject; and the author to whom the credit must be given of first showing how to calculate the value of an annuity on correct principles is Edmund Halley. He gave the first approximately correct mortality table (deduced from the records of the numbers of deaths and baptisms in the city of Breslau), and showed how it might be employed to calculate the value of an annuity on the life of a nominee of any age.

Previously to Halley's time, and apparently for many years subsequently, all dealings with life annuities were based upon mere conjectural estimates. The earliest known reference to any estimate of the value of life annuities rose out of the requirements of the Falcidian law, which (40 B.C.) was adopted in the Roman empire, and which declared that a testator should not give more than three-fourths of his property in legacies, so that at least one-fourth must go to his legal representatives. It is easy to see how it would occasionally become necessary, while this law was in force, to value life annuities charged upon a testator's estate. Aemilius Macer (A.D. 230) states that the method which had been in common use at that time was as follows:—From the earliest age until 30 take 30 years' purchase, and for each age after 30 deduct 1 year. It is obvious that no consideration of compound interest can have entered into this estimate; and it is easy to see that it is equivalent to assuming that all persons who attain the age of 30 will certainly live to the age of 60, and then certainly die. Compared with this estimate, that which was propounded by the praetorian prefect Ulpian was a great improvement. His table is as follows:—

Age	*Years' Purchase*	*Age*	*Years' Purchase*
Birth - 20	30	45 - 46	14
20 - 25	28	46 - 47	13
25 - 30	25	47 - 48	12
30 - 35	22	48 - 49	11
35 - 40	20	49 - 50	10
40 - 41	19	50 - 55	9
41 - 42	18	55 - 60	7
42 - 43	17	60 and upwards	
43 - 44	16		
44 - 45	15		

Here also we have no reason to suppose that the element of interest was taken into consideration; and the assumption, that between the ages of 40 and 50 each addition of a year to the nominee's age diminishes the value of the annuity by one year's purchase, is equivalent to assuming that there is no probability of the nominee dying between the ages of 40 and 50. Considered, however, simply as a table of the average duration of life, the values are fairly accurate. At all events, no more correct estimate appears to have been arrived at until the close of the 17th century.

The first author who fully developed the powers of the table was John Nicholas Tetens, a native of Schleswig, who in 1785, while professor of philosophy and mathematics at Kiel, published in the German language an *Introduction to the Calculation of Life Annuities and Assurances.* This work appears to have been quite unknown in England until F. Hendriks gave, in the first number of the *Assurance Magazine,* an account of it, with a translation of the passages describing the construction and use of the commutation table, and a sketch of the author's life and writings, to which we refer the reader who desires fuller information. It may be mentioned here that Tetens also gave only a specimen table, apparently not imagining that persons using his work would find it extremely useful to have a series of commutation tables, calculated and printed ready for use.

The use of the commutation table was independently developed in England-apparently between the years 1788 and 1811— by George Barrett, of Petworth, Sussex, who was the son of a yeoman farmer, and was himself a village schoolmaster, and afterwards farm steward or bailiff. It has been usual to consider Barrett as the originator in England of the method of calculating the values of annuities by means of a commutation table, and this method is accordingly sometimes called Barrett's method. (It is also called the commutation method and the columnar method.) Barrett's method of calculating annuities was explained by him to Francis Baily in the year 1811, and was first made known to the world in a paper written by the latter and read before the Royal Society in 1812.

By what has been universally considered an unfortunate error of judgment, this paper was not recommended by the council of the Royal Society to be printed, but it was given by Baily as an appendix to the second issue (in 1813) of his work on life annuities and assurances. Barrett had calculated extensive tables, and with Baily's aid attempted to get them published by subscription, but without success; and the only printed tables calculated according to his manner, besides the specimen tables given by Baily, are the tables contained in Babbage's *Comparative View of the various Institutions for the Assurance of Lives*, 1826.

The theory of annuities may be further studied in the discussions in the English *Journal of the Institute of Actuaries.* The institute was founded in the year 1848, the first sessional meeting being held in January 1849. Its establishment has contributed in various ways to promote the study of the theory of life contingencies. Among these may be specified the following:—Before it was formed, students of the subject worked for the most part alone, and without any concert; and when any person had made an improvement in the theory, it had little chance of becoming publicly known unless he wrote a formal treatise on the whole subject. But the formation of the institute led to much greater interchange of opinion among actuaries, and afforded them a ready means of making known to their professional associates any improvements, real or supposed, that they thought they had made. Again, the discussions which follow the reading of papers before the institute have often served, first, to bring out into bold relief differences of opinion that were previously unsuspected, and afterwards to soften down those differences,—to correct extreme opinions in every direction, and to bring about a greater agreement of opinion on many important subjects. In no way, probably, have the objects of the institute been so effectually advanced as by the publication of its *Journal.*

The first number of this work, which was originally called the *Assurance Magazine*, appeared in September 1850, and it has been continued quarterly down to the present time. It was originated by the public spirit of two well-known actuaries (Mr Charles Jellicoe and Mr Samuel Brown), and was adopted as the organ of the Institute of Actuaries in the year 1852, and called the *Assurance Magazine and Journal of the Institute of Actuaries*, Mr Jellicoe continuing to be the editor,—a post he held until the year 1867, when he was succeeded by Mr T. B. Sprague (who contributed to the 9th edition of this Encyclopaedia an elaborate article on "Annuities," on which the above account is based). The name was again changed in 1866, the words "Assurance Magazine" being dropped; but in the following year it was considered desirable to resume these, for the purpose of showing the continuity of the publication, and it is now called the *Journal of the Institute of Actuaries and Assurance Magazine.*

This work contains not only the papers read before the institute (to which have been appended of late years short abstracts of the discussions on them), and many original papers which were unsuitable for reading, together with correspondence, but also reprints of many papers published elsewhere, which from various causes had become difficult of access to the ordinary reader, among which may be specified various papers which originally appeared in the *Philosophical Transactions*, the *Philosophical Magazine*, the *Mechanics' Magazine*, and the *Companion to the Almanac*; also translations of various papers from the French, German, and Danish. Among the useful objects which the continuous publication of the *Journal* of the institute has served, we may specify in particular two: — that any supposed improvement in the theory was effectually submitted to the criticisms of the whole actuarial profession, and its real value speedily discovered; and that any real improvement, whether great or small, being placed on record, successive writers have been able, one after the other, to take it up and develop it, each commencing where the previous one had left off.

VALUATION

The premium for an option contract is ultimately determined by supply and demand, but is influenced by five principal factors:

- The price of the underlying security in relation to...
- The strike price. Options will be in-the-money when there is a positive intrinsic value; when the strike price is above/below (put/call) the security's current price. They will be at-the-money when the strike price equals the security's current price. They will be out-of-the-

money when the strike price is below/above (put/call) the security's current price. Options at-the-money or out-of-the-money have an intrinsic value of zero.

- The cumulative cost required to hold a position in the security (including interest + dividends).
- The time to expiration. The time value decreases to zero at its expiration date. The option style determines when the buyer may exercise the option. Generally the contract will either be American style - which allows exercise up to the expiration date - or European style - where exercise is only allowed on the expiration date - or Bermudan style - where exercise is allowed on several, specific dates up to the expiration date. European contracts are easier to value. Due to the *"American"* style option having the advantage of an early exercise day (*i.e.* at any time on or before the options expiry date), they are always at least as valuable as the *"European"* style option (only exercisable at the expiration date).
- The estimate of the future volatility of the security's price. This is perhaps the least-known input into any pricing model for options, therefore traders often look to the marketplace to see what the implied volatility of an option is — meaning that given the price of an option and all the other inputs except volatility you can solve for that value.

Pricing models include the binomial options model for American options and the Black-Scholes model for European options. Even though there are pricing models, the value of an option is a personal decision, requiring multiple trade offs and depending on the investment objective.

Because options are derivatives, they can be combined with different combinations of

- Other options
- Risk free T-bills
- The underlying security, and

- Futures contracts on that security to create a risk neutral portfolio (zero risk, zero cost, zero return). In a liquid market, arbitrageurs ensure that the values of all these assets are 'self-leveling', i.e. they incorporate the same assumptions of risk/reward. In theory traders could buy cheap options and sell expensive options (relative to their theoretical prices), in quantities such that the overall delta is zero, and expect to make a profit. Nevertheless, implementing this in practice may be difficult because of "stale" stock prices, large bid/ask spreads, market closures and other symptoms of stock market illiquidity. If stock market prices do not follow a random walk (due, for example, to insider trading) this delta neutral strategy or other model-based strategies may encounter further difficulties. Even for veteran traders using very sophisticated models, option trading is not an easy game to play.

History of Valuation

Models of option pricing were very simple and incomplete until 1973 when Fischer Black and Myron Scholes published the Black-Scholes pricing model. Scholes received the 1997 Bank of Sweden Prize in Economic Sciences (Nobel Prize of Economics) for this work, along with Robert C. Merton. In a departure from tradition, Fischer Black was specifically mentioned in the award, even though he had died and was therefore not eligible.

The Black-Scholes model gives theoretical values for European put and call options on non-dividend paying stocks. The key argument is that traders could risklessly hedge a long options position with a short position in the stock and continuously adjust the hedge ratio (the delta value – one of the option sensitivities known as "greeks") as needed. Assuming that the stock price follows a random walk, and using the methods of stochastic calculus, a price for the option can be calculated where there is no arbitrage profit. This price depends only on 5 factors: the current stock price, the exercise price, the risk-free interest rate, the time until expiration, and the volatility of the stock price. Eventually, the model was adapted to be able to price options on dividend paying stocks as well.

The availability of a good estimate of an option's theoretical price contributed to the explosion of trading in options. Other option pricing models have since been developed for other markets and situations using similar arguments, assumptions, and tools, including the Black model for options on futures, Monte Carlo methods, Path Integrals, and Binomial options models.

Market interest rates

There are markets for investments which include the money market, bond market, as well as retail financial institutions like banks, which set interest rates. Each specific debt takes into account the following factors in determining its interest rate:

Inflation: Since the lender is deferring his consumption, he will at a bare minimum, want to recover enough to pay the increased cost of goods due to inflation. Because future inflation is unknown, there are three tactics.

- Charge X% interest 'plus inflation'. Many governments issue 'real-return' or 'inflation indexed' bonds. The principal amount and the interest payments are continually increased by the rate of inflations.
- Decide on the 'expected' inflation rate. This still leaves both parties exposed to the risk of 'unexpected' inflation.
- Allow the interest rate to be periodically changed. While a 'fixed interest rate' remains the same throughout the life of the debt, 'variable' or 'floating' rates can be reset. There are derivative products that allow for hedging and swaps between the two.

Default: There is always the risk the borrower will become bankrupt, abscond or otherwise default on the loan. The risk premium attempts to measure the integrity of the borrower, the risk of his enterprise succeeding and the security of any collateral pledged. Loans to developing countries have higher risk premiums than those to the US government. An operating line of credit to a business will have a higher rate than a mortgage.

The credit worthiness of businesses is measured by bond rating services and individual's credit scores by credit bureaus. The risks of an individual debt may have a large standard deviation of possibilities. The lender may want to cover his maximum risk. But lenders with portfolios of debt can lower the risk premium to cover just the most probable outcome.

Deferred consumption: Charging interest equal only to inflation will leave the lender with the same purchasing power, but he would prefer his own consumption NOW rather than later. There will be an interest premium of the delay. He may not want to consume, but instead would invest in another product. The possible return he could realize in competing investments will determine what interest he charges.

Length of time: Time has two effects.

- Shorter terms have less risk of default and inflation because the near future is easier to predict than events 20 year off.
- Longer terms allow for investments in larger projects with higher eventual returns. Contrast this to the lender's preference for readily available cash for contingencies. This is why banks pay higher interest on non-redeemable GICs than on chequing account balances.

Other: Borowers and lenders may face individual tax rates, transaction costs and foreign exchange rate risks. In a liquid market they cannot exert their personal preferences. It is the sum total of the participants who determine rates. The market for financial instruments has moved from the local, to the national, and is now international.

INTEREST RATES

Output and unemployment

Interest rates are the main determinant of investment on a macroeconomic scale. Broadly speaking, if interest rates increase across the board, then investment decreases, causing a fall in national income. Note that if interest rates are high, that means the broad economy is doing well and thus people will be willing to borrow money at higher interest rates.

Interest rates are generally determined by the market, but government intervention - usually by a central bank- may strongly influence short-term interest rates, and is used as the main tool of monetary policy. The central bank offers to buy or sell money at the desired rate and, because of their immense size, they are able to influence in.

By altering in the central bank is able to affect the interest rates faced by everyone who wants to borrow money for economic investment. Investment can change rapidly to changes in interest rates, affecting national income.

Through Okun's Law changes in output affect unemployment.

Open Market Operations in the United States

The Federal Reserve (often referred to as 'The Fed') implements monetary policy largely by targeting the federal funds rate. This is the rate that banks charge each other for overnight loans of federal funds, which are the reserves held by banks at the Fed.

Open market operations are one tool within monetary policy implemented by the Federal Reserve to steer short-term interest rates. Using the power to buy and sell treasury securities, the Open Market Desk at the Federal Reserve Bank of New York can supply the market with dollars by purchasing T-notes, hence increasing the nation's money supply. By increasing the money supply or Aggregate Supply of Funding (ASF), interest rates will fall due to the excess of dollars banks will end up with in their reserves. Excess reserves may be lent in the Fed funds market to other banks, thus driving down rates.

Money and Inflation

Loans, bonds, and shares have some of the characteristics of money and are included in the broad money supply.

By setting, the government institution can affect the markets to alter the total of loans, bonds and shares issued. Generally speaking, a higher real interest rate reduces the broad money supply.

Through the quantity theory of money, increases in the money supply lead to inflation. This means that interest rates can affect inflation in the future.

Historical documents dating back to the Sumerian civilization, circa 3000 B.C., reveal that the ancient world had developed a formalized system of credit based on two major commodities, grain and silver. Before there were coins, metal loans were based on weight. Archaeologists have uncovered pieces of metal that were used in trade in Troy, Minoan and Mycenaean civilizations, Babylonia, Assyria, Egypt and Persia. Before money loans came into existence, loans of grain and silver served to facilitate trade. Silver was used in town economies, while grain was used in the country.

The collection of interest was restricted by Jewish, Christian, Islam and other religions under laws of usury (essentially a derogatory term for interest). This is still the case with Islam, which mandates no-interest Islamic finance.

Irving Fisher is largely responsible for shaping the modern concept of interest with his 1930 work, *The Theory of Interest.*

INVESTMENT

Investment or investing is a term with several closely-related meanings in business management, finance and economics, related to saving or deferring consumption. An asset is usually purchased, or equivalently a deposit is made in a bank, in hopes of getting a future return or interest from it. Literally, the word means the "action of putting something in to somewhere else" (perhaps originally related to a person's garment or 'vestment').

Types of Investment

The major difference in the use of the term investment between the economics field and the finance field is that economists refer to a real investment (such as a machine or a house), while financial economists refer to a financial asset, such as money that is put into a bank or the market, which may then be used to buy a real asset.

Business Management

The investment decision (also known as capital budgeting) is one of the fundamental decisions of business management: managers determine the assets that the business enterprise obtains; these assets may be physical (e.g. buildings or machinery), intangible (e.g. patents, software, goodwill), or financial. Whatever the type of asset, the manager must assess whether the net present value of the investment to the enterprise is positive; the net present value is calculated using the enterprise's marginal cost of capital.

Economics

In Economics, investment means the purchase (and thus the production) and/or stock of capital goods and/or technology - goods which are not consumed but instead used in future production. Examples include building a railroad, or a factory, clearing land, or putting oneself through college. In measures of national income and output, investment is also a component of GDP given in the formula GDP = C + I + G + NX. The investment function in that aspect is divided into non-residential investment (such as factories, machinery etc) and residential investment (new houses).

Investment is often modeled as a function of income and interest rates, given by the relation I = (Y, i). An increase in income will encourage higher investment, whereas a higher interest rate may discourage investment as it becomes costlier to borrow money. Even if a firm chooses to use its own funds in an investment, the interest rate represents an opportunity cost of investing those funds rather than loaning them out for interest.

Finance

In finance, investment means buying securities or other monetary or paper (financial) assets in the money markets or capital markets, or in fairly liquid real assets, such as gold as an investment, real estate, or collectibles. Valuation is the method for assessing whether a potential investment is worth its price.

Types of financial investments include shares or other equity investment, and bonds (including bonds denominated in foreign currencies). These investments assets are then expected to provide income or positive future cash flows, but may increase or decrease in value giving the investor capital gains or losses.

Trades in contingent claims or *derivative securities* do not necessarily have future positive expected cash flows - so are not considered to be assets, or strictly speaking, securities or investments. Nevertheless, since their cash flows are closely related to (or derived from) those of specific securities, they are often studied as or treated as investments.

Investments are often made indirectly through intermediaries, such as banks, mutual funds, pension funds, insurance companies, collective investment schemes, or even investment clubs. Though their legal and procedural details differ, an intermediary generally makes an investment using money from many individuals, each of whom receives a claim on the intermediary.

Personal Finance

Within personal finance, money used to purchase shares, put in a collective investment scheme or used to buy any asset where there is an element of capital risk is deemed an *investment*. Saving within personal finance refers to money put aside, normally on a regular basis. This distinction is important as investment risk can cause a capital loss when an investment is realised, unlike saving(s) where the more limited risk is cash devaluing due to inflation.

In many instances the term *saving* and *investment* are used interchangeably which confuses this distinction. For example many deposit accounts are labeled as *investment accounts* by banks for marketing purposes. To help establish whether an asset is saving(s) or an investment you should consider where your money is invested. If the answer is cash then it is *savings,* if it is a type of asset which can fluctuate in value then it is *investment.*

INVOICE

An invoice is a commercial document issued by a seller to a buyer, indicating the products, quantities and agreed prices for products or services with which the Seller has already provided the Buyer. An invoice indicates that, unless paid in advance, payment is due by the buyer to the seller, according to the agreed terms. It contains a serial number and date of issue. Invoices are often called bills.

Variations

There are many *'different'* kinds of invoices:

Credit Memo - If the buyer returns the product, the seller usually issues a *credit memo* for the same or lower amount than the invoice, and then refunds the money to the buyer or the buyer can apply that credit memo to another invoice.

Debit Memo - When a hotel fails to pay or short-pays an invoice, it is common practice to issue a *debit memo* for the balance and any late fees owed. In function debit memos are identical to invoices.

Self Billing Invoice - A *self billing invoice* is when the buyer issues the invoice to himself (e.g. according to the consumption levels he is taking out of a vendor managed inventory stock).

Timesheet - Invoices for hourly services work (such as by lawyers and consultants) often pull data from a *timesheet.*

Invoicing - The term invoicing is also used to refer to the act of delivering baggage to a flight hotel in an airport before taking a flight.

Electronic Invoices

With the popularization of the internet, many invoices are not paper based anymore, but done electronically. It is still common for electronic remittance or invoicing to be printed in order to maintain paper records. The regulation on how to do electronic invoicing varies widely from country to country. B2B standards have created messages and implementation guidelines for electronic invoices.

What is on an Invoice?

A typical invoice contains:

Purchase order (PO), invoice and internal order numbers

Tax ID number and/or Data Universal Numbering System (DUNS)

Entry, Shipped, order and invoice dates

Billing or "sold to", shipping, and "remit to" addresses

Terms of payment including due date, discount due date and discount amount

Line-item list of products, quantities and prices

Shipping method and cost

Total number of items and sum of amount due

PRO FORMA

The term pro forma (occasionally written *proforma*) comes from a Latin phrase meaning, "as a matter of form". Its meaning depends on the context in which it is used.

General

Doing something in a pro forma manner is to do it in a perfunctory way to satisfy the minimum requirements or to conform to a convention. Sometimes a pro forma or proforma, can refer to a partially completed document, designed by one person to be fully completed and returned by a number of others. The aim being to standardise the information returned to the designer. Usually a pro forma would contain pointers guiding a user in its completion.

Business

A pro forma document is provided in advance of an actual transaction. Such a document serves as a model for the actual documents of the transaction. For example, when a new corporation is envisioned, its founders may prepare a business plan containing pro forma financial statements, such as projected cash flows and income statements.

Legal Proceedings

Pro forma court rulings are merely intended to facilitate the legal process (to move matters along). Many companies report pro forma earnings, in addition to actual earnings calculated under the Generally Accepted Accounting Principles ("GAAP"), in their quarterly and yearly financial reports.

The pro forma accounting is a statement of the hotel's financial activities while excluding "unusual and nonrecurring transactions" (unusual and nonrecurring expenses) when stating how much money the hotel actually made. Expenses often excluded from pro forma results include hotel restructuring costs, a decline in the value of the hotel's investments, or other accounting charges, such as adjusting the current balance sheet to fix faulty accounting practices in previous years.

Companies that report a pro forma income statement or balance sheet usually do so because, they say, the unusual events being excluded really were unusual, so the GAAP financial reports required by law are misleading to investors and potential investors. The crisis that happened this last quarter is not going to recur in future quarters, so the pro forma results can be used by investors to forecast what a "regular" quarter might portend in the future.

Critics note that pro forma numbers always look more profitable than GAAP numbers, and state that many companies intentionally use pro forma results in order to mislead investors into believing the hotel is in much better financial shape than it is; that there is no defined meaning or accounting standard for "pro forma" and that it is therefore impossible to make an "apples to apples" comparison between companies with pro forma results in the way that GAAP accounting allows; and that most "unusual events" reported as such are part of the ordinary course of business and should be reported as such. Most companies in most capitalist countries restructure themselves often, for example, so, it is argued, it is dishonest to claim that restructuring charges are unusual, one-time events that investors should not anticipate in the future.

There was a boom in the reporting of pro forma results starting in the late 1990s, with many dot-com companies using the technique to recast their losses as profits, or at least to show smaller losses than the GAAP accounting showed. The U.S. Securities and Exchange Commission requires publicly traded companies in the United States to report GAAP-based financial results, and has cautioned companies that using pro forma results to obscure GAAP results would be considered fraud if used to mislead investors.

Legislation

In certain Commonwealth nations, such as Canada and the United Kingdom of Great Britain and Northern Ireland, *pro forma* bills are introduced immediately before consideration of the Speech from the Throne. *Pro forma* bills are incomplete pieces of legislation and undergo only the first reading stage, in order to symbolize the authority of the Houses of Parliament to discuss matters other than those specified in the reasons for Parliament having been summoned. After first reading, the bill is never considered further.

SPREADSHEET

A spreadsheet is a rectangular table (or grid) of information, often financial information. The word came from "spread" in its sense of a newspaper or magazine item (text and/or graphics) that covers two facing pages, extending across the centre fold and treating the two pages as one large one. The compound word "spread-sheet" came to mean the format used to present bookkeeping ledgers—with columns for categories of expenditures across the top, invoices listed down the left margin, and the amount of each payment in the cell where its row and column intersect—which were traditionally a "spread" across facing pages of a bound ledger (book for keeping accounting records) or on oversized sheets of paper ruled into rows and columns in that format and approximately twice as wide as ordinary paper.

Batch Spreadsheets

One of the first commercial uses of computers was in processing payroll and other financial records, so the programs (and, indeed, the programming languages themselves) were designed to generate reports in the standard "spreadsheet" format bookkeepers and accountants used. As computers became more available and affordable in the last quarter of the 20th century, more software became available for them, and programs to keep financial records and generate spreadsheet reports were always in demand. Those spreadsheet programs can be used to tabulate many kinds of information, not just financial records, so the term "spreadsheet" has developed a more general meaning as information presented in a rectangular table, usually generated by a computer.

The concept of an electronic spreadsheet was outlined in the 1961 paper "Budgeting Models and System Simulation" by Richard Mattessich. Some credit for the computerized spreadsheet perhaps belongs to Rene K. Pardo and Remy Landau, who filed U.S. Patent 4,398,249 on some of the related algorithms in 1970. While the patent was initially rejected by the patent office as being a purely mathematical invention, Pardo and Landau won a court case in 1983 establishing that "something does not cease to become patentable merely because the point of novelty is in an algorithm." This case helped establish the viability of software patents.

Interactive Spreadsheets

It was not until the ready availability of visual display units ("VDU's") that fully interactive spreadsheets became possible. Earlier implementations were mainly designed around batch programs. In the early 1970's text based VDU's began to be used as input/output devices for interactive transaction processes. It was several years later before full function graphic user interfaces were available for spreadsheets.

The generally recognized inventor of the spreadsheet as a commercial product for the personal computer is Dan Bricklin although a fully interactive implementation produced in the United Kingdom at Imperial Chemical Industries, running on an IBM mainframe platform using CICS pre-dated Bricklin's version by several years even featuring shared public spreadsheets from the outset.

Works Records System

The system, known as "The Works Records System", was designed by Robert Mais then an employee of ICI Mond Division in the UK and was implemented in 1974 by a team which included Ken Dakin, author of several successful CICS debugging products which were used extensively during its development to ensure the highest possible performance by detecting "hot spots" (high execution locations) during code execution.

All operations were performed using "double precision" floating point arithmetic and formulae (which performed calculations and linked cells, either in the same spreadsheet or in completely separate spreadsheets) could be entered on multiple lines to aid comprehension. Formulae were converted (compiled) to "machine" language "on the fly" on first use and stored for subsequent executions.This technique is now known as Just-in-time compilation (JIT) or, more specifically, "incremental compilation" - but given no label at the time.

Data including "aged" values was stored using an Adabas database (described as a "Relational Like" database in the Wikipedia article about Adabas, although it was not fundamental to the operation of the system).

The IBM 3270 workstation chosen for its implementation at the time was a new "breed" of not so dumb terminals which had some basic built-in hardware validity checking such as 'numeric only' input fields.

Despite the limitations of the device, the input screens could nevetheless be designed interactively by non programmers by using simple "<" and ">" as "field" (cell) delimiters during "the design phase" (building the spreadsheet). As with modern day word processors, these "tab characters" would not normally be visible during normal usage. The same technique was used to define "on screen" the layouts of printed reports that were not limited to the 80 column screen width of the 3270.

It is interesting to note that the system was capable of detecting some illogical operations because of a "units" attribute (such as "kilograms" , "ounces", "feet" or "inches") for numeric values (analogous to currency symbol attributes in today's spreadsheets). It was impossible therefore to multiply kilograms by ounces or commit similar logic errors.

By contrast, today's commercial spreadsheets will willingly allow a column of mixed currencies (say pounds and dollars) for example, to be summed or multiplied with not even a warning. The Works records system represents the first known use of a shared public spreadsheet since it allowed multiple users to access the linked spreadsheets across a private online network covering many remote locations.

Apldot

Another example of an "industrial weight" spreadsheet produced two years later in 1976 at the United States Railway Association on an IBM 360/91 running at The John Hopkins University Applied Physics Laboratory in Laurel MD. The application, named APLDOT, was used successfully for many years in developing such applications as financial and costing models for the US Congress and for Conrail.All software development was in the public domain. The software system underwent a court challenge in US Government vs PennCentral Et al. in 1978, 1979. It was dubbed a "spreadsheet" because that was what the financial analysts and strategic planners called those green pads they used to do their planning on in 1976.

Visicalc

Dan Bricklin has spoken of watching his university professor create a table of calculation results on a blackboard. When the professor found an error, he had to tediously erase and rewrite a number of sequential entries in the table, triggering Bricklin to think that he could replicate the process on a computer, using the blackboard as the model to view results of underlying formulas. His idea became VisiCalc, the first application that turned the personal computer from a hobby for computer enthusiasts into a business tool.

VisiCalc went on to become the first "killer app", an application that was so compelling, people would buy a particular computer just to own it. In this case the computer was the Apple II, and VisiCalc was no small part in that machine's success. The program was later ported to a number of other early computers, notably CP/M machines, the Atari 8-bit family and various Commodore platforms. Nevertheless, VisiCalc remains best known as "an Apple II program".

The acceptance of the IBM PC following its introduction in August, 1981, began slowly, because most of the programs available for it were ports from other 8-bit platforms. Things changed dramatically with the introduction of Lotus 1-2-3 in November, 1982, and release for sale in January, 1983. It became that platform's killer app, and drove sales of the PC due to the improvements in speed and graphics compared to VisiCalc. VisiCorp was unable to respond competitively, and disappeared within a few years.

Lotus 1-2-3 underwent an almost identical cycle with the introduction of Windows 3.x in the late 1980s. Microsoft had been developing Excel on the Macintosh platform for several years at this point, and it had developed into a fairly powerful system. A port to Windows 3.1 resulted in a fully functional Windows spreadsheet which quickly took over from Lotus in the early 1990s. By the time Lotus responded with a usable Windows version of their own, Microsoft had started compiling their Office suite, which still dominates the industry.

A number of companies have attempted to break into the spreadsheet market with programs based on very different paradigms. Lotus introduced what is likely the most successul example, Lotus Improv, which saw some commercial success, notably in the financial world where its powerful data mining capabilities remain well respected to this day. Spreadsheet 2000 attempted to dramatically simplify formula construction, but was generally not successful. Stories attempted to make it easier to deal with 3-D blocks of data (as opposed to the 2-D nature of most spreadsheets), but appears to have seen little or no use.

Programming Issues

Just as the early programming languages were designed to generate spreadsheet printouts, programming techniques themselves have evolved to process tables (also known as spreadsheets or matrices) of data more efficiently in the computer itself. Spreadsheets have evolved into powerful programming languages; specifically, they are functional, visual, and multiparadigm languages.

Many people find it easier to perform calculations in spreadsheets than by writing the equivalent sequential program. This is due to two traits of spreadsheets. They use spatial relationships to define program relationships. Like all animals, humans have highly developed intuitions about spaces, and of dependencies between items. Sequential programming usually requires typing line after line of text, which must be read slowly and carefully to be understood and changed.

They are forgiving, allowing partial results and functions to work. One or more parts of a program can work correctly, even if other parts are unfinished or broken. This makes writing and debugging programs much easier, and faster. Sequential programming usually needs every program line and character to be correct for a program to run. One error usually stops the whole program and prevents any result. A spreadsheet program is designed to perform general computation tasks using spatial relationships rather than time as the primary organizing principle. Many programs designed to perform general computation use timing, the ordering of computational steps, as their primary way to organize a program. A well defined entry point is used to determine the first instructions, and all other instructions must be reachable from that point.

In a spreadsheet, however, a set of cells is defined, with a spatial relation to one another. In the earliest spreadsheets, these arrangements were a simple two-dimensional grid. Over time, the model has been expanded to include a third dimension, and in some cases a series of named grids. The most advanced examples allow inversion and rotation operations which can slice and project the data set in various ways.

The cells are functionally equivalent to variables in a sequential programming model. Cells often have a formula, a set of instructions which can be used to compute the value of a cell. Formulas can use the contents of other cells or external variables such as the current date and time. It is often convenient to think of a spreadsheet as a mathematical graph, where the nodes are spreadsheet cells, and the edges are references to other cells specified in formulas. This is often called the dependency graph of the spreadsheet. References between cells can take advantage of spatial concepts such as relative position and absolute position, as well as named locations, to make the spreadsheet formulas easier to understand and manage.

Spreadsheets usually attempt to automatically update cells when the cells on which they depend have been changed. The earliest spreadsheets used simple tactics like evaluating cells in a particular order, but modern spreadsheets compute a minimal recomputation order from the dependency graph. Later spreadsheets also include a limited ability to propagate values in reverse, altering source values so that a particular answer is reached in a certain cell. Since spreadsheet cells formulas are not generally invertable, though, this technique is of somewhat limited value.

A cell may contain a value or a formula, or be empty. In addition it can contain information about the data type of the data it holds, or expects when a value is entered. This may determine the format in which a value is displayed, and the allowed operations on it. A formula often contains references to other cells. Such a cell reference is a kind of variable. Its value is the value of the referenced cell. If that cell in turn references other cells, the value depends on the values of those. Note that in general the cell content should be distinguished from the cell value.

A typical cell reference consists of one or two case-insensitive letters to identify the column (if there are up to 256 columns: A-Z and AA-IV) followed by a row number (e.g. in the range 1-65536). Either part can be relative (it changes when the formula it is in is moved or copied), or absolute (indicated with $ in front of the part concerned of the cell reference).

Many of the concepts common to sequential programming models have analogues in the spreadsheet world. For example, the sequential model of the indexed loop is usually represented as a table of cells, with similar formulas.

Shortcomings

While extremely popular, spreadsheets are not without their downsides. Some of the problems associated with spreadsheets include:

Lack of auditing and revision control. This makes it difficult to determine who changed what and when. This can cause problems with regulatory compliance, among other things.

Lack of security. Generally, if one has permission to open a spreadsheet, one has permission to modify any part of it. This, combined with the lack of auditing above, can make it easy for someone to commit fraud.

Lack of concurrency. Unlike databases, spreadsheets typically allow only one user to be making changes at any given time.

Because they are loosely structured, it is easy for someone to introduce an error, either accidentally or intentionally, by entering information in the wrong place or expressing dependencies among cells (such as in a formula) incorrectly.

The results of a Formula (example "=A1*B1") applies only to a single cell (that is, the cell the formula is actually located in - in this case perhaps C1), even though it can "extract" data from many other cells, and even real time dates and actual times. This means that to cause a similar calculation on an array of cells, an almost identical formula (but residing in its own "output" cell) must be repeated for each row of the "input" array.This differs from a "formula" in a conventional computer program which would typically have one calculation which would then apply to all of the input in turn. With current spreadsheets, this forced repetition of near identical formulae can have detrimental consequences from a quality assurance standpoint and is often the cause of many spreadsheet errors.This last problem could be solved conceptually, simply by permitting the specification of a new category of "spatially independent" formula, allowing the "left hand" (target) of the formula to be entered combined with use of "indexed cell addressing" of the generic form:-

while count (A1:A20) > 0), C(i) = A(i)*B(i) where i=incremented row number (1-20)

This theoretical category of formula could reside anywhere within the spreadsheet since its target cell(s) are specified independently of their location in the spreadsheet. (However, for clarity, the "cloned" formula could optionally be shown in each target cell, any change to one affecting all its clones automatically, thereby reducing errors).

or, to conform more to current "spreadsheet like" syntax perhaps:-

=IF(COUNT(A1:A20) > 0, A(i)*B(i),"") where 2nd parameter represents the formula to be applied to each occurence - but entered only in the first cell, the rest of them displaying the cloned formula.

With the recent advent of remote data update of cells, the need to specify conditional formula of this type will assume a new urgency since the precise contents and extents of external spreadsheets may not be fully discernable before execution.

While there are built-in and third-party tools for desktop spreadsheet applications that address some of these shortcomings, awareness of these is generally low, and usage lower still. However, many of these earlier shortcomings can be handled by online spreadsheets such as EditGrid and Google Docs and Spreadsheets.

RISKS

Risk is concerned with the unknown. Upside risk is the possibility of gain. Downside risk is the possibility of loss. One half the reasons to use options (like other derivatives) is to reduce risk. Certainty is exchanged with other players who assume the risk in hope of big gains. It is wrong to state that "options are risky."

- *Reduce risk*: The seller of a covered call exchanges his upside risk (gains above the strike price) for the certainty of cash in hand (the premium). The buyer of a covered put limits his downside risk for a price - just like buying fire insurance for your house.
- *Increase risk*: The buyer of a call wants the upside risk of an asset, but will only pay a small percentage of its current value, so his returns are leveraged.

> The seller of a put accepts the downside risk of locking in his purchase price of an asset, in exchange for the premium.

To understand risk, look at the four standard graphs of options (put-call-buy-sell). The value of the options in the interim between purchase and expiration will not be exactly like these graphs, but close enough. In all cases, the premium was a certainty.

Buyers start out-of-pocket. But going forward, the option buyer has no downsider risk. The graph either flat lines or goes up on either side of the spot price.

Sellers start with a gain. Going forward, they have no upside risk. These graphs either flat line or go down on either side of the spot price.

The extent of risk varies. Buyers/sellers of calls have unlimited upside/downside risk as the asset price increases. Buyers/sellers of puts have upside/downside risk limited to the spot price of the asset (less the premium).

Index

F

G

H

I

J

K

L

M

N

O

V

W

Z